WEAPONS OF MASS DESTRUCTION
Response and Investigation

ABOUT THE AUTHORS

Steven C. Drielak received his bachelor's and master's degrees from John Jay College of Criminal Justice in New York City. As a Senior Investigator with the New York County District Attorney's Office from 1975 to 1978, he investigated cases involving corruption and racketeering. In 1978, he joined the staff of the Suffolk County District Attorney's office. He was assigned to the newly-created Environmental Crime Unit in May of 1984 and has commanded the unit since 1992. During his tenure with this unit, he has collected chemical, biological, and radiological evidence at over 500 crime scenes. Detective Lieutenant Drielak is also a certified instructor for the Criminal Investigations Division of the U.S. Environmental Protection Agency and has been awarded the National Trainer of the Year by the US Environmental Protection Agency's National Enforcement Training Institute. His recent book *Environmental Crime: Evidence Gathering and Investigative Techniques,* has been chosen by the US EPA as the Academy textbook for all incoming Special Agents.

Thomas R. Brandon received his bachelor's degree from St. John's University and juris doctorate from the St. John's University School of Law in New York City. He is admitted to practice law in the state of New York. His law enforcement career with the Suffolk County, New York, Police Department began in 1981 and has included assignments in Patrol, Planning and Research, Legal Bureau, and the Emergency Service Section. He has commanded the Emergency Service Section as a lieutenant since 1992 and has responded to numerous critical incidents involving hazardous materials, explosives, barricaded subjects, and other disasters and special operations. Lieutenant Brandon is a graduate of the US Army/FBI Hazardous Devices School at Redstone Arsenal and a member of the National Bomb Squad Commanders Advisory Board. He is a graduate of the FBI National Academy as well as numerous specialized training courses related to hazardous materials, explosives, special weapons and tactics, and technical rescue. Lieutenant Brandon has received several awards from the Suffolk County Police Department as well as other organizations. He has been a firefighter since 1977 and has served as an instructor for various topics including hazardous materials response and incident command.

WEAPONS OF MASS DESTRUCTION

Response and Investigation

By

STEVEN C. DRIELAK

and

THOMAS R. BRANDON

Charles C Thomas
P U B L I S H E R • L T D.
SPRINGFIELD • ILLINOIS • U.S.A.

Published and Distributed Throughout the World by

CHARLES C THOMAS • PUBLISHER, LTD.
2600 South First Street
Springfield, Illinois 62704

© 2000 by CHARLES C THOMAS • PUBLISHER, LTD.

ISBN 0-398-07091-1 (cloth)
ISBN 0-398-07092-X (paper)

Library of Congress Catalog Card Number: 00-032613

With THOMAS BOOKS *careful attention is given to all details of manufacturing and
design. It is the Publisher's desire to present books that are satisfactory as to their physical qualities and artistic possibilities and appropriate for their particular use.* THOMAS BOOKS
will be true to those laws of quality that assure a good name and good will.

Printed in the United States of America
MR-R-3

Library of Congress Cataloging-in-Publication Data

Drielak, Steven C.
    Weapons of mass destruction : response and investigation / by Steven C.
Drielak and Thomas R. Brandon.
        p. cm.
    Includes index.
    ISBN 0-398-07091-1 (cloth) – ISBN 0-398-07092-X (pbk.)
    1. Offenses against the environment–United States. 2. Criminal investigation–
United States. 3. Bombing investigation–United States. 4. Chemical weapons–
United States. 5. Biological weapons–United States. I. Brandon, Thomas R. II.
Title.

HV 6403 .D77 2000
363.25–dc21   00-032613

This book is dedicated to our families.
If it were not for their patience and understanding,
this manuscript would not have been possible.

PREFACE

Law enforcement has faced many new challenges over the years. Today it finds itself preparing for the unthinkable: the intentional release of a chemical, biological, or radiological substance that may kill or seriously injure innocent civilians on a massive scale. In order to meet this challenge, the law enforcement community must provide its officers with the necessary training, procedures, and equipment to safely respond to such an incident *before* the incident actually occurs.

Law enforcement personnel will undoubtedly be among the first responders to an incident involving the use or threatened use of a weapon involving chemical, biological, radiological, explosive, or incendiary materials. The initial actions that they undertake will have a significant effect on the overall outcome of the incident, including the safety of the public, as well as the responders themselves. Law enforcement must assess the threat within their jurisdiction and begin the process of planning for a WMD event. This should include a determination as to what training will be necessary, what equipment may be required, and what response procedures need to be put in place to insure a safe and efficient response.

Because of the potential magnitude and complexity of a WMD incident, law enforcement must be prepared to work side by side with other agencies and disciplines. These may include the fire and emergency medical service communities, as well as other law enforcement agencies from various levels and jurisdictions. A task such as this will require the use of an effective incident management system involving all of the response agencies working together toward a common objective.

A safe and effective emergency response is just one of the challenges facing law enforcement today. The use or threatened use of a weapon of mass destruction is a *crime* and proper police procedures must be established to safely and effectively gather evidence at a crime scene such as this.

The gathering of chemical, biological, and radiological evidence is not a new science. Verification experts from the Chemical and Biological Weapons Treaty organizations have many established WMD sampling and analytical protocols which may be utilized by law enforcement. The U.S. Department of Energy has also established numerous sampling and analytical protocols for radiological substances. In addition, the criminal environmental enforcement community has developed many safe and legally sufficient procedures for the gathering of chemical, biological, and radiological evidence in a declared hot zone. This book has combined these various scientific and investigative disciplines and in doing so has provided detailed procedures for the gathering of chemical, biological and radiological evidence regardless of its form or matrix. When facing this new challenge, investigative law enforcement personnel must accept the realization that a WMD crime scene is no different from any other type of crime scene *with the exception that the evidence you gather may kill you.*

STEVEN C. DRIELAK
THOMAS R. BRANDON

ACKNOWLDGEMENTS

We would like to thank Kenneth Hill, Director of the Suffolk County Environmental and Health Laboratory, and microbiologist Mike Santerrelo for the gracious assistance in preparing this book. We would also like to thank Steve Centore of the U.S. Department of Energy's Radiological Assistance Program for his time and patience.

CONTENTS

                                                                            Page
Preface vii

Chapter
  1. THE THREAT 3
      Where 4
      Potential Targets 5
      How 6
      Methods of Delivery/Attack 6
      Availability of Materials and Information 9
      Who 10

  2. AWARENESS 11
      Chemical Agents 11
          Nerve Agents 12
          Blister Agents 12
          Blood Agents 12
          Choking Agents 13
          Incapacitating Agents 13
      Biological Agents 13
          Toxins 14
          Bacteria 14
          Rickettsia 14
          Viruses 14
      Recognition of an Incident 14
      Start the Investigation at the First "Positive" Indication 15
      Signs and Symptoms 17
      Recognition of Materials 21
      Recognition of Devices 26

3. FIRST RESPONDER ACTIONS 28
    Recognition 28
    Notification 29
    Putting the "Plan" in to Action 29
    Scene Security 29
    Who Will Be Allowed in What Areas 34
    Document Personnel at the Scene 34

4. PERSONAL PROTECTION 36
    Protective Actions 37
    Routes of Entry 37
    Respiratory Protection 38
        Air-Purifying Respirator 38
        Self-Contained Breathing Apparatus 39
        Supplied-Air Respirator 40
    Chemical Protective Clothing 40
        Level A 42
        Level B 42
        Level C 42
        Level D 43

5. LAW ENFORCEMENT RESPONSE 44
    Scene Assessment 44
    Secure the Site 48
    Limiting the Spread of the Hazard .48
    Begin Aiding the Injured 49
    Initiate the Criminal Investigation .49
    Assist Other Agencies in Performing Their Duties 50
    The Restoring of Order and Public Confidence 51

6. HANDLING THE VICTIMS 52
    Aiding the Injured 52
    Gross Decontamination 54
    Secondary Contamination 55

7. INCIDENT MANAGEMENT 57
    Incident Command System Components 58
        Common Terminology 58
        Modular Organization 59
        Integrated Communications 59
        Unified Command 60

Consolidated Action Plans 61
Manageable Span of Control 61
Designated Incident Facilities 62
Comprehensive Resource Management 63
Functional Roles 63
Incident Commander 63
Operations 64
Planning 65
Logistics 66
Finance 67
Command Staff 68
Safety Officer 68
Liaison Officer 68
Information Officer 68
The Command Post 69

8.   SOURCES OF ASSISTANCE 71
Federal Bureau of Investigation (FBI) 71
Federal Emergency Management Agency (FEMA) 71
Department of Health and Human Services (DHHS) 72
U.S. Environmental Protection Agency (EPA) 72
U.S. Department of Energy (DOE) 72
Department of Defense (DOD) 73

9.   TACTICAL OPERATIONS IN A HOT ZONE 74
Equipment 76
Weapons 78
Training 78

10. PLANNING CONSIDERATIONS 80
LEPC Plan 81
Vulnerability Assessment 82
Existing Capabilities 83
Determining Your Equipment Needs 84
Equipment 84
Response Equipment 85
Investigative Equipment 85
Specialized Equipment 86
Investigation Plans 87
The Investigation Team 87
Who Will Gather the Evidence 88

Inter-Agency Planning 88
Training Considerations 89
  Who Will Be Trained 90
  Joint Investigative and Response Personnel Training 90
  Available Resources 91
  Making the Training Practical 91
  Refresher Training 92

11. POST-INCIDENT OPERATIONS 93
Critique 93
Re-Assessing Training Needs 94
Re-Assessing Equipment Needs 94
Re-Assessing Plans and Procedures 95
Post-Incident Stress Debriefing 95
Medical Screening and Surveillance 96

12. PREPARING FOR THE CRIMINAL INVESTIGATION ...97
Personnel Training 98
  Occupational Safety and Health Administration 98
    Emergency Response to Hazardous Substance Release ...98
    Respiratory Protection 99
    Recognition, Evaluation and Control
      of Ionizing Radiation 99
    Confined Space Entry 99
    Industrial Toxicology 99
    Biohazard 99
  United States Environmental Protection Agency 99
    Advanced Environmental Crimes Training Program 99
    Sampling for Hazardous Matrials 100
    Air Monitoring for Hazardous Materials 100
  Hazardous Materials Incident Response Operations 101
    Emergency Response to Hazardous Material Incidents ...101
    Radiation Safety at Superfund Sites 102
The Equipment 102
Standard Operating Procedures 103

13. THE CRIME SCENE 104
Arrival Procedures 104
  Photography and Videotape 105
  Crime Scene Interviews 106
  Victims' Personal Effects 106

14. THE INVESTIGATIVE TEAM 107
     Crime Scene Coordinator 108
     The Safety Officer 108
     The Safety Team 108
     Decontamination Team 109
     Emergency Medical Assistance 109
     The Sample Team 109
     The Laboratory Team 109
     Hot Zone Investigation Team 110

15. GATHERING EVIDENCE IN A HOT ZONE 111
     Equipment and Procedures 111
     The Crime Scene Notes 115

16. SAMPLING FOR CHEMICAL, BIOLOGICAL,
     AND RADIOLOGICAL EVIDENCE 118
     The Sampling Plan 119
     Chemical Evidence 119
     Chemical Evidence Gathering 119
        Trip Blanks 120
        Field Blanks 120
        Glove Changes 122
        Representative Samples 122
        Control Samples 122
        Sampling Equipment and Containers
           for Chemical Evidence 122
        Sampling for Chemical Agent Precursors 125
        Sampling for a Suspected Chemical Agent 126
           Liquids and Solids 126
           Victims'/Suspects' Personal Items 126
           Gases/Aerosols 127
           Surface and Dermal Sampling 128
        Sampling for Degradation Products 132
        Chemical Evidence Quality Control 132
        Labeling and Preserving Chemical Evidence 133
        Storage of the Chemical Evidence 135
     Biological Evidence 135
        Biological Evidence Gathering: *Bacteria, Viruses and Toxins* ...137
           Equipment Preparation 137
           Glove Changes 138
           Control Samples 138

Sampling for a Suspected Biological Agent 138
    Liquids and Solids 139
    Victims'/Suspects' Personal Items 140
    Soils 140
    Surface and Dermal 140
    Bioaerosols 141
Labeling and Preserving Biological Evidence 145
Biological Evidence Storage 146
Radiological Evidence 146
    Radiological Evidence Gathering 146
    Trip Blanks 147
    Glove Changes 147
    Control Samples 147
    Sampling Equipment and Containers
        for Radiological Evidence 147
    Sampling for a Suspected Radiological Substance 148
        Airborne Radioactive Material 149
        Solid Sources 149
        Soils 151
        Surface and Dermal 153
        Liquids 154
    Radiological Evidence Preservation and Storage 155
Packaging and Shipping of Hazardous Evidence 156

17. ANALYSIS FOR CHEMICAL, BIOLOGICAL,
    AND RADIOLOGICAL EVIDENCE 161
    Hazardous Evidence Analysis: *Instrumentation
    and Methodologies* 162
        Chemical Evidence Analysis 162
        Gas Chromatography/Mass Spectrometry 162
        Biological Evidence Analysis 163
            Growth Culture Analysis 164
            Immunoassay 165
            Deoxyribonucleic Acid/Polymerase
            Chain Reaction – DNA/PCR .165
    Radiological Evidence Analysis 166
    The Laboratory: *Post Analysis* 166

18. INTERDICTION TECHNIQUES .167
    Chemical Agents: *Manufacturing* .167
        Precursor Container Tracing 168

Biological Agents: *Manufacturing* 173
Radiological Devices: *Manufacturing* 174
Surreptitious Sampling Techniques 176
   Remote Air Sampling 176
   Remote Liquid Waste Stream Sampling 177
   Raman Light Detection and Ranging (Raman LIDAR) 178

19. SEARCHING THE SUSPECT FACILITY 179
   Determining Goals 179
   Equipment Requirements 180
   Personnel Requirements 181
      The Search Team 181
   The Briefing 182
      Chain-of-Command 182
      Safety Officer 182
      Site Investigation Team 183
      The Sample Team 183
      Type of Facility 183
      Suspected Hazards 184
      Expected Protection Levels 184
      Decontamination Requirements 184
      Emergency Medical Requirements 184
      The Sampling Operation 184
      Site History 185
      Photographs 185
      Facility Diagram 185
      Weather 185
      Communications 186
      Search Warrant Review 186
   The Staging Area 186
      Personnel and Equipment Check 186
      Operation's Plan Overview 186
   The Search 187
      Interior Search 187
      Exterior Search 191
      Post-Search Briefing 192
      Sample Point Identification 193
      The Sampling Order 193
      Chain-of-Custody 194
      Pipe Tracing 194
      The Prosecutor 195

The Receipt 195
Closing the Scene 195

Appendices 197
Notes 207
Glossary 213
Index 219

WEAPONS OF MASS DESTRUCTION
Response and Investigation

Chapter 1

THE THREAT

Regardless of the area covered by a law enforcement agency, it must be prepared for a terrorist event to occur within its jurisdiction. There was little shock in the law enforcement community in 1993 when international terrorists attacked the World Trade Center in New York City. Officials felt that the inevitable had finally occurred in the United States.

It was a different story, however, in 1995, when the United States and the world witnessed the bombing of a federal office building in Oklahoma City, the "heartland" of America. This event showed that no one, not even children in a day-care center, is immune from the effects of terrorism. Whether international or domestic terrorism, all jurisdictions are subject to terrorist acts.

The traditional weapons of terrorism have included explosives, incendiary devices, hostage taking, kidnapping, and other obvious assaults designed to in some way enhance the terrorists' goals. Today's threat includes the potential use of weapons that are chemical, biological, or nuclear in nature. For an assortment of reasons, these new threats are also referred to as weapons of mass destruction (WMD) and are likely to

become the choice of terrorists in the near future.

The acronym "B-NICE" is often used to describe the weapons that may be employed by today's criminals. This stands for **B**iological, **N**uclear, **I**ncendiary, **C**hemical, and **E**xplosives. Of these weapons, the use of explosives and incendiary devices still remains the most commonly seen by law enforcement.[1] One of the dangers that exists is that a terrorist may elect to add to the damage and injury caused by a traditional improvised explosive device by adding a biological, chemical, or radiological element to it. This has created significant new challenges for law enforcement officials in both the response to and investigation of these incidents.

Chemical and biological weapons are relatively easy to manufacture in relatively small quantities. Due to today's information explosion where anyone with a home computer and a telephone connection can have access to a world of knowledge, the formulas for WMD are readily available. In many cases, they can be manufactured with limited risk to the manufacturer, unlike traditional improvised explosive devices which frequently took their toll on the bomb maker.

The actual materials needed to create these weapons are also readily available in a variety of places. While some more exotic materials may need to be obtained from laboratories and scientific suppliers, the typical household can yield many of the materials needed. Chemicals found in the typical garage or basement can be the basis for the creation of a WMD. Nature itself can be the source of the pathogens needed for the creation of a biological weapon.

Chemical and biological weapons have been referred to as the "poor man's" choice for terrorism. Because of their being readily available in everyday commerce, the materials to create an effective WMD make it a relatively low cost way to commit an act of terrorism. In many cases, only a small quantity of a chemical or biological agent is needed to achieve the desired effect. This makes them a relatively inexpensive tool; a large cash supply is not necessary to create a biological weapon that can affect an entire community.

Presently, it is difficult to detect the presence of many of the materials that may be utilized in a WMD. Unlike explosives, for which there are now an assortment of detection devices ranging from specially trained dogs to ion detection devices, the chemical and biological elements that may

be used in a weapon are not yet capable of being readily identified. As will be discussed later with regard to responding to a WMD incident, the identification of WMD materials is still in its developmental stage.

As a result of the difficulty in detecting WMD materials, they may be used rather covertly. This creates a host of problems for law enforcement personnel in both preventing a WMD incident and in becoming aware of and responding to a WMD event. A biological weapon could be introduced today, yet its effects may not be realized for hours or even days.

Depending on the objective of the particular terrorist, a WMD may be used to injure a large number of people in a single event. They are well suited to wide spread dissemination via ordinary airflow by either natural means or mechanical ventilation systems. This may result in a large number of casualties that will in turn put a significant burden on the local emergency response system in its attempt to handle the incident. There are very few agencies, whether law enforcement, fire, or EMS that will be able to handle a WMD incident without requesting assistance from other agencies and levels of government beyond their own. The importance of pre-incident planning will be discussed later in order to prepare for a WMD incident (see Chapter 10).

WHERE

Realistically, there is almost no limit to where a WMD incident may occur. Historically, we have seen terrorist acts committed against individuals, organizations, governments, facilities, and a variety of objectives that a terrorist thought worthy of his attention. While "target hardening" will help reduce the opportunity, there is still no shortage of potential terrorism targets.

By their very nature, certain facilities and events are more attractive terrorist targets than others. Law enforcement agencies should do a threat assessment of the potential targets within their jurisdiction. This will serve as a starting place in developing a plan for response to a WMD incident. Once the threat level is identified, steps can be taken to properly train and, if necessary, equip law enforcement officers to safely and effectively respond to and investigate an incident involving the use or suspected use of a WMD.

POTENTIAL TARGETS

The following is a description of potential terrorist targets against which a WMD may be employed. It is by no means to be considered all-inclusive. Unlike law enforcement, which may find itself limited by jurisdictional boundaries, budgetary constraints, and legal restrictions, terrorists are criminals who know no such limits when its comes to target selection.

- Areas where large numbers of people gather, either on a daily basis or for a special event, are potential targets. Shopping malls, transportation centers, theaters, and congested downtown areas may all present an attractive target to a terrorist.
- Special events such as sporting events, concerts, political rallies, and other high-profile events are likely targets. They are particularly appealing because they may already be the subject of intense media coverage. The bombing that took place during the 1996 Olympics in Atlanta took on added significance because of the venue. A pipe bomb in a park in Atlanta would not have received the attention it did had it not been for the time and place.
- Government buildings and facilities are often the subject of protests. They are often open to the public because of the nature of the business transacted there and are therefore somewhat difficult to safeguard. No level of government should be considered immune from the threat of terrorism. Local, state, and federal facilities should all be identified by law enforcement when conducting a threat assessment in their jurisdiction.
- Organizations that do business with the government such as defense contractors and representatives of foreign governments should also be included in the threat assessment. Military facilities and offices must be included in any target list. Recruiting offices have been threatened and targeted in the past as well as places known to be frequented by military personnel.
- Facilities that are critical to public safety and the everyday operation of government and society must be considered. Power plants, sewage treatment facilities, rail lines, shipping terminals, and communications centers are all sites that may be subject to a WMD attack. These are frequently referred to as the infrastructure and may include police and fire facilities.
- Educational facilities such as colleges and special training centers may be potential targets. Research facilities may also be attractive to a terrorist looking for materials to create a WMD.
- Some facilities, such as abortion clinics and labs involved in research which utilize live animals, have already been threatened and acted against by terrorists having a variety of goals and motivations.
- Law enforcement personnel should pay careful attention to local, national, and international events to determine the possibility of terrorist targets within their area of responsibility. A foreign financial institution with an office in your jurisdiction may suddenly become a terrorist target based on political upheaval on the other side of the world. In today's world of instant communications and world travel, law enforcement officials cannot afford to be unaware of how events occurring else-

where may be related to their own jurisdiction.

• Religious institutions have often been the targets of terrorist actions for a variety of reasons. They are usually highly visible in a community and may be involved in controversial issues that evoke strong emotions. In some cases, religious sites are also centers for community and political activity. Churches, synagogues, mosques, temples, and other places of worship should all be considered possible sites for a WMD event. Other facilities associated with religious groups such as schools, medical facilities, and social centers should also been included.

HOW

One of the aspects of chemical and biological weapons that law enforcement personnel must be aware of are the potential methods of dissemination. These methods may range from simply introducing the substance into an air intake to be spread throughout a facility such as a shopping mall to a more complicated spraying device designed to distribute the material over a large area.

The material to be distributed as well as the intended target will help influence the method of dissemination that a terrorist elects to use. In most cases, the product will have to be transformed into an aerosol state for the most efficient distribution. Some products lend themselves more easily to this than others based upon their physical nature. As with WMD in general, there are various methods of dissemination that can be easily assembled after a visit to the local hardware store. More complicated devices may require an additional trip to a hobby shop or electronics supply store.

METHODS OF DELIVERY/ATTACK

Generally speaking, there are five different types of dissemination devices. Law enforcement personnel should be made aware of these methods as part of their awareness training so that they may recognize them in the course of their response to a WMD incident or take preventative actions before an incident takes place. Investigative personnel in particular should be familiar with these devices to enable them to properly collect and secure valuable evidence left behind at a WMD crime scene.

Due to the nature of the WMD attack, valuable evidence will often remain at the scene in the form of the actual dissemination device or the method used to transport the device. Traditional crime scene evidence such as fingerprints, tire and shoe impressions, and other trace evidence can be recovered at a WMD crime scene in the same manner as a traditional crime scene. The main difference is the potential danger to the investigator when he or she enters the scene. Proper training and the use of personal protective equipment by investigative personnel can, however, reduce this risk.

One type of dissemination device that may be encountered is a spraying device. These devices may employ pressure to spread the agent. Depending on the size of the device, the agent may be spread over a rather large area, particularly if the wind or other air movement is factored into the operation. These devices can be used directly by the terrorist or they may be set up to function with a time delay or be remotely activated. A common seltzer bottle may also be used to spread a chemical agent.[2]

Another dissemination device involves the use of an exploding or bursting device to spread the material into the atmosphere (see Figure 1). Bomb technicians should be called upon to assist with a device such as this if it is located or intercepted before it is activated. In addition to the traditional hazards that are normally associated with improvised explosive devices such as heat, concussion, and shrapnel, these devices may spread the material over a large area. On the positive side, the explosion may consume a portion of the hazardous substance, thus reducing the spread of contamination. Investigators at the scene of a "bombing" must now be concerned with possible chemical, biological, or radioactive contamination being left behind by a terrorist. This adds another dimension of risk to an already hazardous crime scene. Personnel should be particularly wary of this when the device does not appear to have completely functioned or exploded as might have been expected. Witnesses may report hearing a popping sound or a muffled explosion that may be associated with this type of dissemination.

A very basic method of distribution is to employ a simple breakable container (see Figure 2). This device will usually require the terrorist to actually be present to deploy the device, thus creating a more significant risk of injury and capture. Balloons, glass containers, light bulbs, and thermos bottles may be successfully employed as a dissemination device. A possible variation of this device is to create a "binary" device that

Figure 1. Explosives may be adapted to disseminate chemical, biological or radiological materials.

Figure 2. An ordinary light bulb, filled with a hazardous substance, can be used as an improvised dissemination device.

requires the mixing of two materials to create the desired hazardous substance. The materials are then mixed by breaking the containers or causing the materials to come together in some manner. A binary device may be the choice of a terrorist because it is safer to carry and put in place rather than a device in which the hazardous substance is already mixed and ready for dispersal (see Figures 3 & 4).

A device may be employed to use a chemical or biological agent directly against a specific individual. These "surgical strike" type devices do not present the hazards to others in the immediate area that the above-described devices do. These devices are not unlike those described in spy novels that were employed in assassination plots. Instructions are available that show how to modify a dart that is normally used to tranquilize animals to inject a subject with a hazardous substance. These darts can be fired from a distance using an air-powered gun or they can be used at close range similar to a hypodermic syringe (see Figure 5).[3]

The dissemination method that is least accurate and most difficult to control is the vector method. A vector is a carrier of bacteria and may include insects or items that have been contaminated. The English employed this method in the French and Indian War of 1754 to 1767 when they gave blankets that were infected with smallpox to the Indians who were loyal to the French.[4]

Figure 3. Readily available materials (i.e. balloons, cardboard box) can be used to create a binary device.

Another example of this would be the forwarding of letters through the mail or other carrier services that are alleged to have been contaminated with the deadly anthrax bacteria. Because it is difficult to determine exactly where the vector will carry the material, this method is not considered to be favored by a terrorist.

One possible use of the vector method would be in what might be considered "agricultural" terrorism. In this case, a nation's ability to produce food and feed its citizens would be attacked by introducing organisms that would damage crops or livestock. This would impact the economy as well as the ability to feed the people. Law enforcement officials who have agricultural resources within their jurisdiction should be aware of the threat that this type of WMD incident may pose in their area.

AVAILABILITY OF MATERIALS AND INFORMATION

As mentioned earlier, the above dissemination devices can be created rather easily. The only real limits are the ingenuity and resourcefulness of the terrorist.

The nature of the product to be disseminated will influence the type of device to be employed. Some products, such as those involving corrosive materials, may break down certain materials used to contain them. Other products may require specific

Figure 4. Once assembled, the binary device can be transported in a relatively safe and inconspicuous manner.

dissemination methods because they are viscous and not easily spread. First responders and investigators should keep an open mind when processing a WMD crime scene. They should also remember that more than one device may be employed in the same incident or that a device may have been created employing more than one type of design feature.

Ordinary garden sprayers may be utilized and a more extensive dissemination may be sought by employing a compressor or other mechanical advantage. Law enforcement and security personnel should be aware of these various potential devices when engaged in operations at an event that may present an attractive terrorist target or when conducting a search in response to a reported threat.

WHO

Who will launch the next terrorist threat that requires a law enforcement response is anyone's guess. The attack may come from an organized group, an individual, a foreign source or domestic source. Law enforcement intelligence sources on all levels may provide valuable information when planning for a WMD incident, when assessing the validity of a WMD threat and/or responding to an actual WMD incident.

While an organized group of foreign or domestic terrorists may present a significant threat to a particular community or locale, a lone terrorist, such as the Unabomber, can be just as dangerous. The incident in which followers of an Indian guru poisoned several hundred residents of Oregon in order to influence a local election is a prime example of biological terrorism being used in the United States by an organized group. In this case, Salmonella (food poisoning) bacteria were used to contaminate salad bars in local restaurants, thus causing over 700 people to become ill.[5]

Regardless of who is behind the attack and whatever their motivation might be, the law enforcement response in the initial stages of the incident will most likely be determined by the nature of the attack rather than the group or individual behind it. As the investigation progresses and information is developed, the who and why will become more significant.

Figure 5. This syringe, used to tranquilize animals, can be used for a "surgical strike."

Chapter 2

AWARENESS

In all likelihood, the first law enforcement personnel to respond to an incident involving a WMD will not be aware of that fact until they are on the scene. With the exception of an event such as an explosion or other obvious assault, a WMD incident may not present itself as such. The original call may be dispatched as a request to assist a sick person or to identify a suspicious package left in a public place. Notwithstanding how it originates, the first emergency response personnel on the scene, regardless of their affiliation, must correctly assess the situation and initiate the proper procedures. Their lives and the lives of the public and the subsequent responders may depend upon it. Regardless of the size of the agency, the type of jurisdiction it protects, and the perceived level of threat, all law enforcement agencies and their personnel must be aware of the potential for a WMD incident and know the proper response procedures to follow.

CHEMICAL AGENTS

In general, there are five different classes of chemical agents that may be encountered as a result of a WMD incident. These agents are classified according to the manner in which they affect their victims, including blister agents, blood agents, nerve agents, choking agents, and incapacitating agents. They may be designed to kill, cause injury, or incapacitate their victims.

When describing chemical agents, the terms persistent and non-persistent are used to describe one of the qualities of the agent. Persistent describes an agent that remains in an area or on a surface for an extended period of time. Non-persistent describes an agent that dissipates or evaporates in a rather short period of time.

Another factor to be considered when examining the potential effects of a WMD incident involving a chemical agent is the amount of time that it takes for an agent to begin affecting a victim. The time that it takes for a material to begin affecting a victim is known as the *onset time* and can vary according to several factors. The strength of the material, the duration of the exposure, the size of the dose, and the medical and physical condition of the victim may affect onset time. Many chemical agents are relatively fast acting (i.e. nerve agents) while others such as blister agents have a slower onset time.

Nerve Agents

Nerve agents describe materials that attack the nervous system of a victim when they are inhaled, absorbed, or ingested into the body. Nerve agents are frequently referred to as nerve gas but are actually viscous liquids that give off potentially lethal vapors.

Nerve agents may be referred to by their common name or by their abbreviation. Law enforcement personnel should be familiar with the names and abbreviations in the event they appear in the form of a threat or warning. Some of the more common agents are as follows:
• Tabun (GA)
• Sarin (GB)
• Soman (GD)
• VX

Nerve agents act by inhibiting certain enzymes that are required for normal nerve and muscle function in humans. The number of symptoms and the severity of the symptoms will depend upon both the quantity and route that the agent takes to enter the body. For example, exposure via the eyes results in a rapid onset of symptoms, as does exposure via inhalation, whereas an exposure via the skin may take longer to manifest itself and may be less severe.

Blister Agents

Blister agents, also known as vesicants, are intended to damage any tissue they come in contact with such as the eyes, lungs, and skin. While they may cause death under certain circumstances, they are primarily designed to injure victims and cause pain and discomfort. These agents can penetrate skin as well as other materials such as wood, leather, and rubber. These products are very persistent and have been known to last for years.

Blister agents can act either immediately upon their victim or have a delayed reaction. As with the nerve agents, law enforcement personnel should be familiar with the terms and abbreviations associated with blister agents, including the following:
• Mustard (H)
• Distilled Mustard (HD)
• Lewisite (L)
• Phosgene Oxime (CX)

Lewisite is actually an ***arsenical*** and phosgene oxime is an ***urticant***. These products are similar in effects to mustard and are usually included when discussing blister agents.

Blood Agents

Agents that contain cyanide and enter the body primarily by inhalation are known as blood agents. These agents affect the ability of the body to transfer oxygen from the blood to body tissues. Blood agents are known to be highly volatile and are therefore considered to be non-persistent.

Hydrogen cyanide (AC) is a blood agent that can quickly cause death when victims are exposed to high concentrations. It has an odor similar to bitter almonds that can sometimes not be detected. Hydrogen cyanide has various industrial uses and is commercially available. It is lighter than air and will move up into the atmosphere faster than other chemical agents.

Cyanogen chloride (CK) is a blood agent that is highly irritating to the respiratory tract as well as the eyes and nose. It also acts as a choking agent. It is a quick acting agent and is considered to be non-persistent. Unlike hydrogen cyanide, cyanogen chloride is heavier than air and the vapors may linger for a longer period of time.

Choking Agents

Choking agents act upon victims via their respiratory tract, including the nose, throat, and lungs. They actually produce what is known as "dry-land drowning," in which the victim's lungs become filled with fluid as a result of inhaling the chemical. Phosgene (CG) and chlorine (CL) are the two most common choking agents that may be used in a WMD. Both were used during World War I.

Phosgene is a non-persistent, colorless gas that is heavier than air and will linger near the ground. It has an odor that has been described as that of newly mown hay or grass. The effects of exposure to phosgene may not be immediately obvious and symptoms may not be apparent for several hours.

Chlorine is a choking agent that has many industrial uses and is readily available on the commercial market. It has a distinctive odor of bleach or swimming pool chemicals.

Chlorine reacts with the moisture in the mucous membranes of the victim's lungs and forms hydrochloric acid resulting in the above-mentioned dry land drowning.

Incapacitating Agents

Temporary disability may be caused by chemical agents that produce mental or physiological effects. Incapacitating agents produce effects that may last for a period of time that varies from hours to days after the exposure. The results are not permanent and are created by altering or disrupting the functioning of the victim's central nervous system. Incapacitating agents differ from riot control agents normally used by law enforcement agencies in that the effects are much shorter in duration.

BZ is an incapacitating agent that is a white crystalline solid, usually distributed as an aerosol. The respiratory system is the primary route of entry and the digestive tract is the secondary route. If used in conjunction with solvents, it may be absorbed through the skin. If left untreated, a victim of exposure to BZ may take three to four days to fully recover. Because of its physical state, it is considered to be persistent.

BIOLOGICAL AGENTS

Unlike chemical agents, the presence of biological agents at the scene of a WMD incident will not be obvious and will be more difficult to detect. Most biological agents will also have a delayed effect ranging in time from hours to days as opposed to chemical agents whose effects are usually more immediate.

Biological agents cannot penetrate unbroken skin by themselves and must therefore be inhaled or ingested. Biological agents are not volatile like many chemical

agents and will usually be disseminated as either liquid or solid aerosols (particulates). Once released into the environment, biological agents are subject to temperature and humidity as well as sunlight (ultraviolet rays) which will help to kill them.

In general, there are three types of biological agents including bacteria, viruses, and toxins. Both bacteria and viruses are living organisms and require an environment in which they can both live and reproduce. They can enter the body through ingestion, inhalation, a break in the skin, or through other body openings. Some biological agents, such as smallpox and viral hemorrhagic fevers, can be transmitted from one human being to another.

Toxins

Toxins are poisonous substances that are produced by a microorganism, plant, or animal and are not living organisms themselves. They usually enter the body in the same way as other biological agents and are not contagious from one human being to another. Neurotoxins attack the nervous system, while cytotoxins attack the cells. The venom of a poisonous snake and ricin, which is produced from the castor bean, are examples of toxins.

Bacteria

Bacteria include anthrax and plague. Anthrax naturally occurs in hoofed animals and is usually transmitted to humans through cuts and abrasions on the hands of those working with infected animals and their by-products such as wool. When in its spore form for use as a biological weapon, anthrax is transmitted to man through the inhalation route of exposure. It is most dangerous if found in a solid form.

Inhalation anthrax is not transmitted from one human to another.

Plague, also known as "Black Death," is a bacteria that is usually transmitted to humans via rats or fleas; pneumonic plague is an aerosolized version that can be transmitted from man to man via inhalation. Other bacteria that may be found in a WMD incident include tularemia, rabbit fever (deer fly fever), and typhoid fever.

Rickettsia

Rickettsia is an organism that possesses the characteristics of both bacteria and viruses. Typhus and Q Fever are examples of rickettsia. Q Fever is found in animals and can be transmitted to man through inhaling particles contaminated with the organisms. It is usually not fatal and most infected victims will recover without treatment.

Viruses

Viruses are the simplest type of microorganism. They lack a system for their own metabolism and are dependent on their host cells for survival. Viruses require living cells in order to multiply. Smallpox and Venezuelan equine encephalitis (VEE) are examples of viruses that could be employed as biological weapons.[6]

RECOGNITION OF AN INCIDENT

Law enforcement personnel, particularly those who may be considered to be "first responders," must be trained to recognize the indicators of a WMD attack. These primary indicators may include one or more of the following:

• The existence of the signs and symptoms of a chemical or biological agent having been released.

• The presence of mass casualties.
• Numerous victims suffering from the same signs and symptoms.
• The presence of a dissemination device or the apparent remnants of one.
• A warning having been given or credit being taken for the incident.
• Positive readings from a detection device or direct reading instrument at the scene.

- The type of location or occupancy where the incident is occurring.
- Materials, odors, liquids, or other items that are out of place or otherwise unexplainable.

From the time they arrive at the scene, law enforcement personnel must be aware of the possibility of a second device being present at the scene or in the immediate vicinity. This second device may have been left at the scene with the intention of killing or injuring law enforcement, fire, and EMS personnel. It may also be one of several devices that didn't go off as planned and must then be rendered safe. An article such as this may be of great investigative value and should be handled as such. A series of bombings occurring in the Atlanta area involved secondary devices being left at the scene with the apparent intention of killing and injuring emergency personnel. In the first incident, the device exploded at the scene of a bombing while emergency personnel and investigators were on the scene. Serious injury from this secondary device was avoided because parked emergency vehicles absorbed most of the impact and shrapnel. In the subsequent incidents, response personnel, based on their recent experience, conducted a thorough search and discovered the additional device and were able to keep people out of harm's way. The device exploded while being handled by the bomb squad's robot.

Response personnel must keep in mind that the last person to occupy what is now the crime scene may have been the terrorist. Until they are able to secure that scene and take the necessary steps to make it safe, they must proceed as if they are in "enemy territory." Activity within the crime scene area should be limited to that necessary to preserve life until the area can be examined by trained personnel and made as safe as possible. Depending on the hazards discovered at the scene, it might take an extended period of time before the scene can be brought to a level of safety that allows a proper investigation. Building stabilization, decontamination, and bomb searches may have to be conducted before the investigation is undertaken within the affected area.

Law enforcement personnel may be in the best position to observe and recognize the above indicators and initiate the proper response to a WMD incident. The importance of training communications personnel must also be emphasized. The same indicators of a WMD attack that greet response personnel upon their arrival may be recognized by communications personnel as they receive the initial reports from the scene. Their ability to recognize a potential WMD incident in its earliest stages may save the lives of emergency personnel. While the protection and preservation of life, including their own personal safety, must be paramount, law enforcement personnel must approach the incident as they would any other crime scene where a crime against a person appears to have been committed. This approach must include preserving the scene in as intact a condition as possible for the subsequent investigation that will inevitably follow.

START THE INVESTIGATION AT THE FIRST "POSITIVE" INDICATION

In reality, the investigation must commence upon the first "positive" indications of a WMD attack. This may not seem feasible, particularly if the incident involves a large number of casualties, but it must be a consideration if the incident is to be successfully investigated and the appropriate parties held accountable. Even though safety concerns may initially restrict the access of investigative personnel to the actual crime scene, the investigation need not stand idle. Observations made from a safe area can form the basis of the investigation that will follow. The properly trained investigator should begin accumulating information long before he collects his first item of physical evidence.

Among things to be considered early in the incident are the identity of the victims, witnesses, bystanders, and other emergency response personnel who are at the scene. All of these individuals may provide valuable information in the subsequent investigation and their presence at the scene as well as their activity should be properly documented for future reference. The use of video and still photography throughout the incident to record the people at and near the scene should be considered. In addition to images recorded by law enforcement personnel, photos and video recorded by news personnel and private citizens should also be reviewed. Security cameras that may have recorded the incident should also be examined.

Figure 6. Emergency response personnel using Level A protection practice packing a dissemination device in an overpack drum to prevent the further spread of contamination.

Consideration should be given to the use of instant or digital cameras to record dissemination devices or other obvious physical evidence. These instant photos may be used to show other personnel the type of evidence to be on the look out for during the search of the crime scene for additional devices and evidence. These photos may be of particular value in the event that an explosive device is found. If the device is destroyed in the course of rendering it safe, some record will exist for immediate reference. It is also possible to transmit photographic images to specialists (i.e., bomb technicians) who are not at the actual scene. This procedure will allow for their input and guidance.

Physical evidence that may have been left at the scene must also be preserved. Dissemination devices may be found in relatively intact condition unless the use of explosives was employed to spread the hazardous substances. Responders should look for damaged packages, broken containers, and other items that seem out of place and therefore suspicious. Personnel should be trained to identify and isolate potential evidence without actually touching it or getting too close to it. Besides the danger of impairing its evidentiary value, these items may still be dangerous and should only be handled by properly trained and equipped personnel (see Figure 6).

Items left behind at the scene by the terrorist may contain valuable evidence such as fingerprints, fibers, and other items that may link them with the crime. Unlike a fire or explosion scene where much of the evidence is destroyed or contaminated, the aftermath of a WMD attack may leave an even greater wealth of valuable evidence.

Traditional evidence such as footprints, tire tracks, and other similar items should not be overlooked. The possible existence of evidence such as this is another reason for stressing the importance of preserving the integrity of the crime scene from the very beginning.

While it is likely that evidence will be lost or destroyed in the process of rescuing and treating the victims of a WMD attack, a significant amount of evidence may be preserved by simply limiting access to the scene to only those absolutely necessary for lifesaving efforts.

The clothing and outer apparel worn by the victims should be gathered and maintained as evidence until it can be examined by trained investigative personnel (see Chapter 16, Sampling for Chemical, Biological and Radiological Evidence). These items should be treated as being hazardous until it can be proven otherwise by proper testing and examination. Law enforcement personnel should be immediately assigned to the hospitals that are receiving the victims of a WMD incident for a variety of reasons including gathering the clothing of the victims as well as obtaining preliminary identification information. Personnel assigned to the hospitals should be aware of the fact that the terrorist(s) may be among the victims. Ultimately, investigative personnel will assume the evidence collection role. They will accompany the victims through the autopsy stage, if necessary, in order to insure that physical evidence is not overlooked.

SIGNS AND SYMPTOMS

Personnel must be aware of the signs and symptoms that may be exhibited by a victim of a WMD attack. These may be the only indication that a WMD incident is underway. It is also important for their own safety that they recognize the signs and symptoms and are able to diagnose their own exposure.

Each of the various chemical and biological agents present its own set of signs and symptoms. Responders must first understand the difference between signs and symptoms. Signs are indicators that can be observed by the responder without necessarily communicating with the victim. Vomiting, seizures, coughing, and drooling are an example of signs of exposure to a chemical agent.

Symptoms are sensations that are experienced by the victim and must be expressed by the victim because they may not be readily visible to another person. Symptoms may include dizziness, vision impairment, headaches, and nausea. Note that vomiting is a sign while nausea is a symptom.

It should be noted that the onset of signs and symptoms is dependent upon the type of material employed as well as such variables as the strength of the substance, the duration of the exposure, and the medical history of the victim. Some victims, such as the elderly and children, may be more susceptible to the attack than others because of their physical condition. Some chemical agents may begin to have an effect within seconds after a victim is exposed, while some biological agents may require an incubation period of several days before signs and symptoms manifest themselves.

The following chart provides a listing of some common chemical agents and their associated signs and symptoms as well as the physical characteristics of the material. Reference is also made to the appropriate *Guide in the North American Emergency Response Guidebook* (NAERG) (see page 19).[7]

The NAERG will provide quick actions to be taken in the event of an incident involving the above-described agents. This manual is meant to provide guidance for the first emergency response personnel on the scene of a hazardous materials incident and includes information on evacuation distances, first aid procedures, and other protective actions.

With the exception of some relatively fast-acting toxins, an exposure to a biological agent will not usually result in the immediate onset of signs and symptoms. The period of time between when a victim is subjected to a biological agent and when the signs and symptoms appear is referred to as the incubation period. It is during this time that the agent is reproducing in the body and defeating its natural defense systems. It should also be noted that the incubation period for a given biological agent may be dose related.

Healthcare providers will most likely be the first to become aware of the possibility that a WMD incident involving a biological weapon has occurred. When considering a patient's status, epidemiological principles should be employed to assess the possibility that the condition may be the result of an act of terrorism. The following features may alert healthcare providers that a bioterrorism attack may have taken place:

- A normally healthy population experiences a rapidly increasing incidence of disease (within hours or days).
- Within a short period of time, an epidemic curve that rises and falls.
- An unusual increase in the number of people seeking treatment with fever, respiratory, and gastrointestinal complaints.
- A single locale producing a significant number of patients.
- Large numbers of rapidly fatal cases.
- A patient with a disease that is relatively uncommon and has the potential to be used in a terrorist event such as pulmonary anthrax, tularemia, and plague.[8]

Law enforcement should meet with representatives of the local healthcare system to develop a level of awareness on the part of the healthcare system with regard to the recognition of a WMD incident. The healthcare providers should be aware of the above-described factors and know how and when to report their suspicions to law enforcement. With regard to a bioterrorism incident, medical personnel will usually be in the best position to uncover the early signs of an attack.

Some jurisdictions have set up a monitoring system that reviews the cases handled by the local emergency medical system and the hospitals or other medical treatment facilities. This may take the form of daily or weekly reports that are reviewed for the factors described previously. Cases handled by the medical examiners or coroners office should also be reviewed and may be a valuable source of information. Interaction

Common Name	*NAERG Guide #*	*Signs & Symptoms*	*Physical Characteristics*	*Agent Type*
Tabun (GA) Sarin (GB) Soman (GD) VX	153	Pinpoint pupils Dimness of vision Difficulty breathing Runny nose, salivation Vomiting, incontinence Convulsions	Colorless or light colored liquid at normal temperature G-agents slightly less volatile than water V-agents as volatile as motor oil	Nerve
Mustard H,HD,HN	153	Reddening of skin Blisters Eye damage and pain Airway irritation and coughing	Garlic odor H, HD freeze at 57 F Volatile at room temperature	Vesicant (Blister Agent)
Lewisite (L)	153	Immediate pain and skin irritation	Oily, colorless liquid Geranium smell More volatile than mustard	Vesicant
Phosgene Oxime (CX)	153	Immediate burning Weal-like skin lesions Eye and airway irritation and damage	Solid below 95 F, can vaporize	Vesicant
Phosgene (CG) Chlorine (CL)	125 124	Eye and airway irritation Dizziness Tightness of chest Delayed pulmonary edema	Rapidly evaporating liquid Odor of newly-mown hay Gas at normal temperature	Choking
Hydrogen Cyanide (AC) Cyanogen Chloride (CK)	117 125	Cherry red skin or lips Dizziness Nausea and vomiting Headache Convulsions	Rapidly evaporating liquids	Blood

with the medical system as a way of detecting a bioterrorism event at its earliest possible stages should be included in the planning process when preparing to respond to a WMD incident (see Chapter 10,

Planning Considerations).

The following chart lists some biological agents and their signs and symptoms. The possible routes of entry are also listed.[9,10]

Agent/Disease	Exposure Route	Signs & Symptoms	Treatment
Anthrax	Skin, Direct contact, Respiratory	Fever, malaise, fatigue, cough, respiratory distress	Antibiotics before symptoms develop
Plague (Yersinia pestis)	Vector, Respiratory	High fever, chills, headache, respiratory difficulty	Antibiotics
Q Fever (Coxiella burnetli)	Vector, Respiratory	Fever, cough, chest pain (pleuritic)	Antibiotics
Smallpox	Respiratory	Malaise, fever, rigors, vomiting, headache, backache, lesions	Supportive
Viral Hemorrhagic Fevers Ebola, Marbug, Lassa, Rift Valley, Dengue	Direct contact, Vector, Respiratory	Easy bleeding, hypotension, shock, flushing of face and chest, edema, malaise, headache, vomiting, diarrhea	Supportive Antiviral therapy
Venezuelan Equine Encephalitis (VEE)	Respiratory, Vector	Malaise, spiking fevers, rigors, severe headache, vomiting, nausea, cough, sore throat, diarrhea, photophobia	Supportive
Tularemia	Respiratory, Vector	Local ulcer, fever, chills, headache, malaise, fever	Antibiotics
Botulinum Neurotoxins	Digestive system, Respiratory	General weakness, dizziness, dry mouth and throat, blurred vision, respiratory failure	Antitoxin Ventilatory assistance
Ricin	Digestive system, Respiratory	Weakness, fever, cough, hypothermia, hypotension, cardiovascular collapse	Supportive Symptomatic

Because exposure to a biological agent may not be obvious to personnel and victims at a scene, it may be difficult to convince people of the need for decontamination and the possible need for prophylactic medical treatment. It may be necessary to recruit the assistance of medical experts to explain the need for these procedures. For many of these agents, if treatment is withheld until the signs and symptoms manifest themselves, the health damage is irreversible.

Exposure to radiological materials will also go undetected in the initial stages of the incident. Radiological contamination is colorless, odorless, and tasteless and is not detectable by the human senses as a chemical exposure may be. Radiological detection and monitoring instruments will be necessary to detect the presence of these materials and to assess the level of exposure and danger.

RECOGNITION OF MATERIALS

Law enforcement personnel should become familiar with the chemicals, otherwise known as precursors, that may be used to develop or manufacture chemical weapons. The presence of one or more of these items in a non-traditional environment may indicate the presence of illegal activity.

For example, finding hydrogen fluoride and phosphorus trichloride in a private auto or in a residential setting should arouse suspicions. These materials may be used to produce the nerve agents sarin and soman (see Table1).

Table 1

Chemical Agent Precursors[i]	C.A.S. #	CW Agent
Arsenic Trichloride	7784-34-1[†]	Arsine Lewisite Adamsite (DM)
Benzilic Acid	76-93-7	BZ
2-chloroethanol	107-07-3	Sulfur Mustard (HD) Nitrogen Mustard (HN1)
2-Chloro-N,N-diisopropylethylamine	96-79-7	VX VS
Diethyl ethylphosphonate	78-38-6	Ethyl Sarin (GE)
Diethyl methylphosphonite	15715-41-0	VX
Diethyl N.N- dimethyl Phosphoramidate	2404-03-7	Tabun (GA)

Diethyl phosphite	762-04-9	Sarin (GB) Soman (GD) GF
Diisopropylaminoethanethiol	5842-07-9	VX VS
Dimethylamine	124-40-3†	Tabun(GA)
Dimethylamine HCI	506-59-2	Tabun (GA)
Dimethyl ethylphosphonate	6163-75-3	Ethyl Sarin (GE)
Dimethyl methylphosphonate	756-79-6	Sarin (GB) Soman (GD) GF
Dimethylphosphite	868-85-9	Sarin (GB) Soman (GD) GF
Ethylphosphonous difluoride	430-78-4	Ethyl Sarin (GE)
Hydrogen fluoride	7664-39-3	Sarin (GB) Soman (GD) GF
Methyl benzilate	76-89-1	BZ
Methylphosphonate difluoride	676-99-3	Sarin (GB) GF Soman (GD)
Methl phosphonic dichloride	676-97-1	Sarin (GB) Soman (GD) GF
Methylphosphonous dichloride	676-83-5	VX
Methylphosphonous difluoride	753-59-3	Sarin (GB) Soman (GD) VX GF
N,N-diisopropyl -2-aminoethanol	96-80-0	VX
N.N-diisopropyl -2-aminoethyl chloride	96-79-7	VX
O-ethyl methylphosphonothioic acid (EMPTA)	18005-40-8	VX

O-ethyl-2-diisopopyl aminoethyl methylphosphonate (QL)	57856-11-8	VX
Phosphorous oxychloride	10025-87-3[†]	Tabun (GA)
Phosphorous pentachloride	10026-13-8	Tabun GA
Phosphorus pentasulfide	1314-80-3[†]	VX
Phosphorus trichloride	7719-12-2[†]	VG – salt process Tabun (GA) – salt process Sarin (GB) – salt process Soman (GD) – salt process GF – salt process
Pinacolone	75-97-8	Soman GD
Pinacolyl alcohol	464-07-3	Soman (GD)
Potassium cyanide	151-50-8[†]	Tabun GA & hydrodgen
Potassium Fluoride	7789-2-3	Sarin (GB) Soman (GD) GF
3-Quinuclidone	1619-34-7	BZ
Sodium bifluoride	1333-83-1[†]	Sarin GB& Soman GD& GF
Sodium cyanide	143-33-9[†]	Tabun GA & Hydrogen Cyanide, Cyanogen chloride
Sodium sulfide	1313-82-2	VX
Sulfur dichloride	10545-99-0	Sulfur Mustard HD
Sulfur monochloride (sulfur chloride)	10025-67-9 (12771083)[†]	Sulfur Mustard HD
Thiodiglycol	111-48-8	Sulfur Mustard (HD)
Triethanolamine	102-71-6	Nitrogen Mustard & HN3
Triethanolamine Hydrochloride	637-39-8	Nitrogen Mustard

[1]First Responder Chem-Bio Handbook: Practical Manual for First Responders   [†]40 CFR 302.4: Hazardous Substance List

Finding laboratory equipment in a location might arouse suspicion. Chemical containers, laboratory glassware, and other items involved in the chemical process should be considered suspicious when found outside their normal environment. Extreme caution must be exercised if any of these items or materials are found. Many chemicals may be classified as being ***Immediately Dangerous to Life and Health (IDLH)*** and should only be handled by those with adequate training and equipment.

The same can be said for the presence of materials used to assemble improvised explosive devices. Electronic components, gunpowder, power sources, and timing devices may be evidence of materials being gathered to create a bomb. Commercial explosives, blasting caps, and other such materials may also be used in the creation of an improvised explosive device or a dissemination device. The personal background of the individual who is in possession of the materials and the circumstances may either explain their presence or cause further investigation. Finding pieces of steel pipe in a handyman's workshop may be under-standable while finding the same items in the possession of a high school student may not (see Figures 7, 8 & 9).

Military items such as hand grenades, mortar shells, and other devices, usually referred to as ordnance, may also be involved in the development of a WMD device. These items may be used as a source of explosives or they may be modified for use as a dissemination device. Even items that are designated as "training" devices can be dangerous if mishandled. Military ordnance should only be handled by bomb technicians or military personnel. In most cases, military ***EOD (Explosive Ordnance Disposal)*** personnel will respond to handle dangerous military items.

Items that indicate the presence of biological materials may also arouse suspicions. Petri dishes, incubators, and other laboratory equipment associated with biological sciences may be cause for concern based on the given circumstances. Law enforcement personnel should note their observations and forward the information to the appropriate investigative unit or agency.

Radiological materials and their posse-

Figure 7. Black powder is a commonly available explosive material that can be use to create an improvised explosive device (IED).

sion are highly regulated. The presence of these materials in other than a location such as a medical facility or research facility should be cause for concern. Possession of radiological material by anyone not authorized should warrant an immediate investigation.

The possession of personal protective equipment or scientific instruments by those without a legitimate need for these items may be considered suspicious. A subject who possesses chemical protective clothing, air-purifying respirators, or radiological monitoring instruments should be worthy of at least a cursory follow-up investigation. These items may be possessed for legitimate reasons and merely having them is not a crime; the person who possesses them and the circumstances of the possession, however, may indicate a potential WMD plot.

Figure 8. Law enforcement personnel should be aware of the fact that explosives come in a variety of sizes, shapes and packages.

Figure 9. Electric blasting caps may be used in building improvised explosive devices as well as dissemination devices for a WMD.

RECOGNITION OF DEVICES

The need to recognize the devices used in weapons of mass destruction must exist before, during, or after the actual event. The training in this area must be updated and reinforced on a regular basis as new intelligence becomes available and more is learned about the techniques actually being utilized by terrorists around the world and locally. Traditionally, law enforcement personnel have been trained to recognize improvised explosive devices. This training must now be expanded to include WMD devices and materials.

Law enforcement personnel may be called to a scene before the device has functioned. This may be in response to a threat, a warning, or as a result of a suspicious device or package having been discovered. Regardless of what has brought them to the scene, they must realize how dangerous these devices may be. The injury inflicted by exposure to a weapon of mass destruction may be fatal.

Personnel must be taught to recognize the above-described devices. Additionally, they must be familiar with the concepts involved in disseminating hazardous substances so that they might recognize a technique being employed by a terrorist for the first time. For example, they must be aware of the desire to distribute the material in an aerosol state, not just the fact that a garden sprayer may be a dissemination device. This will help them to be on the lookout for more than just previously identified items. Items such as containers, gas cylinders, and laboratory equipment may all be considered suspicious under the proper set of circumstances.

The search for a weapon of mass destruction should be conducted in a fashion similar to a search for an improvised explosive device. Personnel conducting the search should be instructed to look for items that are out of place or otherwise unaccounted for in the area in which they are located. People who are familiar with the location and would therefore be in the best position to determine what belongs and what doesn't belong should conduct area searches. Personnel involved in such a search should be instructed not to touch or otherwise handle or disturb any item that they consider suspicious. This should be left to the specialists who have been trained to handle these items in as safe a manner as possible.

When available, the use of detection devices such as canines, chemical agent detectors, direct reading instruments, or radiological detection equipment may be of great value. Personnel must understand that in most cases these tools are limited to detecting specific items such as explosives, a specified chemical, or nuclear material. The fact that these particular items are not found should not be used to classify a building or other search site as being "safe." It should be reported that "nothing was found" during the search.

The successful use of detection devices depends on the training and skill of the person employing the device. The best explosive detection dog available is only as good as the handler he is working for. The best chemical detection device on the market will not be completely effective if the person using it has not been adequately trained in its use. The devices themselves have certain limitations that must be known and understood by the user in order for them to be utilized in the safest and most effective manner.

Personnel involved in searching for a suspected weapon of mass destruction should be given the following instructions:

• Do not touch or otherwise disturb anything they consider to be suspicious; secure the immediate area and call for expert assistance.

• Do not become complacent while searching.

• Do not stop searching or become less vigilant when a suspicious item is located; there may very well be additional devices.

• Those conducting the search should not use devices such as radios and cellular phones.

• The search should be conducted in a methodical manner so that no area is over-looked.

• Do not overlook obvious locations where a device may be located.

Personnel must also be trained to recognize a device if found "during" an incident. Upon arrival at the scene or in the course of assessing the incident, they may come across a device that is still functioning. For example, they may discover a package that is still leaking or an aerosol device that is still in operation. They must avoid these, note their location and description, and be alert for other devices of a similar nature. Other responders should be made aware of its presence and properly warned to stay away. No attempt should be made to render safe such an item by other than properly trained personnel. Move any victims away from the device rather than attempting to move the device.

Personnel conducting an investigation after an incident has occurred must be alert for additional dissemination devices (see Figure 10). Investigators may come across devices that were overlooked in the chaos of the incident and that may still pose a significant threat. Again, an item should be isolated until qualified personnel can examine it. At this stage of the incident, time is no longer as vital as when victims are being evacuated and treated. The scene can then be secured until it is made as safe as possible.

Emergency medical personnel should be aware that items and devices may be found on "victims" that may be dangerous as well as being of significant evidentiary value. It is possible that emergency medical personnel may end up treating one of the terrorists who may have become a victim of his own device. They must also be reminded of the potential for secondary devices to exist within the confines of the crime scene.

Figure 10. This aerosol dispenser, originally manufactured to disperse tear gas in a crowd control operation, could be modified to disseminate WMD agents.

Chapter 3

FIRST RESPONDER ACTIONS

When discussing the actions to be taken by first responders, regardless of their occupation or field of expertise, certain priorities must be established and maintained throughout the incident. The first and foremost priority is the protection and preservation of life. Responders must be taught that their lives and physical well-being are included in this priority and must be protected. The protection of the environment and property is secondary. The protection of human life must always take precedence.

If an incident is not life-threatening, emergency personnel should not create a life-threatening situation by placing themselves in unnecessary danger. For example, if an improvised explosive device has been located and the area has been secured and evacuated, the incident will not become life-threatening until someone approaches the device. This should be the responsibility of a trained bomb technician who will use whatever tools and techniques are available to protect himself.

RECOGNITION

As stated earlier, it is extremely important that first responders be trained to recognize the existence of a WMD incident. Their safety and the safety of any subsequent response personnel will depend on their ability to recognize the incident and be aware of the hazards that may be associated with it. They must recognize the limitations of what actions they can take based on the availability of protective equipment. They must be trained to control the scene as quickly and effectively as possible in the early stages in order to keep the materials involved from spreading and affecting even more potential victims.

Because the severity of a WMD incident may not be readily apparent, responders must be taught to err on the side of caution and safety when securing the scene. For example, when establishing an inner perimeter or what will be known as the "hot zone," responders should take control of as large of an area as possible. If it later is determined that the danger is less than originally thought, it is easier to reduce the hot zone than to expand it once resources have begun to be put in place. When a question exists as to what level of personal protective equipment is necessary; the safer approach is to go with a higher level.

The previously discussed topics including dissemination devices, signs and symptoms of exposure to WMD materials, the identification of precursor materials are all factors that should be familiar to first responders so that they may be able to recognize a WMD incident as early in the response as possible. The earlier the scene is secured and the incident is identified as a WMD incident, the more likely that injuries will be reduced and evidence will be preserved.

NOTIFICATION

At the point when first responders begin to suspect that they may be dealing with a WMD incident, they must know what notifications need to be made. These will usually begin within the responder's own agency and will either be done by the responder himself or via his agency's communications system. Individuals and agencies that will be notified during the course of the incident should be addressed in the pre-planning stage (see Chapter 10, Planning Considerations).

Initial notifications should include those trained personnel who will be able to determine if, in fact, the incident involves a WMD. This will most likely include a unit capable of handling hazardous materials, or in the case of explosives, improvised explosive devices. The units that can meet these needs should be identified beforehand and their capabilities and responsibilities delineated. These units should be included in the planning process to insure that the proper units are used to the best of their abilities.

PUTTING THE "PLAN" INTO ACTION

First responding law enforcement personnel must be familiar with the response plan for their agency and know how to activate it. In many cases, this will be the simple matter of making the above-described notifications from the field and initiating protective actions such as evacuation and securing the scene.

SCENE SECURITY

When dealing with ordinary improvised explosive devices (IED's), the rule of thumb for initial isolation of the device is 300 feet in all directions and under or behind cover. In the event the device is suspected to be larger (i.e., a vehicle bomb), a greater area would be evacuated and isolated. For pre-planning purposes and for reference during an incident, there are informational sources available to provide estimates of the harm that may be caused by explosives based upon the type and amount (see Figure 11).

The rules are different, however, when dealing with a hazardous device that contains suspected chemical, biological, or radiological materials. When determining

Weapons of Mass Destruction

the initial isolation area for a suspected WMD, the initial area should be 700 feet in all directions for incidents involving "small packages" (i.e., less than 55 gallons).[11] This is the recommended action to be taken when faced with an incident involving an unknown poisonous material. As more information is developed regarding the nature and identity of the hazardous substances involved, this book may be used as a reference to either expand or reduce the initial isolation area.

The isolation area may be reduced if it is believed that the material can be adequately contained and that it will not be released into the atmosphere. Specialists, upon reviewing the available information and intelligence, should make this determination.

The initial isolation area will be referred to as the ***Hot Zone*** or "Restricted Zone."[12] Access to this area will be limited to those

emergency or investigative personnel who are properly equipped with protective equipment and have a legitimate need to be in this area. This would include the need to rescue injured victims and the collection of evidence during the investigation. If a suspected WMD device is located before it has activated and released its hazardous materials, access to the hot zone will usually be limited to those personnel absolutely necessary to render the device safe. This entry will usually consist of bomb technicians, hazardous materials technicians, or a combination of these specialists. The use of a robot may also be employed to render the device safe. Regardless of the tactics employed to render the device safe, the number of personnel in the hot zone must be kept to an absolute minimum to reduce the number of people at risk (See figure 12).

Immediately beyond the hot zone will be

ATF	VEHICLE DESCRIPTION	MAXIMUM EXPLOSIVES CAPACITY	LETHAL AIR BLAST RANGE	MINIMUM EVACUATION DISTANCE	FALLING GLASS HAZARD
	COMPACT SEDAN	500 Pounds 227 Kilos (In Trunk)		1,500 Feet 457 Meters	1,250 Feet 381 Meters
	FULL SIZE SEDAN	1,000 Pounds 455 Kilos (In Trunk)		1,750 Feet 534 Meters	1,750 Feet 534 Meters
	PASSENGER VAN OR CARGO VAN	4,000 Pounds 1,818 Kilos		2,750 Feet 838 Meters	2,750 Feet 838 Meters
	SMALL BOX VAN (14 FT BOX)	10,000 Pounds 4,545 Kilos		3,750 Feet 1,143 Meters	3,750 Feet 1,143 Meters
	BOX VAN OR WATER/FUEL TRUCK	30,000 Pounds 13,636 Kilos		6,500 Feet 1,982 Meters	6,500 Feet 1,982 Meters
	SEMI-TRAILER	60,000 Pounds 27,273 Kilos		7,000 Feet 2,134 Meters	7,000 Feet 2,134 Meters

Figure 11. Decisions regarding evacuation distances are made based on factors including the size of the explosive device and reference to established data bases such as this information provided by the Bureau of Alcohol, Tobacco, and Firearms.

the area referred to as the ***Warm Zone***. This area may also be referred to as the "Limited Access Zone"[13] or the "Contamination Reduction Zone." Access to this area will also be limited to properly equipped, trained, and necessary personnel. The decontamination process will take place in this zone. Entrance and exit corridors must be laid out to ensure that those entering the hot zone are properly documented upon entering and exiting the crime scene and to ensure that they are properly decontaminated (see Chapter 6, Handling the Victims). The size of this zone will depend upon the extent of the decontamination process that must be employed as well as the hazardous materials involved. Within this zone, an effort will be made to set up the decontamination line in an area that is upwind and uphill from the hot zone.

The area outside the warm zone will be referred to as the ***Cold Zone***, "Support Zone," or "Safe Zone." It is in this area that the command post will be located, as well as other operations necessary to support the operations taking place in the hot zone and the warm zone. This may include the staging area, the media area, medical facilities, and other sites as required by the nature and magnitude of the particular incident. This area is also restricted to those necessary to the incident. Law enforcement personnel securing the outer perimeter should control access to the cold zone. The Incident Commander, with input from technical personnel, should establish the criteria for entry into the cold zone. Because the incident must be treated as a crime scene, all subjects entering the cold zone should be identified and documented. The documentation should be repeated as a subject passes from the cold zone to the warm zone and eventually the hot zone (see Appendix 4).

As with the decontamination line, the activities in the cold zone should be set up in an area that is upwind and uphill from the

Figure 12. The perimeter must be secured as soon as practical to preserve evidence.

source of the hazard. The atmosphere and weather conditions must be monitored throughout the incident to ensure that the cold zone remains in a safe location. This will protect the personnel operating in this area who will not be utilizing personal protective equipment.

After the initial isolation area has been established, the protective action area must be calculated and determined based on the information available and by the guidance provided by the North American Emergency Response Guidebook. This is the area downwind of the incident in which people will be endangered should there be a release of hazardous materials into the atmosphere.[14] The area to be protected downwind for a small (i.e., less than 55 gallons) release in the daytime will be 1.2 miles; the same release at night will require an area of 5.5 miles.[15] These areas may be reduced if the device can be adequately contained in a building or other location that will keep the material from being released into the open atmosphere (see Figure 13).

Once the endangered area is determined, a decision must be made with regard to the people within this area who may be in danger. In many cases, the best course of action will be to evacuate those in danger to a safe area until the danger can be neutralized or until it passes. For example, if an explosive device is located, people should be evacuated to a safe area. How far to evacuate people from an explosive hazard will depend on several factors including the size and estimated strength of the device as well as the location of the device and any natural cover provided. The natural cover may include any substantial buildings or the topography of the land. The presence of gas storage tanks or other hazards may also effect the area to be evacuated.

Before an *evacuation* is undertaken, officials should ascertain that the area to be occupied by the evacuees is safe. This may

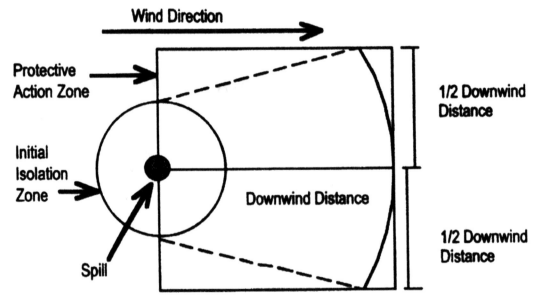

Figure 13. This diagram found in the North American Emergency Response Guidebook is used to help calculate and plot the downwind hazard area in the event of a release of a hazardous substance into the atmosphere.

necessitate sweeping the area for explosives or other hazards, as well as providing security for those being moved into this area. Care must also be taken not to expose the evacuees to additional danger by moving them passed dangerous items or exposing them to other hazards such as gunfire.

A viable alternative to evacuation may be the process known as ***sheltering in place*** or "protection in place." There may be situations where people are actually safer if they remain in a secure environment rather than moving them through a dangerous area or atmosphere as part of an evacuation process. Sheltering in place involves advising people who are located in an area near chemical, radiological, or biological contamination to remain in place until the hazard passes or dissipates. This may be necessary when the area to be evacuated includes a facility such as a hospital or nursing home that would be extremely difficult to evacuate with existing resources.

If the decision is made to shelter in place, those involved must be advised to shut off the ventilation system within the building. If any heating and air conditioning systems involve bringing in outside air, they should be shut down. Emergency response officials must also establish and maintain communications with a competent person within the building. Occupants should also be advised to remain away from the windows. Keep in mind that the interiors of vehicles will offer only limited protection from WMD hazards.[16]

Evacuation and shelter in place decisions should be made based on input from technical experts such as bomb and hazardous materials technicians. Factors such as the presence or absence of wind and the potential for the agent to mix with the atmosphere must be considered. Weather conditions will need to be considered in the determination of where and how far to move peo-ple. Existing weather conditions at the scene must be considered when making these types of decisions. It should be noted that the weather at the scene may differ significantly from the information obtained from a weather source away from the incident (i.e., a nearby airport). Whatever course of action is decided upon, law enforcement will play an important role in controlling exit routes, notifying the public, and providing security for evacuated areas.

The following are some of the factors that should be considered in determining the protective actions to be taken in the event of a release or threatened release of a hazardous substance as a result of a WMD incident:

• The materials involved:
  • Degree of hazard to health.
  • Amount of the product involved.
  • The ability to contain or control the release.
  • The rate of the movement of the vapor.
• The population at risk:
  • The location in question.
  • The number of people potentially at risk.
  • The time available to evacuate or shelter in place.
  • The ability to actually control the evacuation or sheltering in place.
  • The type and availability of buildings and other structures.
  • Special populations and considerations such as hospitals, schools, nursing homes, etc.
• Weather conditions at the site:
  • The effect of the weather on vapor and cloud movement.
  • The potential for the weather to change.
  • The effect of the weather on evacuation or sheltering in place.[17]

When using the NAERG evacuation tables, it should be noted that the tables show the distances for the first thirty minutes after the release of the product into the atmosphere. These distances may increase with time. Many HazMat teams and environmental agencies have programs available to plot the movement of chemicals in the atmosphere. These may be valuable in determining evacuation and isolation distances and areas. They can also be used to determine required protective actions that may need to be taken prior to the actual release of the hazardous material.

WHO WILL BE ALLOWED IN WHAT AREAS

Access to the hot zone will be limited to personnel who are properly trained and equipped to a level that will protect them from the known or suspected hazards. During the earliest stages of the incident, unprotected personnel may find themselves working in a contaminated area while assisting injured victims and securing the area. They must be removed to a safe area as soon as possible and decontaminated as necessary.

Once trained personnel have arrived on the scene, they may eventually enter the hot zone to gather evidence, render safe any additional devices, contain released materials, and/or perform other tasks necessary to bring the incident to a safe conclusion. In all instances, the number of responders entering the hot zone should be limited to the minimum necessary to do the job safely and properly.

The hot zone should be controlled like any other crime scene of this magnitude. All movement in and out of the hot zone should be documented for later reference. Access and egress should be through one control point at which those entering the hot zone are recorded including their time in and out. When personnel are using breathing apparatus with a limited air supply, the Safety Officer will also be involved in keeping track of the time they spend in the hot zone.

DOCUMENT PERSONNEL AT THE SCENE

All law enforcement personnel at the scene should be recorded in an incident log. Many departments already have forms that are used for this purpose (see Figure 14). Once a sense of order and command is established at the scene, all responding personnel should be directed to a central reporting site (i.e., command post or staging area) where they will be "logged in" and their presence documented.

When an incident involves the presence or suspected presence of hazardous materials, it is essential that a strict system of accountability be employed for all emergency response personnel at the scene. This will help determine who may have been exposed or contaminated. It will also assist in determining which individuals are in need of critical incident stress debriefing. It may also assist in identifying those individuals who may possess additional information that investigative personnel may be unaware of. Strict accountability is also necessary for the safety of all those at the scene in the event there is a second event such as a building collapse, detonation, or activation of a secondary device. This procedure will assist in the subsequent search and rescue efforts.

SCENE LOG

LOG INITIATED		LOG TERMINATED	
DATE:	TIME:	DATE:	TIME:
CC#:	Command:	Pct/Occ:	Sector:
Report Date:		Date/ Time of Inc:	
Victim's Last Name:		Victim's Address: (#/ St./Town/ State/ Zip)	
First Name:	M.I.		
Incident:		I/L (#/ St./ Town/ State/ Zip)	
Recorder's Name/Rank/Shield Command			

NOTE: LIST ANY CHANGES IN THE RECORDERS ON THE LOG

Date	Time	Last Name	First Name	Title/Rank Shield	Unit	Cmd. Name	Agency/ Affil.	Remarks

Reporting Officer's Signature	Supervisor's Signature

PDCS-1060   Page _____ of _____ Pages

53-0574::9/94

Figure 14. A pre-printed form may be used to document personnel at the scene of a WMD incident.

Chapter 4

PERSONAL PROTECTION

There are several ways that hazardous materials may harm an individual at the scene of a WMD incident. In order to determine the proper methods of protection to be employed by response personnel, it is necessary to have an understanding of these types of threats. HazMat response personnel use the acronym TRACEM[18] that includes the following:

• Thermal
• Radiological
• Asphyxiation
• Chemical
• Etiological
• Mechanical

Thermal harm refers to injuries caused by temperature extremes. This may include either extreme heat from an explosion or incendiary fire or extreme cold from contact with a cryogenic liquid (i.e., liquid oxygen).

Radiological harm refers to injury caused by contact with (or exposure to) alpha particles, beta particles, or gamma rays. This may occur if the WMD incident involves the use of radiological material.

Asphyxiation will occur when there is not enough oxygen in the air to support life. This type of harm is usually associated with an enclosed or confined space in which a hazardous material such as carbon dioxide exists and displaces enough oxygen to create a hazardous atmosphere. This may be a hazard faced by investigators searching a confined space (i.e., sewer system) for evidence after a WMD incident.

Chemical harm is caused when there is exposure to or contact with hazardous chemicals. This can be caused by corrosive materials (i.e., sulfuric acid) being added to the contents of an incendiary device or by toxic materials such as "nerve gas."

Etiological harm is caused by an exposure to a biological organism. This type of harm comes from disease-causing organisms such as bacteria and viruses. It may also originate from toxins that are derived from living organisms.

Mechanical harm is caused by physical trauma associated with a WMD detonation. This may include injuries from explosives (i.e., wounds caused by shrapnel) or the damage to internal organs that may result from the blast pressure wave caused by an explosion. Many of the victims of the 1995 Oklahoma City bombing received injuries that would be classified as "mechanical harm."

PROTECTIVE ACTIONS

The basic principles of protection from the TRACEM types of harm include **Time**, **Distance**, and **Shielding**. These principles were originally taught with regard to protective actions for incidents involving radioactive materials. As hazardous materials training evolved, they were adapted for use in HazMat response. They can be easily adapted to most incidents involving the use or suspected use of a WMD device.

Time refers to the principle of limiting exposure to the item or device that may cause harm. The less you are exposed in terms of time, the less likely you are to be harmed. The less time a bomb technician spends in close proximity to the hazardous device, the less likely he or she is to be injured by it. Conversely, the more time a person is exposed to (or in contact with) a hazardous substance, the more likely they are to be injured.

Distance involves staying as far away from the materials that may cause harm as possible. The exclusionary zones that have been described are an example of using distance to provide a basic level of protection from potential harm. The further you are from the danger, the safer you will be.

Shielding results from placing something between you and the hazard. A ballistic vest used by tactical personnel who may encounter gunfire is an example of shielding. The personal protective equipment, including chemical protective clothing and respiratory protection used by HazMat response personnel, is an example of the shielding that is likely to be used at a WMD incident. Using a vehicle to protect personnel from the effects of an improvised explosive device is another example of shielding.

ROUTES OF ENTRY

In order to determine what type of protective equipment is necessary for a given incident, responders must consider how the toxic or hazardous materials may enter their system and thus cause illness or injury. The four most common "routes of entry" include inhalation, ingestion, absorption, and injection.

The most frequent route of exposure is inhalation. The toxic material will enter the victim through the normal course of breathing when the material is present in the air. The material is then transferred into the blood via the lungs in the same manner that oxygen is absorbed. As discussed earlier, many WMD agents must be aerosolized in order to distribute them thus making inhalation a primary danger to victims and responders alike. Biological agents in particular

present an inhalation hazard. For this reason, dry products are considered to be a greater hazard than wet products.

Ingestion occurs when a toxic material enters via an oral route. This may take place when someone eats or drinks a substance that has been contaminated. This may be a primary concern when biological agents are used or in the case of radiological contamination of water, milk, and food supplies. Other acts, such as biting one's nails, holding a pen or pencil in one's mouth, or using one's teeth to remove a glove may also result in ingestion of a toxic material. In order to avoid these types of exposures, proper decontamination and personal hygiene practices must be followed.

Toxic materials may also enter the body via absorption. Materials that come in contact with unprotected skin may eventually pass this barrier and enter the bloodstream. The physical state of the material (i.e., solid or liquid) will have a significant effect on its ability to be absorbed, as well as, the speed with which it is absorbed. Other aspects of the material, including its ability to adhere to the skin and its chemical makeup, will determine how much of the material and how quickly the material is absorbed. The exposure location on the body, how much skin area has been exposed, and the length of time of the exposure will also be significant.

The eyes are very sensitive to exposure to chemical agents and biological materials. Responders should be aware of the potential for hazardous substances to be absorbed via the eyes and take appropriate precautions (i.e., protective glasses or shields).

The most rapid and direct route of entry is injection. In cases such as these, the toxic material is injected directly into the bloodstream. This may be caused by the intentional use of a dart or hypodermic syringe. It may also be caused by a subject receiving a cut or puncture wound. This may be a result of a cut caused by a contaminated object.[19] The spread of a biological agent via a vector (i.e., infected insect) that bites the victim is another example of this type of direct entry.

When examining the type of hazard that may be presented by a particular WMD agent, personnel must be aware that a toxic material may present more than one type of hazard and thus attack more than one route of entry. For example, a mustard agent may attack the skin as well as the respiratory system. Therefore, more than one type of protection may be needed at any given incident.

One thing that all the above routes of entry have in common for the responder is that they can be protected against. The first line of protection will be maintaining a safe distance and avoiding contact with suspect items or materials. The next line of protection is to select and use the proper personal protective equipment based upon the perceived or known danger.

RESPIRATORY PROTECTION

Because the greatest risk of exposure to a WMD comes via inhalation, steps must be taken to provide respiratory protection for those operating in a potentially hazardous environment. There are various levels of protection available depending upon the risk. When selecting the method of respiratory protection to be employed by response personnel, consideration must be given to the applicable regulations as established by OSHA in the Respiratory Protection Standard.[20]

The OSHA standard addresses such topics as respirator selection, training for users, medical clearance, fit testing, and other pertinent aspects of respiratory protection. As with other standards applicable to HazMat operations, law enforcement personnel operating at a crime scene involving hazardous materials must comply with this rule.

There are basically three types of respiratory protection available to personnel who must operate in a contaminated atmosphere. These include *air-purifying respirators* (APR), *self-contained breathing apparatus* (SCBA), and a *supplied air respirator* (SAR). Each one of these has advantages and disadvantages, many of which are dependent upon the nature of the incident being handled and the operational requirements of the user.

Air-Purifying Respirator

An air-purifying respirator purifies the

existing air in the atmosphere by filtering it, neutralizing the air-borne contaminants, or by absorbing the contaminants. This equipment is relatively lightweight and easy to use. It is the least expensive of the three choices. This type of respiratory protection is very limited in its use in emergency situations for a variety of reasons. These reasons include:

- The proper cartridge must be employed to protect against the hazard being faced. In most WMD incidents, the actual material may not be identified until some time into the incident, thus making the APR impractical during the early stages of the incident. There is no single cartridge available that will provide protection from all possible contaminants.
- The APR can only be used in an atmosphere where the concentration of the contaminant is known; this will rule out its use in most WMD incidents.
- The APR can only be used in an atmosphere where the contaminant has a warning property such as an odor that is detectable if it penetrates the respirator.
- The APR cannot be used in an oxygen deficient atmosphere. There must be sufficient oxygen content in the atmosphere to support life.

A variation of the APR is the "Powered Air Purifying Respirator" or PAPR. This device is an APR with a blower that forces air into the mask. It has the same limitations as the standard APR with regard to the type of atmosphere in which it may be used, but it creates a positive pressure environment for the user similar to an SCBA. An intrinsically safe motor that uses batteries that can last up to 11 hours powers the blower.

The PAPR does not supply breathable air with the proper oxygen content thus making them unusable in an atmosphere that may be oxygen deficient. The atmosphere must contain at least 19.5 % oxygen. A meter to determine the oxygen content must be used when entering an atmosphere that may not contain the proper level of oxygen.

The PAPR may be advantageous for investigators who need to operate for extended periods of time in a contaminated atmosphere that has been properly identified and is oxygen sufficient. It may also be useful for law enforcement personnel providing support services (i.e., inner perimeter security) in close proximity to the hot zone.

There may come a point in the investigation when the above limitations are overcome and investigators may utilize an APR. If this point is reached, investigators must still make sure that all Respiratory Protection Standards are complied with.

Self-Contained Breathing Apparatus

The most popular type of respiratory protection device used in emergency response is the self-contained breathing apparatus. This equipment provides the user with his own supply of breathing air to be used in a hostile environment. Even though it is the device of choice by most emergency responders, the SCBA has several limitations. These limitations include:

- The unit is heavy and somewhat cumbersome, weighing 20-30 pounds.
- The user's working time in the hazardous atmosphere is limited by the amount of air in the tank. The tanks are usually rated at either 30 or 60 minutes, but in reality, only offer 15-45 minutes of actual use.
- The user must be properly trained in the use of the SCBA. This includes emergency procedures in the event difficulties are encountered while in the contaminated area.
- The physical condition of the wearer will affect the duration of the air supply. A person in poor condition will not have the

same working time as someone in good physical condition.

• SCBA requires regular inspection and maintenance to insure that it is ready for use in case of an emergency.

Despite these limitations, the SCBA still provides the highest level of respiratory protection available to emergency personnel who must work in an atmosphere that is suspected to be contaminated as the result of a WMD incident. The SCBA provides respiratory protection in an atmosphere involving unknown concentrations of unknown contaminants. This is the type of scenario most likely to be encountered when a WMD is employed.

Supplied-Air Respirator

A variation of the SCBA that may be used in a hazardous atmosphere is the supplied-air respirator system. The SAR equipment requires the user to operate in the hazardous environment while attached to an umbilical cord that draws an air supply from a remote location outside the contaminated area. This equipment is not normally used in the early stages of an emergency response but may be useful during the later stages which may involve cleanup and/or investigation. The SAR offers the advantages of being lighter in weight than the SCBA and offering extended operating times.

Once again there are disadvantages to the system. The disadvantages of the SAR include the following:

• Movement is restricted by the airline. The maximum length of the airline is 300 feet from the point of connection to the air source; this may not be long enough to be effective at many scenes.

• The airline may become damaged or contaminated by chemicals.

• The extended air supply may actually cause personnel to remain in a hazardous atmosphere and work for too long a period of time thus creating the risk of problems such as heat stress and fatigue.

CHEMICAL PROTECTIVE CLOTHING

In addition to respiratory protection, law enforcement personnel operating at the scene of a WMD incident may also require clothing that will protect them from contaminants. There are many factors that must be considered when selecting the type of *chemical protective clothing* (CPC) to be employed at an incident. The use of chemical protective clothing, combined with other protective equipment, creates the "Level" of protection (i.e., Level A, B, C, and D). Both OSHA and the EPA have established standards regarding these levels of protection.

When selecting the type of chemical protective clothing to be worn by personnel entering the hot zone, it is important to note that the material must be "compatible" with the suspected hazardous materials. The manufacturer of a protective suit should supply information regarding the type of materials the suit will protect against and the duration of the protection. Based on the available information regarding the suspected hazards and the information regarding the suit's material, the decision will be made as to what type of suit will be used to enter the hot zone.

The same selection criteria will be employed with regard to chemical resistant boots and gloves. As an added measure of protection, both inner and outer gloves are utilized to provide multiple barriers. Boot covers may also be use to raise the level of protection. Because of the stress placed upon these items in the course of operations within the hot zone, the gloves and boots are subject to damage and therefore may require this extra level of protection.

It should also be noted that chemical protective clothing does not provide protection in the event of a fire or explosion. A special suit (i.e., flashover) may be worn over the chemical resistant suit to protect the emergency responder from a flash fire when operating in a flammable atmosphere. This suit is cumbersome and greatly restricts the ability of the wearer to function adequately. This is particularly true when investigative functions, such as photography and sampling, are to be done. A better course of action might be to ventilate the location and wait until the flammable atmosphere becomes safe to enter without the use of the extra suit.

Another factor to be considered is the effect of heat stress on the person using the protective clothing. By its very nature, chemical protective clothing will not allow the body's natural cooling mechanism to function properly. Because of the stress placed upon the body while working in chemical protective clothing, the amount of time that a person is able to work without a rest period for rehabilitation and fluid replenishment is limited. Actual work times will be short in warmer climates. However, heat stress-related conditions may occur in any climate at any time of the year. The physical condition of the individual wearing the clothing will also significantly affect the length of working time.

Figure 15. The Level A protective ensemble provides the highest level of protection against exposure to hazardous substances including dermal and respiratory protection. It is cumbersome and difficult to work in.

Level A

The highest level of protection must be employed when entering an atmosphere that contains a product that is highly toxic and may enter the body via the respiratory system, skin, eyes, and/or mucous membranes. Level A protection may also be employed when dealing with unknown materials that are suspected of being highly toxic (see Figure 15). Level A protection consists of the following:

• Positive pressure, self-contained breathing apparatus (SCBA).
• Fully-encapsulating, chemical-resistant suit.
• Chemical-resistant, inner and outer gloves.
• Chemical-resistant boots.
• Optional equipment includes long, cotton underwear; hardhat; and coveralls.
• Two-way radio communications. This system must be intrinsically safe if used in a flammable or explosive atmosphere.

Level B

When the highest level of respiratory protection is needed but a lesser level of skin and eye protection is needed, Level B protection may be utilized. Level B is the minimum level recommended for initial entry into the site until the hazards have been better identified and determined through monitoring and field testing (see Figure 16). Level B consists of the following:

• Positive-pressure, self-contained breathing apparatus (SCBA).
• Chemical protective suit (not fully-encapsulating).
• Inner and outer chemical-resistant gloves.
• Chemical-resistant boots.
• Two-way radio communications. This must be intrinsically safe if the atmosphere is flammable or explosive.
• Optional equipment may include a hardhat and coveralls.

The main difference between Level A and Level B is the fact that the chemical resistant suit used in Level A operations is fully-encapsulating. The SCBA in Level B is not covered. From a practical standpoint, Level B is much easier to work in and does not place as much physical and psychological stress on the wearer.

Level C

If the type of hazardous substance involved in the WMD incident is known and identified, it may be possible to use the level of protection known as Level C. This level utilizes an air purifying respirator instead of the SCBA normally associated with Level A

Figure 16: Level B protection provides respiratory protection and a reasonable level of dermal protection. It allows greater mobility than Level A.

and B operations. When the decision has been made to equip personnel with Level C protection, the atmosphere must be continually monitored to insure that it remains safe to use an air-purifying respirator (see Figure 17). Level C consists of the following:

• Full-face, air-purifying respirator.
• Chemical-resistant clothing.
• Chemical-resistant gloves.
• Chemical-resistant boots.
• Optional equipment includes hardhat, coveralls, escape mask, inner gloves, and radio communications.

Level D

Personnel who will not be exposed to skin or respiratory hazards may use the level of protection known as Level D. This consists of ordinary work clothes. The use of Level D protection is usually restricted to personnel working in the safe area or cold zone.[21]

Figure 17. Response personnel may utilize Level C protection after the hazards have been identified and this degree of protection is deemed adequate for the existing hazards.

Chapter 5

LAW ENFORCEMENT RESPONSE

The actual response by law enforcement to an incident involving the use or suspected use of a WMD will vary from agency to agency based on several different factors. These factors include:

- The size of the agency and the resources that it has readily available. These resources may include manpower, equipment, and specialists.
- The magnitude and scope of the WMD incident.
- The primary responsibility of the agency. This may be restricted to response, investigation, incident management, mitigation, and rescue.
- What role has the agency been designated to play within the entire emergency response plan.
- The jurisdiction of the agency. The authority of the agency and what laws it has been charged with enforcing.

Once an agency has reviewed the above factors, it can then begin formulating its response to a given incident. The pre-incident planning that is necessary to successfully handle a WMD incident will also be based upon the above elements. However, there are several aspects that will be common to the response of most law enforcement agencies to a WMD incident.

The following are the basic tasks that a law enforcement agency should be expected to handle in response to a WMD incident:

- Scene assessment.
- Site security.
- Stopping further harm from occurring.
- Aiding the injured.
- Initiating a criminal investigation.
- Assisting other agencies in performing their duties.
- Restoring order and public confidence.

SCENE ASSESSMENT

The initial actions taken by the first law enforcement officials at the scene of a WMD incident will help determine the overall outcome of the incident. Based on their training and experience, they must recognize the signs that a WMD incident has occurred or is in the process of occurring. The longer it takes to recognize a WMD incident, the more difficult it will be to mitigate and investigate. Lives may be lost and valuable evidence destroyed if the incident is not recognized as early as possible.

The first officials on the scene must do an accurate initial assessment and communicate the following information as soon as possible:

- What type of WMD incident is suspected (B-NICE)?
- How many victims are present and their apparent condition?
- Is the event still going on or has the event already taken place?
- What other resources are needed (i.e., fire, EMS, etc.)?
- The exact location of the incident.
- The safest approach route for other responders.
- Have other WMD devices been located?
- Is the terrorist at the scene or is their location known?

This information must be communicated as soon as it is gathered and updated on a regular basis. Consideration should be given to using a secure means of communication (i.e., a telephone) to avoid making sensitive information available to those who may be monitoring public safety radio bands. Prompt availability of vital information will also help expedite the response of specialized resources that will be necessary to handle a WMD incident.

When assessing a threat that involves a suspected biological agent, several specific questions should be asked in order to gather the information necessary to make a reasonable assessment. The following questions will be useful in determining the proper course of action to be followed when biological agents are suspected:

- Is there an agent or munition present?
- Is the suspected device capable of producing an aerosol that may be inhaled?

- Is the agent in a liquid or dry form?
- Has the device already detonated or functioned?
- Is the item located inside or outside of a building or other structure?
- What are the weather conditions at the scene?
- Are there people in the downwind or danger areas?
- Can the agent be contained?
- Can the agent be decontaminated where it is located?[22]

These questions can also be used to assess other threats associated with weapons of mass destruction. The information obtained in response to these inquiries can then be analyzed by a team of specialized personnel assembled for this purpose. The following is a model of such a team developed by the FBI:

- Threat Evaluation Team
- Law enforcement
- Microbiologist
- Chemist
- Psychologist
- Forensic expert
- Public health officer
- Veterinarian[23]

In situations in which an actual or suspected device *has not* been found, the first law enforcement officers on the scene must begin to assess the scene in terms of the threat. The person who received the threat must be interviewed as soon as possible to begin the assessment process. Law enforcement officers are usually very adept at handling this portion of the assessment. This is due to of their practical experience in interviewing people on a regular basis. This interview should consist of the basic investigative questions of *who, what, where, when, why,* and *how.* This interview will also help to initiate the investigation and the responses should be properly documented in accordance with local procedures.

Exact time of call _____

Exact words of caller _____
_____
_____

QUESTIONS TO ASK

1. When is bomb going to explode? _____

2. Where is the bomb? _____

3. What does it look like? _____

4. What kind of bomb is it? _____

5. What will cause it to explode? _____

6. Did you place the bomb? _____

7. Why? _____

8. Where are you calling from? _____

9. What is your address? _____

10. What is your name? _____

CALLER'S VOICE (circle)

Calm	Disguised	Nasal	Angry	Broken
Stutter	Slow	Sincere	Lisp	Rapid
Giggling	Deep	Crying	Squeaky	Excited
Stressed	Accent	Loud	Slurred	Normal

If voice is familiar, whom did it sound like? _____

Were there any background noises? _____

Remarks: _____
_____

Person receiving call: _____

Telephone number call received at: _____

Date: _____

Report call immediately to: _____
(Refer to bomb incident plan)

Figure 18. A card containing important information to be gathered in the event of a WMD threat should be available to those likely to receive such a threat. This card is produced by the FBI's Bomb Data Center.

With minor variations, the procedures for assessing a WMD threat will be the same as assessing a bomb threat. The person who communicates the threat is often the best source of information about the device. There are written materials available that can be provided to those individuals (i.e., 911 operators, switchboard operators) who are likely to receive these types of threats (see Figure 18). These aids will be useful when debriefing those who had contact with the person communicating the threat.

Personnel assessing the threat should pay particular attention to certain aspects of the threat including the following:
• *When* is the device going to be activated?
• *Where* is the device or hazardous substance?
• *What* does the device look like and what type of device is it?
• *What* kind of device is it and what will cause it to explode or disperse the materials?
• *Why* was the device or material placed?[24]

The input of those specialists who will be responding to a WMD incident should also be sought with regard to the debriefing of any witnesses or those who received the threat. This may include bomb technicians, hazardous materials specialists, investigators, and health department officials. These specialists may be able to obtain information, unique to their needs, from the people being interviewed that may otherwise have gone unnoted by the first responder doing the interview.

Based on the threat information available, there are three basic courses of action that may be taken:
• Ignore the threat.
• Evacuate immediately.
• Search and evacuate if warranted.

To ignore the threat completely may not be the best course of action. Should a WMD event take place, there may be serious liability issues raised if a threat is received and not acted upon. As mentioned, law enforcement agencies should review their existing bomb threat procedures and modify them as necessary to meet the new demands of a WMD response.

Choosing to conduct an evacuation in response to every bomb threat or WMD threat is a course of action that is employed in many jurisdictions. This takes much of the need for decision making out of the hands of the first responders but may actually result in the very disruption of activity and business that the person making the threat desired. There is also the possibility that a criminal looking to cause injuries may use the threat process to cause potential victims to be moved to an area where they are more vulnerable to an attack.

In many jurisdictions, the more desirable approach is to conduct a search in response to a threat and evacuate when a suspected device is located. This prevents the disruption of the business or whatever event is underway while the search is being conducted. In the event a suspicious item is located and an evacuation is necessary, this procedure allows the evacuees to be moved away from the suspicious item and thus reduces the possibility of further exposure to the potentially harmful item.[25]

With regard to the actual search for a suspicious item, the best course of action usually involves the use of personnel familiar with the location being searched. These people will be most familiar with what is considered "normal" and will therefore be more likely to recognize something as being suspicious or out of place. They will also have the ability to identify potential hiding places or other strategic locations that should be searched. Before allowing anyone to conduct a search for a bomb or other WMD device, the searchers should be briefed on what to look for based on the threat. These searchers should avoid touching or disturbing any suspicious items they find.

Depending on local policy and procedures, specialists may elect to use dogs capable of detecting explosives or field instruments capable of detecting the presence of chemicals or radioactive materials. In most cases, these techniques will be used to supplement the search by those responsible for the building. These specialized search techniques may be reserved for high-risk locations or where there are other extenuating circumstances (i.e., prior incidents).

SECURE THE SITE

One of the most important roles to be played by law enforcement at the scene of any critical incident is to provide scene security. Uniformed personnel with law enforcement powers are in the best position to provide this vital service. As with any crime scene or other major incident, it is important to establish a secure perimeter as early in the incident as possible. A secure scene will accomplish many objectives including the following:

• Prevent potential witnesses and/or suspects from leaving the scene without being identified.
• Preserve evidence in its original place and condition.
• Prevent others from entering a dangerous scene and being exposed to whatever hazards maybe present.
• Provide a safe working environment for other emergency response personnel (i.e., fire and emergency medical personnel).
• Limit the spread of WMD materials beyond the original scene.

Because of the possible presence of hazardous materials, the securing of a WMD incident scene may require more manpower than a typical crime scene. Responders must be careful to secure a large enough area to avoid being contaminated themselves. When explosives are suspected, responders must always be aware of the possibility that there may be additional devices intended to injure emergency personnel.

Law enforcement must also provide secure routes in and out of the site for other emergency personnel. If the incident involves a large number of casualties, transportation routes must be established to move the victims to medical treatment areas and facilities. Traffic control must be established as early in the incident as possible. Staging areas should be established early in the incident to prevent the scene from becoming congested with vehicles. Once control of the access routes is lost at a major incident, it is almost impossible to regain control.

Access routes for those entering the scene may be defined using devices such as barricades and barricade tape. Once a safe path in and out of the scene has been established, it should be clearly marked and its integrity should be maintained by security personnel.

LIMITING THE SPREAD OF THE HAZARD

First responders can take action to prevent further harm from occurring after the initial WMD event. One of the first actions that will accomplish this is the act of securing the scene. By preventing others from entering the hazardous area created by the WMD, the spread of the materials and the injury of additional victims will be reduced.

When a device that is still disseminating its hazardous material is found at the scene, further harm can be reduced by isolating the device, moving others away from it or by preventing others from being exposed to it. This can be accomplished without unnecessarily exposing the first responder to harm by giving directions and commands from a safe distance. A loud speaker or public address system may be employed for this purpose.

Where the safety of the scene is questionable, subjects found within the site should be moved to a location that is determined to be safer and kept there until released from the scene. There may be instances where a mass evacuation of an area may not be the safest and most effective course of action. There have been situations where terrorists have used one terrorist act to move people into another area for the purpose of attacking them.

BEGIN AIDING THE INJURED

In addition to the above actions, law enforcement personnel may be expected to begin aiding the injured within the scope of their training. Personnel will have to determine what actions should be taken that will be helpful to the largest number of victims. The securing of a vital traffic control point at a mass casualty incident may be more important to the overall success of the incident than the limited first aid that may be provided by a law enforcement official. The task of caring for the injured should be transferred to the appropriate agency responsible for this as soon as possible. This will allow law enforcement personnel to attend to their other duties at the scene.

When time and resources permit, law enforcement personnel may begin aiding the injured by assisting in evacuating them from the scene. This may include moving them away from hazardous materials by directing them toward triage areas or decontamination areas. When possible, non-injured, non-contaminated victims should be kept in an area where they will not have a view of the triage and treatment areas. This will reduce the possibility of *psychogenic illness* among otherwise healthy individuals (see Chapter 6, Handling the Victims).

INITIATE THE CRIMINAL INVESTIGATION

The earlier in the response that a criminal investigation is initiated the more likely it will be successful. Law enforcement personnel should be aware that regardless of the type of WMD incident they are confronted with (B-NICE), the one thing that they will all have in common is that a violation of law has occurred. The scene and its victims should be treated with the same degree of attention to details as all other types of violent crimes.

First responders should begin identifying witnesses and suspects, avoid the destruction of evidence, and limit unnecessary and unauthorized access to the scene. Those responsible for the investigation of a WMD incident should be notified at the earliest possible point in the incident. This will allow them to begin their investigation before witnesses move on and evidence is lost.

These same principles may be applied to incidents that appear to be "hoaxes" or where the existence of a WMD is suspected but not confirmed. It is better to handle the incident as a crime scene from its onset. A crime scene cannot be recreated when witnesses and suspects are unidentified and evidence is disposed of or destroyed.

ASSIST OTHER AGENCIES IN PERFORMING THEIR DUTIES

There are many different agencies, with varying disciplines, that may be brought together at a WMD incident. They will each have different responsibilities and duties to perform. In many instances, they will require a safe and secure environment in which to work.

Law enforcement will be in a unique position to provide the security necessary for these other agencies to accomplish their individual tasks. The previously described functions of securing the site and stopping further harm from occurring are part of the process of providing a secure and safe environment. Law enforcement personnel will be able to provide a visible, uniformed presence at the scene of a WMD incident. This is essential to securing the perimeters, preventing unauthorized access to the scene, and gaining control of the civilians who may be in a state of panic. While fire and emergency medical personnel will be primarily concerned with evacuating, rescuing, and providing emergency medical treatment to the victims, law enforcement will be concerned with securing and controlling the scene.

In addition to establishing a secure perimeter, law enforcement may be called upon to guard against further attack. Law enforcement personnel should be alert to the possibility of an armed assault, explosive devices, or other WMD devices. By providing a visible, armed, and organized presence, an additional attack may be prevented. Specialists such as bomb technicians, special weapons teams, and counter-snipers may be called upon to provide the high level of security necessary to handle a WMD incident.

Law enforcement may be needed to assist emergency medical personnel in gathering information from victims or others who may have been exposed to hazardous substances. The interviewing skills possessed by law enforcement personnel, as well as, their obvious authority may elicit the cooperation of otherwise reluctant subjects. In many cases, law enforcement personnel possess the authority to order evacuations or hold people in "quarantine" until the situation can be resolved or at least accurately assessed.

The role to be played by law enforcement, whether it is patrol officers or specialists, with regard to enabling others to do their jobs, should be addressed in the planning stage. Where limited law enforcement resources are available, particularly in the early stages of a WMD incident, priorities may have to be established with regard to what activities will take place first. For example, the evacuation of unexposed subjects to a safe area may have to wait while law enforcement provides security for the rescue of those in immediate danger.

In the event of an incident involving the use of a biological agent where the potential exists for widespread illness, law enforcement may be called upon to provide security for medical facilities and associated sites such as pharmacies. The supplies of antibiotics and other specialized medications that may be needed in the event of a large-scale biological incident are somewhat limited and may need to be tightly controlled by public health authorities. Fear and panic may require that law enforcement provide a highly visible presence at pharmacies and other similar facilities to prevent theft and civil disorder.

THE RESTORATION OF ORDER AND PUBLIC CONFIDENCE

One of the possible effects of a WMD incident is the destruction of public confidence in the ability of the government to protect its citizens from terrorist attacks. The fear of additional attacks and the sense of panic associated with this fear are as harmful to a community as any actual attack. In order to negate or counteract this state of mind, law enforcement must project a feeling of confidence in their ability to handle the incident and, at the same time, prevent other attacks from occurring. A highly visible and organized law enforcement presence will help accomplish this goal.

Law enforcement must be prepared to respond to the public's questions regarding the events associated with the WMD incident in a manner that inspires both confidence and a sense of security. Law enforcement must begin the process of restoring order at the earliest possible stage in the incident.

Part of law enforcement's obligation to help restore confidence in the government's ability to protect and care for its citizens will be the ability to investigate the crime and bring the criminals to trial. The sooner the crime is solved, the quicker the public will regain confidence in the government. A well-planned response by law enforcement, including a properly trained and equipped investigative element, will greatly enhance law enforcement's efforts in restoring order and public confidence. By successfully meeting the preceding goals, law enforcement will also help deter future attacks.

Chapter 6

HANDLING THE VICTIMS

AIDING THE INJURED

First responders, including law enforcement personnel, will frequently be called upon to provide assistance to those that may have been injured in the course of a WMD incident. Usually, providing first aid to an injured victim at the scene of a crime does not involve a significant risk to the responder other than the danger of exposure to bloodborne pathogens. However, this is not the case with a WMD incident. At this type of incident the victims themselves may present a significant hazard to the rescuers.

Those attempting to aid the victims of a WMD attack may face the following immediate dangers in the course of their response:

• Chemical, biological, or radiological materials may contaminate victims. This contamination may be passed from victim to responder in the course of providing treatment.

• The area in which the victims are found by the responders may be within the hot zone. This presents a danger to rescuers who enter the area to assist the injured.

• When a weapon such as an explosive or incendiary device has been used, there

may be structural damage making it hazardous to access and render aid to victims.

• Additional (secondary) devices may be present that can harm those responding to the scene.

In order to minimize the risk to response personnel, procedures should be established that call for the rapid removal of victims from the hot zone. Rather than assisting the injured where they are found and attempting to treat them in a potentially dangerous location, the victims should be moved as quickly as possible to a safe area before beginning first aid. While this may not be the most medically advantageous course of action for the patient in terms of preventing further injury, it may be necessary to save their lives and minimize the exposure of the rescuers.

This approach to rescue is frequently referred to as "scoop and run" and is somewhat different from usual emergency medical procedures that usually emphasize stabilizing the patient before attempting to move them. The scoop and run acknowledges the dangers that may be associated with the scene after an attack employing a WMD (see Figure 19).

Responders should be trained in the process referred to as Simple Triage Rapid Treatment (START). In this procedure, victims who are ambulatory are quickly identified and then lead out of the hot zone where they will then be individually triaged. The ambulatory victims are rapidly triaged as either requiring immediate or delayed transport from the scene based on the nature and severity of their injuries.[26]

Victims who are obviously deceased should be left in the position in which they are found. They should be moved only if necessary to ascertain their status or to assist or gain access to other victims. Responders must remember that they are working within a crime scene at all times.

Response personnel should also make an effort to minimize their actual physical contact with the victims until they can be decontaminated. Where there is obvious contamination of victims, responders should be trained to avoid this contamination and thus placing themselves at risk and removing themselves from future activity. Responders should employ the protection principles of **time**, **distance**, and **shielding** with regard to those injured in a WMD attack. The use of loudspeakers or other similar devices should be considered to give instructions to victims from a safe distance and thus avoid unnecessary contact and contamination.

Figure 19. Victims may require rescue by emergency response personnel in chemical protective clothing.

GROSS DECONTAMINATION

One of the first actions that may be necessary at the scene of a WMD incident is the initial or "gross" decontamination of those victims suspected of having been exposed to chemical or biological agents. Most contamination occurring as the result of a WMD attack will be surface contamination. The act of removing a victim's clothing will usually remove as much as 75 per cent of the contamination. This initial decontamination will usually consist of drenching the victims with large amounts of water in order to attempt to remove the surface contaminants. Under optimum conditions, a diluted bleach solution should be employed to increase the effectiveness of the decontamination process. A soap solu-

tion may also be used in this process. The victims' clothing may also be removed at this stage to insure that all contaminants are left at the scene. This should be done within the hot zone or the warm zone.

From a law enforcement perspective, the decontamination process, though necessary to save lives and reduce injuries, presents several problems. First and foremost is the need to control the victims and assist other responders in getting them through the decontamination process in an orderly and controlled manner. Depending on the perception of the danger in the eyes of the victims, they may be reluctant to submit to the decontamination process unless ordered to do so by law enforcement personnel.

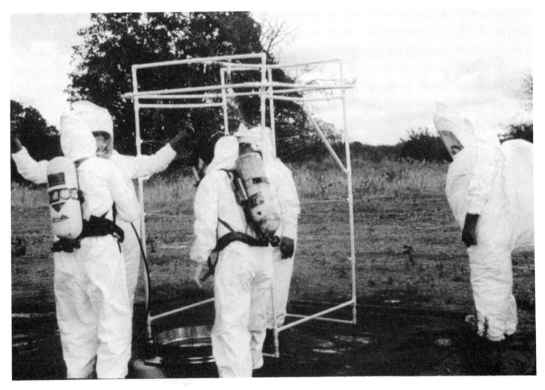

Figure 20. Victims of a WMD attack, as well as first responders, may require decontamination by a hazardous materials response team

The act of decontaminating victims using large amounts of water may destroy or wash away evidence. In addition, the chemical or biological agents may be carried from the scene unless responders have the time and the resources to contain the runoff. The evidence may also be diluted and thus more difficult to obtain as a result of the decontamination process. Despite its effect on the evidence and the subsequent investigation, the investigators must realize that the decontamination process may be essential to saving lives and reducing the impact of the attack. Investigators should examine the runoff water from the decontamination process, as well as any clothing that was removed from the victims.

Investigative personnel should be told what specific decontamination solution has been used in order to determine its possible effect on the evidence that is being gathered (see Figure 20).

Whether or not a WMD agent is water-soluble will determine the method of decontamination. An example of this is sulfur mustard. It is described as being slightly soluble in water and very soluble in isopropanol and in organic solvents. The recommended procedure for decontamination of victims exposed to sulfur mustard is to pre-treat their skin with detergents if using water and then use a solution of 0.5% bleach.[27] Information such as this should be provided to those responsible for the sampling and other evidence gathering.

Law enforcement personnel should attempt to secure the clothing and personal effects of the victims as they are decontaminated. The clothing and other items obtained as a result of the decontamination process may provide a direct link to the person(s) responsible for the attack. Valuable evidence may be found in the scientific examination of these items. These items should be separated by victim, placed in a plastic bag, and labeled for future reference. In order to provide a proper chain of custody for these items, they should be kept under the supervision of a law enforcement official. The person responsible for the security of these items should be aware of the fact that they may still contain sufficient amounts of the hazardous material and may be harmful to those who may handle them if they do not employ proper protective measures (see Chapter 16, Sampling for Chemical, Biological and Radiological Evidence).

Law enforcement personnel, particularly those first on the scene, may be required to go through the decontamination process. Unless they were properly equipped and were wearing the proper level of protective clothing and respiratory protection, they will in all likelihood have to be decontaminated. This will help to ensure that they do not carry the agents from the scene.

SECONDARY CONTAMINATION

Secondary contamination occurs when contaminants are passed from one person or object to another. Contamination such as this can occur when an emergency medical technician becomes contaminated as a result of handling a victim who has not been properly decontaminated. Another example of this is when a police officer becomes contaminated as a result of handling contaminated evidence.

Secondary contamination from a victim can be avoided by the process of decontaminating the victim prior to treatment and by using the proper type and level of personal protective equipment. First responders should be taught to avoid contact with victims until they are decontaminated or until the proper personal protective equipment can be obtained. First responders should remain a safe distance from the victims until proper safety precautions can be taken.

The risk of contamination from contaminated evidence is best reduced by the use of protective equipment and proper safety practices. The evidence at the scene of a WMD incident may dissipate quickly after its release. In terms of incident safety, the dissipation of the evidence will normally help make the scene safer for those responding to assist the injured and otherwise mitigate the incident. However, in terms of the investigation, the dissipation of evidence may be very damaging. Investigators must balance the need to collect evidence in a timely fashion with the need to do so in a safe and proper manner.

Chapter 7

INCIDENT MANAGEMENT

An incident involving chemical, biological, or radiological materials used as a weapon will undoubtedly involve various agencies representing different disciplines and multiple levels of government. Regardless of the magnitude or severity of the incident, it will be essential to implement an incident management system in the earliest stages of the incident to insure that the incident is brought to a safe resolution as efficiently and expeditiously as possible.

Unless an incident management system is activated at the beginning of the response process, resources will not be used to their maximum effectiveness, incident goals will not be met, and the safety of both the response personnel and the public may be unnecessarily endangered. Most agencies that will be involved in responding to and mitigating a WMD incident are already familiar with the principles of incident management (incident command). Part of the pre-planning process should be to determine what systems are already in place and the development of procedures that will meet the needs of the jurisdiction in the event of a WMD incident (see Figure 21).

Incident command as we know it today has its origin in the large brush fires that

occurred in the western United States in the early 1970s. These fires frequently crossed jurisdictional boundaries and involved vast resources to control them. The *Incident Command System* (ICS) was developed to manage these resources effectively and efficiently despite the fact that multiple layers of government may be involved as well as different disciplines.[28]

The system has grown and been refined to the point where it is a universally accepted principle that emergencies should be managed by an Incident Command System of some type. In fact, federal regulations regarding the response to hazardous materials incidents mandates the use of a system.[29] Personnel receiving hazardous materials training pursuant to OSHA standards are trained in the basics of incident command.

In addition to the above-mentioned OSHA requirements, the Commission on Accreditation for Law Enforcement Agencies calls for the use of this system. This standard calls for plans that will identify the person in command of law enforcement operations during what are described as "unusual occurrences."

One of the principles behind incident

command that makes it so useful is the fact that it can be employed for any type of incident or hazard, regardless of the magnitude, no matter what emergency response organizations are involved. It can also be employed in the pre-incident planning stage in order to develop an effective plan for responding to various emergencies that may occur within a given jurisdiction.

INCIDENT COMMAND SYSTEM COMPONENTS

In order to be effective in coordinating and making the best use of the law enforcement resources during a WMD incident, there are several basic components that should be utilized when developing a plan for response. These components include the following:
• Common terminology.
• Modular organization.
• Integrated communications.

• Unified command structure.
• Consolidated action plans.
• Manageable span of control.
• Designated incident facilities.
• Comprehensive resource management.

Common Terminology

Because a critical incident, such as a WMD attack, will bring together different

Figure 21. The command post during the initial phases of a WMD incident may be established using available vehicles and personnel from various agencies.

disciplines, it is essential that a common language be used by all those involved. Plain language should be used whenever possible in interagency communications to avoid confusion and misinterpretation. Common names should be used for both equipment and personnel resources. All involved should have a common understanding of such terms as *task force, response team,* and other terms that may be used in the course of a critical incident. When possible, these terms may be predefined in the plans developed to direct the response to a WMD incident.

The use of agency specific radio codes should be avoided. While the "ten codes" may facilitate intra-agency communications on a daily basis, they may create potentially dangerous conflicts if all the agencies involved do not use exactly the same codes. This is particularly true if the agencies do not realize that there are differences in their radio code systems.

In the event there are multiple incidents occurring simultaneously, each incident should be given an identifying name to minimize confusion. An example of this would be if an explosion occurs at the Central City Mall, while simultaneously a package suspected of containing anthrax is found at an IRS Facility. These two incidents would be referred to as *Central City Mall Command* and *IRS Facility Command* by those involved in the response. This is especially helpful where common radio channels are being used for multiple incidents.

Modular Organization

Incident management is designed and intended to be developed from the arrival of the first unit (regardless of agency) through the conclusion and final resolution of the incident. The various functional components of the Incident Command System are designed to be implemented as needed and then de-activated when they are no longer required.

The only component that will always be established is the *command function.* Even in an incident classified as "minor in nature," someone must be in charge. Theoretically, this starts with the first arriving emergency responder and is passed on up through the chain of command as the scope of the incident increases. The command function must be flexible and may pass from one agency to another and from one discipline to another as the incident progresses.

The modular components of the Incident Command System can be looked at as a set of building blocks that can be used as the Incident Commander sees fit in order to develop the organization he needs to effectively handle the incident. Not all elements of the system will be needed at every WMD incident but remain available should the Incident Commander choose to implement them.

Integrated Communications

Communications is frequently viewed as one of the biggest problems in critical incident management. There must be a good exchange of information between the management and command level of the incident and the operations level. As the scope of the incident increases and more people from various agencies become involved, information exchange becomes both more difficult and more important. Integrated communications will involve the management of incident communications through the use of a common communications plan.

Plans must be developed before the incident actually occurs in order to facilitate effective communications during an actual incident. The compatibility of radio systems should be determined. Common channels for interagency use and tactical channels for intra-agency use should be designated in advance whenever possible. As stated earlier, the use of plain language should also be addressed in the communications plan.

Unified Command

By its very nature, a WMD incident will most likely involve many different agencies, multiple disciplines and numerous jurisdictions. If one agency encompassing a single jurisdiction were able to respond to and resolve all the aspects of a WMD event, then one Incident Commander could manage the incident from start to finish. It is difficult to envision an incident involving the use or threatened use of a weapon that has a chemical, biological, or radiological element to it that will not initiate a response from fire, police, and emergency medical agencies thus requiring a unified command structure.

Unified command is used when the incident is multi-jurisdictional or multiple agencies contribute to the command process. Under the concept of unified command, all the involved agencies contribute to the command and management process by determining the overall goals and objectives of the incident and in jointly developing tactical objectives (see Figure 22).

Command personnel operating in a unified command structure must be aware that the various agencies may have different goals and objectives that they may desire to meet. An example of this would be when a

Figure 22. Law enforcement, fire, and emergency medical personnel must coordinate their actions to insure a successful outcome to a WMD event. These responders are shown planning a large-scale evacuation during a hazardous materials incident involving a large amount of flammable materials.

fire department's main objective is to rescue the injured victims, while the law enforcement agency's objective may to locate and arrest the person(s) responsible for the incident. Both of these objectives must be met in order for the incident to be brought to a successful conclusion. The commanders must develop a plan and course of action that will enable both of these objectives to be met as efficiently as possible.

The unified command structure will usually consist of one key official from each agency or jurisdiction that will act together to develop an action plan. The Operations Officer will usually accomplish the actual implementation of this plan. The Operations Officer will usually represent the agency with the greatest involvement in that particular portion of the incident activities. An example of this would be when, in the initial stages of the incident, the agency responsible for search and rescue may assume the role of Operations Officer. After the viable victims have been removed, a law enforcement agency may assume this position to initiate the investigation. On occasion, this position may be occupied by several different people throughout the course of an incident.

Consolidated Action Plans

One of the primary duties of the unified command group will be to develop what is known as the *consolidated action plan* for the incident. Where a pre-existing plan has been developed, it will form the basis for the action plan. The consolidated action plan should include strategic goals, tactical objectives, and those support activities necessary to meet these goals and objectives.

A consolidated action plan is important when the resources of multiple agencies are involved and when more than one jurisdiction is involved. It is also important in inci-dents that will involve changes in personnel or equipment as the incident extends beyond normal operation periods or shifts. WMD incidents can be expected to be prolonged operations due to the extensive investigation that will most likely be undertaken. The investigation of both the 1993 World Trade Center and 1995 Oklahoma City bombings took extended periods of time that required the creation of investigative plans.

All action plans should be in written form. This will help minimize confusion and misunderstanding when the plans are passed from one shift to the next or from one group to another in the course of an incident. An action plan will help maintain some degree of continuity throughout the incident. It will also provide a reference point when the event is reconstructed and critiqued at a later point in time.

Manageable Span of Control

Most command and supervisory personnel are already familiar with the concept of *span of control.* It is a management principle that is defined as the number of subordinates that a supervisor can effectively manage. Usually, the desirable range is considered to be from three to seven people, with five being the optimum number.

There are various factors, however, that will determine the optimum number for a particular scenario. These factors include the nature of the work being done, the complexity of the tasks, the geographical area being covered, and the hazards associated with the job being performed. The capabilities of both the supervisor and the subordinates must also be considered.[30]

One of the objectives of the Incident Command System is to limit the number of people reporting to the Incident Commander to a manageable number. No matter how talented a commander is, he can only effectively process a limited amount of information at one time. By limiting the number of people with direct access to the commander, he or she, in all likelihood, will receive a manageable amount of input and thus be able to make the best possible decisions.

Sector officers are utilized to keep the span of control manageable. Individuals are placed in charge of various tasks or geographic areas.

Designated Incident Facilities

A command post must be established at the scene of a WMD event. This will be the location from which all incident operations will be directed. There should be only one command post per incident. Where multiple agencies bring their own mobile command posts to the scene, they should be located as close as possible to each other; one of these should be designated as the incident command post. The others may be used by individual agencies to manage their operations and activities during the incident.

The unified command team should be located in the command post. It is from the command post that the direction, coordination, control, and management of the incident resources will emanate. The communications for the incident should also flow through the command post in order to insure that the command staff is adequately informed.

When pre-plans are developed to address the possibility of a WMD incident, incident facilities should be identified. When a plan is developed with regard to a particular location, command posts may be designated as well as staging areas and perimeters. An example of this would be the development of a plan in the event that a local courthouse experiences a bombing. A suitable location for a command post and staging area can be identified and should be included in the plan.

Whenever pre-designated incident facilities are established, alternative sites should also be designated. Because of the unpredictable nature of a WMD attack, an alternative command post and staging area should be identified and selected. When choosing alternative sites for a command post and staging area, planning personnel should keep in mind the extent of the damage that may be caused by the WMD incident. This damage may force operations personnel to go beyond the routine evacuation areas and distances in order to insure the safety of emergency responders.

Many terrorists and criminals are also familiar with emergency response procedures. In some cases they have used false alarms to test and observe the response of emergency personnel before actually committing their crime. Because of this, law enforcement personnel should be aware of seemingly innocent false alarms occurring at high-risk locations (i.e., government buildings). These false alarms may be part of the criminal's planning process.

Where high-risk locations are involved, it may be advisable for emergency personnel to vary their responses in terms of where the command post is established and the location of staging areas for personnel and equipment. A terrorist planning an attack may notice that the first officer on the scene always enters through the same door after parking his patrol car in the same location. This information could be used by the terrorist if he or she were to place a secondary explosive device. Officers should be trained to vary their routine and not become complacent in their responses.

Because law enforcement facilities themselves may be the target of a WMD attack, plans should be developed that will enable the agencies to continue to function and provide a minimum acceptable level of service. An example of this would be an attack upon a local police department's communications system.

Comprehensive Resource Management

The efficient use of available resources in the management of an incident is one of the main reasons that the concept of incident command exists. It can be expected that a WMD incident will require the use of significant resources to mitigate the event. In a worst case scenario, responders may be faced with hundreds or thousands of victims requiring rescue, decontamination, treatment, and transportation. This will require obtaining and distributing large amounts of resources in an efficient manner to insure that all the needs of the incident are met.

The incident command structure will allow the commanders to manage the available resources as effectively as possible under the given circumstances. Resource management will address the acquisition, distribution and accountability for the resources needed for the incident.

FUNCTIONAL ROLES

Incident Commander

Depending on the local plans that are developed regarding scene management and incident command, a law enforcement officer may find himself in the role of Incident Commander at some point during the course of a WMD event. This, in all likelihood, will occur when it is determined that the incident is in fact a crime scene and control of the overall operation will rest with the lead law enforcement agency.

There are several areas of responsibility that the Incident Commander will have to address at various times throughout the incident. The responsibilities of the Incident Commander include:

• The Incident Commander must assess the priorities of the given incident and, based on this assessment, determine the strategic goals. Normally, there will be three main priorities for the WMD Incident Commander. These priorities will include *life safety, stabilizing the incident*, and *minimizing property damage*. Strategic goals, broad in nature, will make up the overall plan to

handle the incident.

An example of a strategic goal during a WMD incident would be the development of a criminal case that could be used to successfully prosecute the subject or subjects responsible for the WMD attack.

• Once the strategic goals have been determined, tactical objectives must be ascertained. The objectives are the specific steps that must be taken to achieve the goals. The objectives should be measurable so that the progress of the plan may be monitored and adjusted if necessary.

Some examples of tactical objectives during a WMD incident would be establishing a secure inner perimeter, obtaining physical evidence that will be admissible during a trial, identifying witnesses, and conducting witness interviews.

• Once the goals and objectives are determined, the Incident Commander will be responsible for the development of the incident action plan. In some cases, the Incident Commander's staff may actually develop this plan. However, final approval of the plan is still the Incident Commander's responsibility.

• As the incident progresses and becomes resource-intensive, an organizational structure must be developed. This will begin at the command level and expand to meet the needs of the incident. One of the important aspects of the organizational structure will be the establishing of a manageable span of control for the Incident Commander and others in supervisory roles within the structure. A manageable span of control is essential for a successful operation. A manageable span of control is particularly important during the early stages of a WMD incident when large amounts of resources may be flowing into the incident.

• The Incident Commander will be responsible for coordinating the activities of the various agencies and disciplines that become involved in the WMD incident. This responsibility will include the management of the resources that are necessary to resolve the incident. This will require the Incident Commander to continually monitor the status and progress of the incident to ensure that efforts are not being duplicated or that opposing activities are not taking place. The command of a WMD incident will require coordination to ensure that all life-saving priorities are met, as well as any crime scene considerations.

• The safety of the response personnel who are involved in the incident is also the ultimate responsibility of the Incident Commander. He or she will rely heavily on the command staff to meet this responsibility. However, it should be noted that all those involved in response to a WMD incident must be aware of the dangers involved and should contribute to the overall safety of the operation. Safety must be the responsibility of everyone, not just the incident command staff and the Safety Officer(s).

• The Incident Commander will also be responsible for the release of information to the media and other outside agencies. Dealing with the flow of information to the media during the course of a WMD incident, and the subsequent investigation, is extremely important and will require a coordinated effort between the various response agencies. The Incident Commander must be able to balance the requests and demands of the media with the needs of the investigators. It is possible to give the media sufficient information to do their job yet, maintain the integrity of the investigation. Personnel experienced in dealing with the media during critical incidents should be included in the Incident Commander's command staff. Those responsible for the investigation of the WMD incident should be included in the process of determining what information should be released to the media.

In addition to Command, there are four other functional areas of incident command that may be utilized during a WMD incident. The activation of these functional areas will depend upon the complexity and magnitude of the incident. These functional areas include *Operations*, *Logistics*, *Planning*, and *Finance*.

Operations

The Operations element is responsible for the direct management of the tactical operations needed to bring the incident to a successful conclusion. The Operations Officer will report directly to the Incident Commander and is responsible for the actual implementation of the incident plan. The Operations Officer insures coordination of the various tactical activities that may be undertaken during a WMD incident.

The Operations Officer must keep the Incident Commander informed of the progress of the incident and the need to develop or change the strategic goals and/or tactical objectives. One of the main reasons for the Operations Officer existence is to limit the span of control of the Incident Commander and thus increase his ability to properly manage the incident.

A supervisor from the agency or discipline that has the greatest functional involvement in the incident will usually fill the Operations Officer position. Based on these criteria, the position may change hands as the incident progresses through its various stages. An example of this would be during the initial moments of the incident, when the rescue of injured victims is the top priority. In this situation, the fire/rescue service may provide the Operations Officer. When the focus of the incident changes from a rescue operation to a criminal investigation, the Operations Officer position may then be staffed by a law enforcement official from the agency having jurisdiction.

Another duty of the Operations Officer is the management of the staging areas. He or

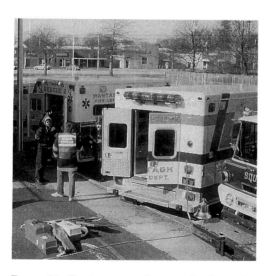

Figure 23. Equipment such as medical supplies may also be assembled for distribution at a large scale incident.

she will usually designate a *"Staging Area Manager"* to actually perform this duty. In an incident covering a large geographical area, this may require the designation of several staging areas with a corresponding number of managers (see Figures 23 & 24).

In a WMD incident involving a large amount of resources, the establishment and management of staging areas will be vital to the successful management of the incident. Incoming resources should be directed to the appropriate staging area and be assigned from there. This will enable the command personnel to control the allocation and distribution of resources and will also help to minimize *"free-lancing"* (i.e., independent action taken by responders not at the direction of the Incident Commander). As the incident progresses, competition for resources may become intense. An effective management system, employing the use of staging areas, will help properly distribute these resources.

Planning

The Planning Officer is responsible for collecting, evaluating, and disseminating information pertaining to the incident. This includes an assessment of the incident, as well as any necessary projections based upon available information. Information regarding resources is also the responsibility of the Planning Officer. This includes the availability and status of the various resources needed to handle the incident such as manpower and specialized equipment. The managers of the staging areas, as well as those responsible for logistics will supply this information to the Planning Officer.

The Planning Officer will play an integral part in the development of the incident action plan. The Planning Officer may be asked to provide information regarding the effects of a particular hazardous substance suspected of being used in the WMD attack. This may also include health hazards, environmental impact, and decontamination procedures. The Planning Officer will usually have a staff of technically competent people to assist him in these duties.

The Planning Sector may have several smaller units under it in order to enable the Planning Officer to more efficiently manage the Planning function. These individual units may be highly specialized and can be added or subtracted from the command structure as the incident progresses. These units may include *Situation Status, Demobilization, Weather,* and *Scientific Information and Research.*

Logistics

The Logistics Officer has the responsibility of providing material, facilities, and services for the incident. In a WMD incident, the Logistics Officer may have a tremendous amount of work and responsibility. As has frequently been mentioned, a WMD incident may require a significant commitment of resources. Many of the resources necessary to handle a WMD incident may not be readily available. Also,

when resources are available, they may not be available in sufficient quantities. The Logistics Officer and the Logistics staff have the task of locating, procuring, and distributing the resources under the direction of the Incident Commander.

To enable the Logistics Officer to efficiently handle this vital function, he or she may establish several branches and units within this functional area. The logistics function can be divided into *service* and *support* branches. The service branch would be responsible for activities at the incident such as communications, emergency medical services for emergency response personnel and the feeding of response personnel.

Within the service branch, the *communications unit* would develop a plan for communications during the incident. This unit would be responsible for obtaining the necessary equipment and distributing it as needed. The communications unit will also be responsible for staffing the incident communications center and for maintaining the communications equipment.

The *medical unit* within the service branch will be responsible for developing the plan

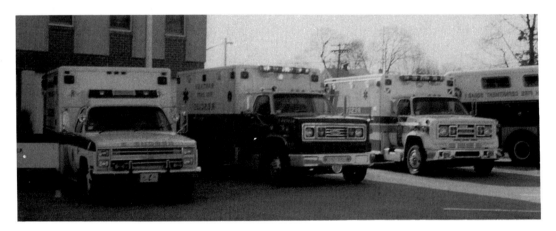

Figure 24. Vehicles should be assembled in a staging area until needed for an assignment. These ambulances are ready to respond to the scene of a mass casualty incident to transport patients to local hospitals.

for emergency medical treatment for the emergency personnel operating at the incident. This is separate from the emergency medical care of the victims of the WMD attack. This unit will also be responsible for preparing any reports and maintaining any records that may be required. This unit should establish dedicated resources for the safety and well-being of the personnel assigned to the incident, including those providing emergency, mitigation, and investigation services.

The *food unit* of the service branch will handle the responsibility of feeding the personnel working at the incident. Determining the food needs, planning the various menus, and preparing and serving the food will be done by the food unit. The food unit will also be responsible for supplying fresh drinking water.

In addition to the service branch of the logistics section, a support branch may be necessary to provide the necessary personnel, equipment, and supplies to support the incident operations. The supervisor of the support branch of the logistics section should establish supply, facilities, and ground support units to assist in his or her duties.

The *supply unit* will actually order the equipment and supplies and will maintain an inventory. The *facilities unit* establishes and maintains the various facilities (i.e., command posts and staging areas) that may be needed to conduct operations at a WMD event. The facilities unit may be asked to supply sanitation facilities, as well as sleeping accommodations. The *ground support* unit will handle the fueling, maintenance and repair of vehicles, as well as, the transportation of personnel and supplies.

Finance

The Finance Section is established to handle the financial aspects of the incident. This includes payments, budgeting, and the tracking of personnel costs. Cost recovery for expenses accrued in the handling of a WMD incident may be possible and will be handled by the Finance Section. There may be instances where resources from the private sector may be utilized. The payment for these types of resources will also be the responsibility of the Finance Section.

There may already be personnel within the law enforcement agency who are currently performing some of the above-described functions (i.e., transportation, supply, and finance. These individuals should be employed in these roles during the WMD incident in order to provide for the most efficient and effective use of available manpower. An example of such an individual would be the person who normally obtains supplies for the agency. He or she will most likely be familiar with the available vendors, as well as, the necessary purchasing procedures.

In the event of a significant WMD incident, it is unlikely that a small- to medium-size law enforcement agency will be able to staff all of the above incident management positions. This may require utilizing personnel from other agencies and from other levels of government. An example of this would be a law enforcement agency that does not have its own emergency medical service. In situations such as this, the Logistics Service Branch role of managing the medical unit should be assigned to a qualified representative of the local emergency medical service agency. While a WMD incident is undoubtedly a criminal event, it is obvious that the management of the incident may require input and assistance from a variety of non-law enforcement agencies and disciplines. Each of these must learn to work together toward a common goal.

COMMAND STAFF

In addition to the above described positions (Operations, Planning, etc.), the Incident Commander may require additional assistance in managing the incident and meeting his or her responsibilities. To help the Incident Commander manage the incident as it becomes more complex, a command staff consisting of Safety, Liaison, and Information Officers may be established. This staff will work directly for the Incident Commander and assist in maintaining a manageable span of control.

Safety Officer

The Safety Officer will monitor the scene and assess safety hazards to personnel operating at the incident. This is extremely important in a WMD incident where operations may be taking place in an environment that is hazardous to personnel. The Safety Officer will keep the Incident Commander informed of existing safety problems and potential threats as they develop. He should be involved in the planning process to ensure that safety issues and concerns are addressed at all stages of the incident.

The Safety Officer will have the authority to take immediate action to correct an unsafe activity. For example, if the Safety Officer observes personnel operating in an area at the scene of a bombing that is in danger of imminent collapse, he or she must have the authority to order personnel to cease operations and leave the danger zone. For actions not requiring immediate action, the Safety Officer should go through the chain of command to have them corrected. When immediate action is taken, the Safety Officer should inform the Incident Commander as soon as practical.

Liaison Officer

An incident involving a WMD will result in numerous agencies and disciplines responding to the scene. The Incident Commander can easily be overwhelmed by the influx of these people into the command post seeking his attention. A *Liaison Officer* should be designated by the Incident Commander as a point of contact for those arriving at the scene. It is conceivable that at a large-scale incident, agencies could arrive and begin to perform activities without the knowledge of the Incident Commander and without working within the Incident Command System (i.e., free-lancing). The Liaison Officer should be a visible point of contact for those arriving at a WMD incident.

The Liaison Officer's most important responsibility is to coordinate the management of assisting agencies and departments. It will require the services of someone who is thoroughly familiar with the Incident Command System, as well as having a familiarity with the agencies involved. This should include a working knowledge of their functions, responsibilities, resources, and capabilities. The Liaison Officer will help communicate with assisting agencies that have not previously trained with the agencies already working at the incident. He or she will also assist agencies that are not familiar with the Incident Command System. This will require a Liaison Officer who is an experienced supervisor and who has an adequate rank or level of authority to help direct the other agencies to work within the system.

Information Officer

An incident involving the use of a WMD

or the threatened use of a WMD will undoubtedly attract the attention of the media. While it is important to keep the public informed, particularly to avoid panic and rumor, the Incident Commander will not, in all likelihood, be able to address the media directly. The Information Officer will be responsible for coordinating all activities with the media, as well as any releases of information with regard to the incident. Many law enforcement agencies have a full-time public Information Officer or other designated spokesperson. Where such a person does not already exist, the Incident Commander must assign someone to this role as early in the incident as possible.

When multiple agencies are involved in a WMD incident, it is essential that any and all releases of information be coordinated by the Information Officer with the approval of the Incident Commander. Personnel working at the incident should be directed to refer all requests for information to the Information Officer. This will help insure that accurate and consistent information is disseminated.

The Information Officer will also be responsible for establishing an area for the media to assemble. The size and specific needs of this area will be determined by the magnitude of the incident. Local regulations or policies may dictate where the media is positioned, as well as the extent of the access that they are allowed. The Information Officer should be familiar with existing laws and policies regarding the media and release of information.

Because a WMD incident is a criminal event, the investigators must have input into the amount and details of the information to be released to the media at various stages of the incident and the investigation. While all releases of information must be coordinated with the Incident Commander, the investigators must also be involved in the information process.

It is essential that the information being disseminated is as accurate and consistent as possible. The Information Officer should have the ability to function under extreme pressure and not yield to the demands of the media.

If the incident is extensive enough to require more than one Information Officer, these officers must coordinate with each other and function at the direction of the lead Information Officer. A situation such as this could arise when a WMD incident has affected multiple locations or has resulted in a massive interest by the media.

Because of the importance of the role to be played by the Information Officer at a WMD incident, those who may be expected to fill this role in the Incident Command System should be included in both the planning and training phases. WMD plan development should include an element to deal with the media and the release of information. Information Officers should be included in the WMD training process. This training should be, at a minimum, to the Awareness Level. This will enable them to more effectively and intelligently do their job in the event of a WMD incident. This will enable them to be familiar with the terminology involved, as well as, with the procedures being employed in handling the incident.

THE COMMAND POST

The command post at an incident involving the use or threatened use of a WMD will become the on-scene center for managing the incident. The command post should be highly visible to those responding to the scene (see Figure 25). Command posts can be as simple as an Incident Commander working from his vehicle to elaborate, mobile command centers specifically designed for emergency management. Regardless of the size and design of the command post, there are certain basic needs that the command post must meet.

The command post should be positioned upwind and uphill of the incident to avoid becoming part of the problem. The safety of those working in and around the command post must be considered at all times. The location of the command post should be in an obvious place so that incoming resources can readily identify it. Ideally, the command post should have as good a view of the incident location as possible, but this may not always be practical. The type of hazard suspected and the local geography may require that the command post be placed out of site of the incident. The area should be checked for secondary devices and secured before the command post is established.

Figure 25. Flags can be used to mark the location of the command post for responding personnel.

The command post will usually become the center for communications. This will include on-scene communications as well as communications between the scene and other locations (i.e., public safety dispatch center and the emergency management center). The command post should therefore be equipped with adequate communications equipment, including radios, telephones (both portable and hardwire), FAX machines, and other items. For example, portable computers may be invaluable during a WMD incident. Many command posts also contain equipment that enables video recording and playback, as well as television reception.

The command post should provide command personnel with a place to conduct operations that offers protection from the weather. It should be free from distractions and provide workspace for staff personnel to write and prepare records as necessary.

The security of the command post should be considered and access to the command post should be controlled by law enforcement personnel, preferably in uniform. Only those with an absolute need to be present in the command post should be admitted. The Liaison Officer should be enlisted to help determine who is needed in the command post. Because a WMD incident is a crime scene that may attract significant attention, the security of command post is essential.

As discussed previously, the command post may be pre-designated when plans are developed for a WMD incident. The above factors should be taken into consideration when deciding where to locate the command post.[31]

Chapter 8

SOURCES OF ASSISTANCE

There are many sources of assistance available to those local authorities charged with the responsibility of responding to a WMD incident. These resources include law enforcement, as well as a variety of other specialists who may be of value in the event of a WMD incident. Those involved in the planning process should determine the availability of such resources and the procedure necessary to actually obtain them.

FEDERAL BUREAU OF INVESTIGATION (FBI)

The FBI has been designated as the lead federal agency for *crisis management* in the event of a WMD incident. This is primarily a law enforcement response and involves the measures necessary to prevent and/or resolve a terrorism threat or incident.[32]

While the agents from the local FBI field office will most likely be the first FBI resources on the scene, the FBI has developed other specialized resources to respond and assist at a WMD incident. The FBI's Hazardous Materials Response Unit (HMRU) has sampling, detection, and identification capabilities that may be used regarding suspected WMD agents. They also have the capability to collect forensic evidence at a WMD crime scene.

The FBI maintains Evidence Response Teams (ERT) throughout the country that are capable of evidence collection and crime scene documentation. These teams are capable of supporting criminal investigations involving acts of terrorism.

FEDERAL EMERGENCY MANAGEMENT AGENCY (FEMA)

The lead federal agency for *consequence management* in the event of a WMD incident is FEMA. Consequence manage-ment involves the measures that are necessary to protect the safety and health of the public. This includes rescue, treatment of victims, evacuation, and preventing the spread of any contamination. Consequence management is also concerned with providing relief and assistance to government, businesses, and individuals affected by the incident.

FEMA also administers the Urban Search and Rescue Teams (USAR) that are available to assist local jurisdictions in the event of building collapses.[33]

DEPARTMENT OF HEALTH AND HUMAN SERVICES (DHHS)

The health and emergency medical concerns that arise during a WMD incident may be significant in terms of both complexity and number of victims. The volume of requests for services may quickly overwhelm local resources. Metropolitan Medical Strike Teams (MMST) are available to assist local governments with agent identification and detection, decontamination of patients, triage and medical treatment. These teams are organized similar to the USAR Teams.

The Center for Disease Control (CDC) is available to provide both on and off site technical consultation and can also provide response support for health agencies at the state and local level. The Epidemiological Intelligence Service (EIS) is also maintained by the CDC.

U.S. ENVIRONMENTAL PROTECTION AGENCY (EPA)

The EPA has the statutory authority to respond to incidents involving the release of hazardous substances into the environment. This would include the release of certain radiological substances, as well as chemical agents such as Sarin, Chlorine, and Hydrogen Cyanide. The EPA's responsibilities are primarily in relation to natural and industrial incidents but also include those caused by an act of terrorism. The EPA can provide technical support and immediate assistance in terms of cleanup and mitigation.

U.S. DEPARTMENT OF ENERGY (DOE)

The DOE is responsible for incidents involving the release of threatened release of radioactive materials. The DOE has established the Radiological Assistance Program (RAP) that will provide the initial DOE response to an incident involving radiological materials. This team will assist in identifying the presence of radiological contamination on personnel, equipment, and property at the scene of an incident. They will also provide assistance with regard to personnel monitoring, decontamination and containment, and recovery of radiological materials.

The Nuclear Emergency Search Team (NEST) is available to provide technical assistance and response to incidents involving improvised nuclear devices and radiological dispersion devices. This team has the ability to search, locate, and identify radiological devices or materials. They also have the capability to transport, render safe, or disable such devices once they have been identified.

The DOE also has numerous other resources that are available to assist local jurisdictions with WMD incidents that involve or are suspected to involve radiological materials. These resources are strategically located throughout the country and can be accessed on a 24-hour basis.

DEPARTMENT OF DEFENSE (DOD)

The "National Defense Authorization Act for Fiscal Year 1997" assigns the primary responsibility for incidents involving chemical, biological, or other related materials to the Department of Defense, while the Department of Energy is responsible for incidents involving nuclear or radiological materials.[34]

There are numerous resources available through the Department of Defense to assist in response to WMD incidents. Some of these specialized units and their capabilities are as follows:

- U.S. Army Technical Escort Unit (TEU) – Field sampling, monitoring, recovery, rendering safe, and decontamination.
- U.S. Army Military Research Institute for Infectious Disease (USAMRIID) – Technical consultation, biological assessment and identification.
- U.S. Marine Corps Chemical Biological Incident Response Force (CBIRF) – Rapid response force, agent identification, hazard prediction, decontamination, medical treatment, and security.

Chapter 9

TACTICAL OPERATIONS IN A HOT ZONE

There may come a point in the response to a WMD incident where traditional tactical operations (i.e., Special Weapons and Tactics – SWAT) may have to be performed within the boundaries of a suspected hot zone. An example of this would be when an investigation determines that a subject is in the process of assembling a WMD device or developing the materials needed for such a device. This may require an effort to interdict before the device is complete and capable of being used as intended. Traditional tactics will have to be modified in order to provide the greatest level of safety for those conducting the operation, as well as the public who may be effected.

Law enforcement tactical teams have had limited training and experience with regard to this type of operation. It will require bringing together the expertise of both tactical and HazMat personnel to create a reasonable procedure. Bomb technicians should also be consulted because of the likelihood that explosives would be a part of a WMD scenario.

Preparation for a tactical operation in a hazardous atmosphere will require attention to several factors not normally considered in day-to-day SWAT activities. These factors will include the use of chemical protective clothing, body armor, respiratory protection, the type of weapons that may be safely deployed in the given environment, and the tactics to be employed by a team utilizing HazMat equipment.

While tactical personnel will be familiar with performing their duties while using respiratory protection (i.e., tear gas situations), this experience will most likely be limited to the use of an air-purifying respirator. Unless the material in question is identified and known in advance of the tactical operation, it is more likely that the tactical team will be entering an atmosphere contaminated by unknown hazardous materials. This will require the highest level of respiratory protection which is provided by a SCBA (see Chapter 4, Personal Protection).

The intelligence gathered that will be used in planning the tactical operation will be critical. The more that is known about the target, including the type of materials that may be encountered, the more successful the operation will be. Because it is virtually impossible to provide maximum protection against all possible hazards, command personnel will focus on providing the highest level of protection that is possible against the perceived threat. Investigative personnel should be taught that the evidence they are gathering as part of their forensic investigation, either before or after an incident has occurred, might be used by other law enforcement personnel conducting a tactical operation. This situation is similar to a narcotics investigator who realizes that his or her investigation may culminate in the execution of a search warrant based upon the information gathered.

Evidence gathered by investigative personnel in the course of their investigation may provide valuable information in planning a tactical operation when a WMD may be involved. For example, sampling done to establish probable cause for a search warrant may provide information regarding the chemical or biological hazards to be faced by the tactical team. Sampling done by remote means or at a safe distance from the site may be of particular value in determining the types of hazards that may be encountered within the suspect location. By reviewing this information, tactical personnel, in consultation with HazMat personnel, will be better able to decide upon the proper type and level of protective equipment necessary to complete their required tasks.

When planning for tactical operations within a HazMat environment, it will be necessary to balance the perceived risk and the level of protection employed. There may come a time in tactical operations where a higher level of protection, based upon the perceived WMD threat, may actually create a greater risk from the tactical perspective. For example, the perceived risk of chemical exposure may, in a normal HazMat incident, call for an entry to be made while wearing a Level A, fully encapsulating, chemical protective suit. Unfortunately, tactical operations in this ensemble would be so

difficult as to become ineffective and dangerous. It would be more prudent to use a lesser level of protection (i.e., Level B) and increase the level of tactical effectiveness and thus the overall margin of safety.

Prior to any operation involving a WMD scenario, tactical personnel must be adequately briefed on the hazards they may encounter and the necessary safety measures. The goal of the tactical operation should be to secure the premises as quickly and safely as possible and to remove any subjects found within as soon as possible. Once this is accomplished, the scene can be properly assessed as to the hazards present and handled in a controlled and orderly manner. Tactical personnel should be briefed regarding the following:

- *Do not* turn any switches on or off. They could be booby-trapped, cause sparks, or interrupt a chemical or biological process.
- *Do not* unplug or disconnect any equipment.
- *Do not* open refrigerators, freezers, or any other containers.
- *Do not* move containers that are in the way. Go over them or around them. Avoid contact with containers and equipment within the location.
- *Avoid* the use of any items that may produce a flame or spark.
- *Do not* taste, smell, or touch any substance.
- *Do not* eat, drink, or smoke within the hot zone.
- *Minimize* contact with subjects found in the location.
- *Do not* touch your mouth, eyes, or other mucous membranes with your hands until you have been decontaminated.
- *Do not* allow a subject found within the location to touch or handle anything. Secure and remove him or her from the scene as quickly as possible.

When planning a WMD tactical operation, an effort should be made to minimize the number of personnel who will actually enter the location during the operation. Utilizing a large number of tactical personnel does not necessarily guarantee a safe and successful operation and may actually hinder the operation. The number of entry personnel should be based upon factors including the size of the location, the number of suspects that may be encountered, and any other special circumstances that exist (i.e., the presence of weapons, dogs, and/or innocent subjects). The team should be of sufficient size to enter and quickly secure the site while not being so large that tactical personnel are getting in each other's way. By keeping the entry team to a minimum, the number of individuals being exposed and requiring decontamination will also be minimized.

The type of tactical procedures to be employed must be carefully selected based on the available intelligence and the perceived threat. Tactical procedures that rely on high-speed entries may not be practical when personnel must operate in cumbersome protective equipment and in the presence of dangerous materials. A team that normally begins a high-risk entry with the introduction of a distraction device into the target location may not be able to employ this tactic when flammable or explosive materials are suspected to be present. Teams should consider employing tactics that will disrupt the location as little as possible to reduce the chances of items being broken or spilled and thus releasing hazardous materials.

When planning a WMD tactical operation, consideration should be given to involving other non-law enforcement agencies that may have resources and expertise to contribute. The fire department may be of value where HazMat personnel are needed and when the site may contain flammable materials. Both emergency and routine scenarios should be considered and decontamination should be planned for. Emergency medical personnel should be available during the operation. Many tactical teams already incorporate emergency medical personnel into their operations in the form of tactical personnel trained as medics or medical personnel trained in tactical operations. In either case, medical personnel should be fully briefed regarding any possible hazards suspected of being present.

EQUIPMENT

In terms of equipment, there are some items that may not normally be employed in a tactical operation that should be on hand for an operation involving a WMD (see Figure 26). Consideration should be given to having the following items available:
- Fire extinguishers. Dry chemical may be used to suppress a fire occurring during or as a result of the entry. Carbon dioxide (CO2) may be used to suppress fire as well as control dogs found at the site. Water may be used to suppress fires involving paper, wood, etc. or to provide emergency decontamination. Care must be used because of the possible presence of water reactive chemicals.
- First aid kits should be readily available. Equipment for treating burn injuries should be on hand.
- "Less lethal" weapons may be useful in controlling and securing subjects found at the site. "Tasers" or stunning weapons may not be feasible if the location is suspected of containing flammable or explosive

materials.

- Personnel should be equipped with radiological dosimeters to measure individual exposure to radioactive materials encountered in the operation.
- Explosion-proof lights should be utilized when operating in a flammable or explosive atmosphere.
- Disposable clothing should be available for those who require decontamination. This should include disposable clothing for victims and suspects found within the location. The original clothing worn by suspects may provide valuable evidence regarding their activities and link them to the crime. Night vision equipment may be useful for perimeter personnel in night operations, as well as personnel operating in low-light or dark environments.
- Thermal imaging devices may be valuable in searching for suspects. It is also useful in the subsequent assessment of the scene when looking for chemicals that may be

giving off heat or other reactions not visible to the naked eye.

- Video cameras may be used to record the interior of the location before investigative personnel and others enter. Personnel can view the interior from a safe location and make their assessment without exposing additional personnel to the risks associated with entry into a hot zone.
- Video equipped robots employed by bomb technicians may be used to provide a view of the interior. Every effort should be made in operating a robot in the hot zone to avoid moving equipment or materials and disturbing the delicate balance that may exist within the site.
- Fans may be used to provide ventilation of the site once it has been determined that this is a safe and prudent course of action. Keep in mind that while a fan may be described as intrinsically safe and thus approved for use in a hazardous atmosphere, the electrical connections to the fan

Figure 26. Tactical operations may require the use of a specialized vehicle such as this Military surplus vehicle employed by a municipal police department for high-risk operations. It provides limited ballistic protection for its occupants.

may not be safe.
- When available, medical antidotes for chemical exposure should be on hand.
- Only intrinsically safe radios should be used in a flammable or explosive atmosphere. The use of portable phones should also be avoided in a potentially flammable atmosphere.

WEAPONS

The selection of weapons to be employed by personnel making the tactical entry will also require consideration and undoubtedly generate discussion among tactical personnel. As with any "normal" tactical operation, the type of weapons selected for the entry will be based upon several factors that will vary from incident to incident. Factors to be included in weapon selection should include the following:
- The weapons utilized by tactical personnel should be those that they train with and are thoroughly familiar with.
- The type of hazardous atmosphere that may be present. If a flammable or explosive atmosphere is present, weapons that give off the least amount, or ideally, no flash should be selected. A flammable or hazardous atmosphere will also preclude the use of distraction or diversionary devices that produce a flame.
- The anticipated armament of the subjects that may be encountered. This will include the type of weapons suspected of being present and any ballistic protection available to the suspects.
- The type of structure to be entered. This should include an evaluation of how much room is available for the movement of tactical personnel.

The actual tactics to be employed in the operation should be determined on a case by case basis. What is appropriate in one scenario may be inadequate or dangerous in another. Whether a dynamic type of entry or a slow and deliberate entry is used will be based on the dangers that are believed to be present. The tactics to be employed in a given case will depend on a variety of factors, including, but not limited to, the following:
- The perceived level of danger and threat.
- Available intelligence regarding the location and the suspects.
- The level of training and ability of the tactical team.
- The equipment available to the team.

TRAINING

Where there appears to be a threat of a WMD incident that may require operations involving special weapons and tactics, law enforcement personnel will require additional specialized training. Recommended training for SWAT personnel with regard to WMD should include the following:
- Orientation to WMD, biological and chemical nerve agents, and toxins.
- Orientation to Level A with specific emphasis on *MOPP-4 protective equipment*.
- Individual and team communications (both hand signals and electronic communication devices).
- Self-decontamination procedures.
- Arrest and control methods (including handcuffing) in MOPP-4.

- Orientation with chemical detection equipment in MOPP-4.
- Team movement in MOPP-4.
- Firearms manipulation and qualification in MOPP-4.
- Field training exercises (FTX) requiring SWAT (equipped in MOPP-4) to assist non-law enforcement entities inside contaminated areas with evacuation, decontamination lines, and recovery of evidence.[35]

Where MOPP-4 is not available, personnel should train with the safety equipment that will be used in the event of an actual operation (i.e., Level B or Level C).

Chapter 10

PLANNING CONSIDERATIONS

In order for law enforcement to effectively respond to a WMD incident, a certain degree of planning must take place prior to the incident actually occurring. Traditionally, local law enforcement has been known to be more reactive than proactive when it comes to emergency response operations. Command personnel are used to, and quite adept at, reacting to emergency situations as they occur. Because of the potential magnitude of a WMD incident and the danger it may pose to police personnel and the public, law enforcement cannot afford to merely wait for the incident to occur and then react to it. They may find that their existing procedures and training are not adequate to mitigate the WMD event.

The plans for a WMD incident need not attempt to cover every potential event. They should be generic in nature and offer guidance to the first officer on the scene as well as supervisory and command personnel. Those responsible for developing such plans should first check to see what plans already exist within the agency. For example, the department may already have a plan in place that describes the desired response to an incident involving hazardous materials. A great deal of this type of planning has been done pursuant to federal regulations that require local governments to have contingency plans in place for the release of hazardous materials.[36]

The department may have a plan for handling crime scenes. The hazardous materials plan and the crime scene plan should be reviewed with regard to responding to a WMD incident. It may be possible to modify one of these plans to meet the WMD needs or to combine elements from both to create a new plan. Whatever course is taken, the plan must be practical and take into consideration the role that will be played by the agency, the resources of the agency, and the availability of other resources that the agency may have access to.

The role to be played by the law enforcement agency in the event of a WMD incident should be determined prior to actually developing the plans. Certain duties will almost certainly be the responsibility of the law enforcement agency in question. These may include traffic control, crime scene security, and crowd control. Other responsibilities may include evidence preservation and collection, public information, criminal investigation, victim tracking, and other emergency management functions.

The plan should provide a list of units or commands within the department that should be notified in the event of a WMD incident. The notification process should also include outside agencies that may have resources to offer or a role to play in a WMD incident. For example, the FBI has been designated as the lead federal agency for crisis management in the event of a WMD incident and should be notified as early as possible to facilitate their response.[37] Other agencies that may be included in the notification process include:

• Health Department
• Bureau of Alcohol, Tobacco, and Firearms
• U.S. Postal Service
• Other law enforcement agencies with a jurisdictional interest (i.e., state police)
• Fire department
• Emergency medical services
• Emergency Management Office

• Public works
• Local government officials
• Special response teams (i.e., EOD, HazMat, SWAT)
• Environmental agencies
• Intelligence units/agencies
• Agencies that may be affected by the WMD incident or have resources to offer towards its resolution
• Adjoining jurisdictions
• High-profile or high-risk locations that may need to be alerted to the possibility of a WMD event at their site

Plans should be kept simple in order to be effective in the event that a WMD incident occurs. The people who will be expected to put the plan in action and make it work should be aware of both its existence and contents. In-service training should be conducted to make sure that everyone is familiar with the plan and their individual roles and responsibilities.

LEPC PLAN

The Superfund Amendment and Reauthorization Act of 1986 (SARA, Title III) requires local governments to have a plan in place for response to incidents involving the release of hazardous materials that threaten the safety of the public and the environment.[38] States are required to develop contingency plans and maintain information regarding the presence of certain hazardous materials within their jurisdiction. Most states, in turn, passed this responsibility on to smaller government entities such as the counties. The counties responded by establishing *Local Emergency Planning Committees* (LEPC's) consisting of representative from the various government entities and the private sector that may be involved in a release of the hazardous materials that fall within the scope of the law.

The LEPC's throughout the nation have developed extensive local plans addressing the potential problems associated with the release of hazardous materials. These plans offer a great reference source for law enforcement personnel tasked with developing a plan for response to a WMD incident. Many of the elements needed for a WMD plan may already be present in the LEPC plan. Some of these elements may include the following:

• Emergency notifications.
• Command and control.
• Available resources.
• Evacuation procedures.
• Public information.
• Emergency medical response and resources.
• High-risk locations and transportation routes.

VULNERABILITY ASSESSMENT

As part of the WMD planning process a law enforcement agency should examine the locations within its jurisdiction to determine if there are any potential targets for a WMD attack. This analysis can be based on prior incidents occurring in the jurisdiction in question or in other locales. Planning personnel should consult with other agencies and authorities that may be involved in the same planning process to make sure that no potential targets are overlooked. While the potential list of WMD targets is only limited by the imagination and motivation of a terrorist, the following is a list of potential targets that can be found in many communities and are worthy of inclusion in the planning process:

• Areas where large numbers of people gather (i.e., shopping malls, theaters, and sporting events).
• Locations that may be controversial including abortion clinics, foreign government facilities and educational facilities.
• Government facilities of all levels of government.
• Military facilities.
• Transportation facilities including airports, bus terminals, and train stations.
• Public works facilities such as water treatment and sewage plants.
• Water supplies.
• Communications facilities.
• Media facilities.
• Municipal power supplies.
• Corporate, business, and financial centers. Particular attention should be paid to those businesses that are high profile or that have international interests.
• Criminal justice facilities (i.e., courts, detention facilities, and law enforcement facilities).
• Religious institutions and facilities.
• Research facilities.

• Facilities that use, store, or manufacture hazardous materials, explosives, biological materials, and/or radiological materials that may be used in the manufacture of a WMD.

Historically, most of these locations have been the victims of some form of terrorist activity in the past. Law enforcement officials should be aware of their existence within their own jurisdiction and make appropriate plans to deal with a WMD incident occurring there. When developing plans to respond to a WMD incident occurring at one of the above-described locations or facilities, attention should be paid to the following law enforcement concerns:

• Securing access to and egress from the scene for other emergency responders.
• Providing crime scene security for the site.
• Establish evacuation areas that can be secured before being occupied.
• Controlling victim evacuation routes and evacuation centers.

Figure 27. The planning process for a WMD incident may include the establishment of pre-designated incident facilities for responding personnel such as this police staging area.

• Protecting victims and responders from further attacks.
• Notifying other agencies as needed including investigative agencies such as the FBI.
• Preserving the integrity of the crime scene for evidentiary purposes.
• Pre-designating command post and staging areas (see Figure 27).

In addition to the above-described locations, law enforcement may be faced with a special event occurring within their jurisdiction. This may be in the form of a sporting event or high-profile dignitary visits. Other special events may include a controversial criminal trial or other media event that may draw unprecedented attention or crowds to a particular location. Events such as these may tax the resources of most agencies and may require outside assistance just to meet basic manpower requirements. Assistance may also be required for specialized units such as bomb technicians and tactical teams.

These special events may require a significant amount of planning on a relatively short notice. Again, planners should refer to existing plans and modify them as needed for the special event. Coordination with other law enforcement agencies from various levels of government may be required during these events as well as with other disciplines (i.e., fire, rescue, HazMat, and emergency management). It is essential that the Incident Command System be established during the planning phase of the operation to ensure the highest level of efficiency during the operation. By incorporating the Incident Command System into the plan, the participants will have a greater understanding of their role and responsibilities, as well as having an existing chain of command (see Chapter 7, Incident Management).

EXISTING CAPABILITIES

As part of the planning process, law enforcement agencies should first examine their existing capabilities for the handling of a WMD incident. For example, even if an agency does not have its own bomb squad or bomb technicians, they will most likely have a procedure in place to obtain such specialized services in the event of an emergency occurring within their jurisdiction. Existing plans for hazardous materials incidents, bomb and explosives incidents, radiological incidents, and incidents involving mass casualties may serve as the basis for the development of a plan to respond to a WMD incident. These plans should be incorporated into the WMD plan to avoid "reinventing the wheel." These plans may already establish important contacts and relationships that will be essential in the event of a WMD incident.

Local law or custom may require that letters of agreement or mutual aid arrangements be established in order to provide for the services that may be required. These issues should be addressed in the planning process and must be resolved before the actual incident occurs. A law enforcement agency should not wait until a suspected nerve agent has been released within its jurisdiction to discover that the assistance relied upon from a neighboring agency is not available due to the lack of a proper agreement. Even large law enforcement agencies that normally act independently may find themselves in need of assistance in the event a WMD incident occurs. A WMD incident involving the exposure, or suspected exposure, of a large number of victims could easily overwhelm the available resources of even the largest agency.

When determining personnel needs in the event of WMD incident, planners should be realistic in terms of the resources they expect to actually be available at the time of the emergency. When reviewing the availability of off-duty personnel to respond to an emergency, the following factors should be considered:

• Members committed to child-care respon-sibilities may need to find alternatives before reporting for duty.

• Personnel may be involved in other activi-ties in the community such as being a member of the local volunteer fire department or ambulance corps that may be relying on them in the event of a WMD incident.

• A proper and updated mobilization plan must be in place.

DETERMINING YOUR EQUIPMENT NEEDS

It is clear that a WMD incident will require resources beyond the existing capability of most law enforcement agencies. Additional manpower, equipment, supplies, and technical assistance may all be required for a law enforcement agency to successfully respond to, control, and investigate a WMD incident. The availability of these resources and the procedure to obtain them when needed should be addressed in the planning stage (see Chapter 10, Planning Considerations).

Equipment

Equipment needs may be varied depend-ing on the nature of the incident. After assessing the vulnerability of a jurisdiction to a WMD attack, the existing equipment that may be needed by law enforcement to perform their role during the incident should be reviewed (see Figure 28). The following items may be required by law enforcement in the event of a WMD incident:

• Crowd control equipment including barri-cades, loud speakers, and auxiliary lighting.

• Traffic control devices such as road flares, traffic cones, and programmable traffic signs.

• Personal protective equipment may be needed for those aiding the injured, securing the inner perimeter, gathering evidence and conducting the investigation in the hot zone (see Chapter 4, Personal Protection).

• Communications needs such as portable radios, phones, FAX machines, and computers.

• Equipment needed to run the command post and facilitate operation of the Incident Command System.

• Equipment and materials needed to identify, collect, and preserve forensic evidence (see Chapter 16, Sampling for Chemical, Biological, and Radiological Evidence).

In some cases, these items may already be on hand, but not in sufficient quantities to handle a large incident. Provisions should be made to obtain the necessary amounts in the event of an emergency. Some items may be in the possession of other municipal agencies and can be made available during a WMD event. An example of this would be a local highway department that can provide barricades or a department of parks and recreation that may have portable lighting equipment. As stated earlier, the acquisition and distribution of equipment during the actual incident will usually be the responsibility of the Logistics Officer.

Law enforcement personnel who will be responding to a WMD incident will require certain equipment that may not already be available to them. This equipment can range from the personal protective equipment previously described to specialized investigative equipment. Law enforcement equipment needs should be determined *after* a plan has been developed and *after* it has been decided what functions and responsibilities the agency will be undertaking.

Response Equipment

The type and level of protective equipment provided for law enforcement first responders will depend on several factors including the following:

Figure 28. Specialized equipment such as auxiliary lighting may be needed at the scene of a WMD incident.

• The role that the law enforcement responder will be playing. Those who will be expected to have contact with victims and assist in operations in a potentially hazardous environment will require a higher level of protection than those in a safe area manning perimeter positions.
• What will be the level of training for the law enforcement personnel? The use of respiratory protection requires a certain level of training as well as other prerequisites as established by OSHA.
• What level of funding is available to equip law enforcement first responders? Planners and administrators must realize the costs associated with committing law enforcement personnel to safely respond to WMD incidents.
• What is the level of threat that exists within the law enforcement agency's jurisdiction? The planning process should help determine the presence of certain high-risk locations such as government facilities. Officers responding to these locations may need a higher level of protection available to them.

Investigative Equipment

The equipment required by law enforcement personnel responsible for investigating a WMD incident will vary with the nature of the incident. Personnel expected to enter a potentially hazardous atmosphere to gather evidence and conduct a criminal investigation will require the same level of protection that other specialized personnel would use.

Much of the equipment found in a routine criminal investigation will also be found in a WMD investigation. However, the equipment used to properly collect scientific evidence and should be obtained *after* the decision is made regarding the level of involvement the law enforcement agency will have in a WMD investigation.

Specialized Equipment

In addition to the first responders and investigators, other law enforcement personnel may require specialized equipment to handle incidents involving a WMD. Law enforcement specialists such as bomb technicians and tactical personnel may require personal protective equipment, as well as special tools and weapons to properly handle a WMD incident.

Bomb technicians and their unique equipment needs must be considered in the planning stage. This is essential when you consider that explosives are still the primary choice of weapon for a terrorist. Some specialized equipment that may be utilized by bomb technicians includes:

• Standard bomb suits, worn to protect against fragmentation, heat, and overpressure, may not be compatible with chemical protective clothing and respiratory protection. Suits that are designed to be compatible with PPE are available and may need to be acquired.

• Robots that can be used to enter hazardous atmospheres and thus avoid exposing bomb technicians and investigative personnel to danger. Robots can be used to obtain samples, perform video reconisance, monitor a hazardous atmosphere, and perform render safe procedures on suspect devices (see Figure 29).

• Equipment to record a person's exposure to radiological materials in the form of dosimeters or exposure badges may be required for personnel when the presence of such materials is suspected.

Figure 29. Bomb technicians prepare to deploy a robot to investigate an improvised explosive device.

Tactical personnel may require specialized equipment to operate in a hazardous environment (see Chapter 9, Tactical Operations in a Hot Zone). These items may include:

• Special garments that may be necessary when the atmosphere is suspected to contain flammable or explosive materials.

• Respiratory protection that is compatible with both the perceived threat and the other tactical equipment may be required.

• Chemical protective clothing may be necessary in conjunction with the ballistic protection normally employed during tactical operations.

Once the equipment needs have been determined, based on an analysis of the potential threat, the necessary equipment must be funded and procured. However, the process does not end with the delivery of the equipment to the agency. The equipment must be distributed so that it is in the proper place to be utilized by the people who will need it in the event of a WMD incident.

Personnel will also have to be familiarized with the equipment and trained in its proper use. Personnel must be aware of the equipment's limitations and be able to use it under emergency conditions. A program must be developed to maintain the readiness of the equipment and to repair and replace it as needed.

INVESTIGATION PLANS

Part of the planning process for law enforcement should include the determination of who will handle the investigation of the WMD incident. Even though a WMD incident may involve an investigation and subsequent prosecution at the federal level, local law enforcement must also be prepared to investigate the incident with regard to the violation of local and state laws. Some state laws that may be applicable include homicide, assault, weapon violations, arson, and property crimes. Local law enforcement should be prepared to investigate these offenses with the ultimate goal of a successful prosecution.

The Investigation Team

The law enforcement agency in question must decide who within their agency will handle the investigation. Smaller agencies that do not have specialized investigators may assign the responsibility as they would any other specialized crime. Other agencies may divide responsibility based upon crimes against property versus crimes against persons. Whatever criteria an agency relies upon, it will be incumbent upon the agency to insure the designated investigators are properly trained and equipped. Even if an agency decides that it will not conduct a WMD investigation and defers the investigation to another agency, it must still insure that its investigators are familiar enough with the WMD problem to be able to recognize the need to call in the proper people.

Law enforcement agencies may already have valuable investigative resources within their ranks that, with additional training, may be designated to investigate WMD incidents. Law enforcement has been investigating the criminal use of explosives for quite some time and many agencies already have investigators trained in this highly specialized field. This type of training provides an excellent foundation for the future WMD investigator.

In recent years, many law enforcement agencies have also been involved in investigating incidents regarding crimes against the environment. These investigators have been trained to recognize and investigate crimes involving the intentional or negligent release of hazardous materials into the environment. Law enforcement agencies with access to these investigators should consider using their expertise in the investigation of WMD incidents.

Who Will Gather the Evidence

Part of the investigation in the event of a WMD incident will involve the collection of physical evidence. This part of the investigation may require personnel to enter the hot zone and thus require them to be properly trained and equipped. A plan for law enforcement response to a WMD incident should include designating those who will be responsible for actually collecting the physical evidence that will be necessary to conduct a proper investigation. The *forensic evidence* collection that is necessary for a proper criminal investigation should not be confused with the *sampling* and *field testing* done by the first responders as part of their scene assessment. There are specific procedures and protocols that are required to be followed in order to insure the admissibility of the evidence in a subsequent prosecution.

Ideally, the plan should call for the evidence to be gathered at the direction of the investigator designated as the "crime scene coordinator." This individual will be an investigator who is familiar with the evidentiary requirements in question, as well as, the type of evidence that may be present based upon the nature of the event (see Chapter 14, The Investigative Team).

INTER-AGENCY PLANNING

In planning for a WMD incident, law enforcement must engage in planning with the other agencies that will be involved in the response, mitigation, and investigation of a WMD incident. This should include the various levels of government that may be involved in the incident. Law enforcement should be prepared to take the lead within their jurisdiction in bringing together these agencies and disciplines in order to plan for an event such as this. Because of its existing command structure and visible presence within a community, law enforcement is in a unique position to act as the lead agency.

The fact that a WMD incident *will* involve a criminal act places the onus on law enforcement to play an integral part in the planning process. In most cases, even the threat of a WMD attack will be a violation of a statute on the local, state, or federal level. Because of this, law enforcement will be involved in *every* WMD incident. This may not be the case with the other emergency response agencies. For example, when a letter is received threatening to contain anthrax, but there is no apparent material present, there may not be a need for the local fire department to respond.

Some jurisdictions have created a task force or similar committee that meets on a regular basis to discuss the WMD issues within their locale. Some of the issues that may be addressed during these inter-agency sessions include:

• What roles the various local, state, and federal agencies will play during an incident.
• An ongoing assessment of vulnerability and potential targets. This must be ongoing as the population and makeup of an area may change.
• Developing response plans and standard

operating procedures for WMD incidents.

- Establishing equipment needs, training needs, and other requirements for the handling of a WMD incident.
- Determining existing resources.
- Obtaining proper funding levels based on the established needs.
- Bringing all participating agencies up to the proper level of awareness with regard to the potential for a WMD incident and the ability to recognize a WMD incident in its earliest stages.
- All the participants should become familiar with the duties, responsibilities, and capabilities of the other agencies that may be involved in a WMD incident.
- Gathering and sharing intelligence information on a regular basis.
- Reviewing WMD incidents occurring within the jurisdiction and elsewhere.
- Provide an open forum for questions, ideas and suggestions regarding WMD issues.

These planning sessions should be held on a regular basis. Those sent to represent the various participating agencies should possess a level of authority that allows them to provide input regarding their agencies capabilities and policies.

If conducted properly, these inter-agency meetings can have a significant impact on how successfully a WMD incident is handled when it occurs. The interpersonal relationships that are established between the supervisors of the various disciplines will prove to be invaluable in the event a WMD incident occurs

Once the above-described plans have been developed, on both an agency and task force level, it is essential that they be reviewed and modified on a regular basis. In particular, items such as contact names and numbers, potential target locations, available resources, and other similar details need to be updated on a regular basis. Someone within a law enforcement agency should be responsible for keeping the agency's plan updated and current. How often a plan is subject to review depends on the nature of the agency and jurisdiction in question. Large-scale operations where personnel and other elements change on a frequent basis will require a more frequent review than a small agency with minimal turnover.

The plan should also be reviewed as part of the critique process to be conducted upon conclusion of the incident (see Chapter 11, Post-Incident Operations). Plans should also be reevaluated when incidents occur elsewhere. These incidents may provide insight, procedures, or guidelines for handling WMD incidents. As an agency's level of expertise develops with regard to WMD response, their plan should also reflect these positive changes.

TRAINING CONSIDERATIONS

The training needs of the law enforcement agencies should be examined as part of the WMD planning process. The first step in this process will be to determine what specific roles law enforcement personnel will be designated to play in the event of a WMD incident. For example, it must be determined who will be in the hot zone, who will be in close proximity to the hot and warm zones, and who will be in the outermost or safe areas.

Once the roles of the law enforcement personnel have been delineated, the type and level of training necessary to enable them to do their job safely and effectively may be determined. There are existing standards and rules that can then be applied based upon this information. In some cases, an actual job/task analysis may have to be performed to further clarify who will be responsible for specific duties.

Who Will Be Trained

Existing standards already require that all law enforcement personnel that may be the first to respond to or discover an incident involving hazardous materials must be trained to a certain minimum level.[39] This level of training is usually referred to as the "Awareness" level and most patrol personnel should already be trained to this level. Many police academies already include this type of training in their curriculum for recruits. The main emphasis at this level of training is to be able to recognize the existence of a hazardous materials incident, notify the proper people to handle the incident, and to secure the incident to keep others from entering the area.

Patrol personnel, those working at special events, and any other law enforcement personnel who may find themselves at the scene of an incident involving a release or threatened release of a hazardous substance should be trained to this Awareness level. Additional training should be provided to include recognition of WMD devices, the signs and symptoms of exposure to WMD materials, and other essentials regarding the recognition of a potential WMD incident. This training must also include basic procedures to follow regarding scene security, personal protective actions, and what notifications need to be made.

Those who will be involved in actual incident mitigation and defensive actions should be trained to the next level of training. This level of training is referred to as the "Operations" level. Generally speaking, those requiring Operations level training are personnel who will contain the incident from a distance, keep it from spreading, and prevent exposures.[40] Personnel at this level will be familiar with the selection and use of personal protective equipment, perform basic decontamination procedures, and understand the concept of hazard and risk assessment with regard to the hazardous substances involved.

Operations level training will be required, as a minimum, for those law enforcement personnel who will be expected to enter a hazardous environment that requires the use of personal protective equipment. Those involved in handling contaminated injured or deceased victims, gathering evidence near the hot zone, and/or assisting in the decontamination of others should be trained to the Operations level.

Those who respond to a WMD incident for the purpose of minimizing or stopping the release and taking a more aggressive action than the operations personnel should be trained to the "Hazardous Materials Technician" level. Responders at this level will be expected to actually work within the hot zone if necessary.[41]

Hazardous Materials Technicians will be able to use field survey instruments, select and use personal protective equipment, perform containment and control operations, and perform decontamination procedures. Personnel at this level will also be familiar with basic chemistry concepts and have a basic understanding of toxicology. In many jurisdictions, existing hazardous materials response teams will perform this level of activity.

Joint Investigative and Response Personnel Training

In order to ensure optimum performance in the event of a WMD incident, investigative personnel should train with the HazMat response personnel who will be involved in mitigating the incident. This training will help develop a working relationship between the different agencies and disciplines that may find themselves working at a WMD incident.

Personnel will become familiar with the needs and operating requirements of the other groups as well as their procedures and protocols. This familiarization will result in fewer conflicts during the incident and provide for a smoother overall operation. They should become familiar with the equipment that the other units utilize, as well as, any special resources or expertise that may be available for use. As an example, through this joint training, the local HazMat team may become familiar with the capabilities of the bomb squad and, if available, their robot. This may prove to be useful in the future when the HazMat team is confronted with a problem that may benefit from the use of a robot.

In many cases, the interpersonal relationships that develop during these training sessions will be as valuable as any technical training that may take place. Responders and investigators will develop confidence in each others abilities, as well as gaining an insight into the missions that need to be accomplished. This type of training will also help to insure the safety of the public and, at the same time, hold the responsible parties accountable for the crime.

Available Resources

When developing the training program to prepare for a law enforcement response to WMD incidents, all existing training programs should be examined first. Local police, fire, and emergency medical service training academies may already have programs in place that can be utilized to prepare for a WMD incident (i.e., HazMat Awareness and Operations courses).

The United States Environmental Protection Agency offers hazardous materials training courses at the Technician level as well as other specialized classes such as HazMat sampling. There are also correspondence courses available from the Federal Emergency Management Agency (FEMA), as well as the National Fire Academy that address topics that include radiological response, hazardous materials response, and terrorism.

There are many private training entities that provide training in this highly specialized field. As discussed earlier, training should be based on the needs of law enforcement with regard to the roles they will be designated to play in the event of a WMD incident.

Making the Training Practical

When developing WMD training for law enforcement personnel, it is important to make it both practical and relevant. In most instances, training time for law enforcement personnel is an extremely valuable commodity and cannot afford to be wasted. Emphasis should be placed on the skills and knowledge that are essential to the mission. Information that is "nice to know" should be considered a secondary priority.

Training should be related to the jurisdiction in question and should address local scenarios. The information gathered in the vulnerability assessment and planning stage should be utilized in making the training relevant to the locale. For this training to be of value, local problems and available resources should be incorporated into the training. Tabletop exercises may be used to enhance the training and increase the awareness level of the trainees.

Personnel who will be required to function in a hazardous area should receive hands-on training and practice in the use of personal protective equipment, as well as training in the use of the instruments and equipment they will be expected to utilize. Investigative tasks, such as collecting evidence in the hot zone, should be practiced to a point where they can be done under the stressful and adverse conditions that will be found during a WMD incident. Once skills are developed, they must be practiced on a regular basis to maintain the desired level of competence.

Training should also be conducted with regard to the Incident Command System and the WMD plans that are developed. Law enforcement personnel must be aware of their roles and responsibilities before the actual incident takes place.[42] Supervisory personnel should be familiar enough with the Incident Command System and the response plan to enable them to step into any role that may be required of them.

Refresher Training

Existing OSHA requirements require that those trained in accordance with their HazMat standards receive refresher training on an annual basis. This annual training is intended to maintain the competencies established in the initial training that brought them to the Awareness, Operations, Technician, Specialist, and Incident Commander levels.[43]

As with any other training that is undertaken to prepare law enforcement personnel for a WMD incident, refresher training should be documented. Proper documentation of the training process will help to track who is trained to what level, who needs training (either initial or annual refresher), and what the future training needs of the agency are. The proper documentation of the training received by law enforcement personnel may be necessary to establish a responder's or an investigator's expertise in the event that their testimony is required in the trial process. Training documentation will also come under scrutiny in the event that a responder is injured or exposed during the incident and a subsequent inquiry is made with regard to workplace safety.

Chapter 11

POST-INCIDENT OPERATIONS

Once operations at a WMD incident have been concluded, there are several steps that must be taken to insure that the lessons learned from the incident are properly utilized. Regardless of how success- ful an operation was, there will always be things that can be improved upon. This process will also help other jurisdictions in planning their response.

CRITIQUE

Within a short period of time after the termination of a WMD incident, the various agencies that participated in the response should be brought together for the purposes of critiquing the incident operations. The critique should be conducted under the direction of one person acting as a "chair- person." The chairperson should be someone with authority. He or she should have the ability to take an overall view of the entire incident. The Incident Commander should be present at the critique. However, he or she may not be the best person to manage the critique due to his or her personal involvement. Each agency should be prepared to discuss their actions with regard to the incident, as well as make recommendations to improve upon or correct shortcomings that were encountered during the incident. The critique should be conducted within a specified time frame to allow the chairperson to keep the meeting focused and moving.

In order for the critique to be productive, it must be conducted in a professional and non-adversarial manner. All the participants should realize that regardless of how well an incident may have gone, there will always be room for some degree of improvement. In order to accomplish the most during the critique session, it may be advisable for the individual disciplines and agencies to gather beforehand and review their own operations before gathering as a group. For example, all the law enforcement agencies may wish to gather before the general critique to specifi- cally examine the law enforcement response to the incident. There may be some issues that are unique to law enforcement that do not need to be discussed as part of an overall incident critique (i.e., sensitive intelligence issues).

A record should be kept during the critique with the intention of preparing an after action report. This report should be seen as a vehicle to improve incident response in the future, as well as a possible method of sharing information with other agencies and jurisdictions so that others may learn from the incident. It should not be done in a negative manner and should be as thorough as possible, including both positive and negative points of the operation. How extensive the report is will be determined, to a certain extent, by the magnitude or complexity of the incident. Documentation should include photos, diagrams, video, and

other records when appropriate.

There are different formats that may be employed when conducting a critique of a large-scale incident. One technique involves having each individual present a statement regarding his own performance and state what he feels the major issues are. After individual statements are made, the individuals should be surveyed again for comments regarding the strengths and weaknesses or each group's actions and contributions regarding the incident. Following these first two steps, the leader of the critique should elicit discussion and constructive comments concerning the problems and issues that have been presented.[44]

RE-ASSESSING TRAINING NEEDS

The critique and after action report should also examine the issue of training. Specifically, the following questions should be addressed during the critique phase:
• Was the training provided to response personnel before the incident adequate and appropriate?
• What specific topics need to be addressed in future training programs?
• Are there existing programs that will meet the identified needs or is there a need to develop new programs?

• Would training have resulted in a different outcome for the incident or any particular aspect of it? If so, what type of training and how can it be provided?

Because of the importance of training in the future success of any WMD response, those who will be involved in the training process should be represented during the critique. This will give them a better understanding of the overall operation and help them to provide the most effective training.

RE-ASSESSING EQUIPMENT NEEDS

The critique should also examine equipment needs. Regardless of how well equipped and prepared an agency is, there will undoubtedly be some shortcomings discovered in the course of a WMD incident. These should be identified with the goal of being better prepared for the next event.

As with the question of training, specific questions should be addressed regarding equipment. The equipment reassessment questions include:
• Was the existing equipment adequate to handle the various tasks that needed to be accomplished during the incident?
• What specific equipment will be needed to

handle future WMD incidents?
- Did existing equipment function properly and meet the needs it was intended for?
- Were there adequate supplies to support the operation?
- Were the equipment and supplies readily available in a timely manner?
- Was the equipment properly maintained to

insure that it was in optimum operating condition?
- How can identified needs be met to ensure adequate equipment and supplies for future incidents?
- If mutual aid agreements were relied upon for equipment and supplies, did these agreements function properly?

RE-ASSESSING PLANS AND PROCEDURES

The critique process should also examine the plans that have been developed for response to WMD incidents. If these plans have yet to be developed, either by individual agencies or on a jurisdictional level, the critique may serve as both a catalyst and a starting point for the development of such plans. Those who are involved in the planning process should be represented during the critique and should be included in the distribution of any after action reports. There are some specific points that should be addressed with regard to plans and procedures including the following:
- Did the plan provide the needed guidance for the handling of the incident?
- Were the notification aspects of the plan adequate and were they followed?
- Was the command and control portion of the plan adhered to and did it meet the needs of the incident?
- Did any contingencies arise that were not

sufficiently addressed in the plan?
- Was the plan too extensive or too complicated to serve as a useful tool for personnel managing the incident?
- Were the guidelines for first response personnel adequate?
- What additions need to be made to the plan to handle the next incident?
- What part of the plan was ineffective or erroneous and should be replaced or deleted?

These questions should be asked of the plans of both the jurisdiction in general, as well as any specific law enforcement agency's plan. Any negative or otherwise questionable answers to the above questions should result in a follow-up review by the jurisdiction or agency in question. Plans should be reviewed after every incident to see if they are up to date and provide both necessary and accurate information.

POST-INCIDENT STRESS DEBRIEFING

It has been recognized that response to, and participation in, critical incidents (i.e., WMD incidents) places a significant amount of physical and psychological stress upon emergency response personnel. This includes those involved in supervisory, support, and investigative roles. Many law

enforcement agencies have already established procedures to provide critical incident stress debriefing (CISD) services for their employees that have been involved in critical incidents. These programs may be available to employees on a voluntary basis or, in some cases, participation may be mandatory. Some labor unions and other organizations that represent law enforcement personnel also make such services available to their members.[45]

Law enforcement management should be aware of the need for such programs for the benefit of their personnel and their families. There have been examples of law enforcement officers attempting to take their own lives after having been involved in critical incidents. The plans developed by law enforcement agencies for response to WMD incidents should include the provision of CISD services for its members. Where an agency does not have such a capability, the procedure should make provisions for obtaining these essential services.

MEDICAL SCREENING AND SURVEILLANCE

Law enforcement personnel who were involved in the response to a WMD incident may have been exposed to hazardous substances. In some cases, this may be obvious and readily detectable (i.e., chemical splash). Other cases may not be obvious (i.e., anthrax inhalation). In either instance, law enforcement personnel who may have been exposed should be provided with medical treatment in the form of an examination in which the necessary tests to determine and document exposure are provided.

Agencies that already have a medical officer, or an existing medical program, should include this in their planning process and should utilize these resources in the event of an actual incident. Those whose jobs require them to work with hazardous materials should already be participating in a medical surveillance program that consists of an annual medical exam with special emphasis placed on screening for exposure to hazardous substances.[46] Employees who may have been exposed must also be provided with medical treatment as necessary.

All actions taken with regard to exposure to hazardous substances should be carefully documented. This documentation will serve to protect the employee in the event he or she should later become ill as a result of an exposure. It will also protect the employer against employee claims that may arise that are not a result of a WMD incident.

Chapter 12

PREPARING FOR THE
CRIMINAL INVESTIGATION

Law enforcement agencies have several choices available to them when dealing with the investigative issues surrounding the use or the threatened use of a weapon of mass destruction. In many instances, the initial investigation may be handled by a local law enforcement agency.[47] In some instances, federal assistance may be required. The size and scope of the incident may require the Federal Bureau of Investigation to act as the lead investigative agency. However, a full response by the Federal Bureau of Investigation, which would include hot zone evidence gathering capabilities, may take several hours. It is during this critical period of time that certain biological and/or chemical evidence may disperse to such an extent that obtaining a proper sample (for criminal prosecution purposes) may be impossible. However, many incidents of this type may be limited in scale and may not warrant or require an immediate federal response. There are dozens of criminal incidents involving hazardous materials that occur each day throughout this country. Local law enforcement personnel have been called upon many times to investigate these types of incidents. An example of such a limited incident may be a chemical device, containing a simple irritant, which has been brought into a school by a student and then detonated. While this may cause a temporary hospitalization of many students and staff, the criminal investigation may best be handled on a local law enforcement level and may not require a federal response. In another situation, there may be the release of a cyanide gas at a manufacturing facility causing severe injuries both on and off the site of occurrence. A release such as this may be accidental in nature or it may have been caused by the willful act of a disgruntled employee. In another situation, low level radiological sources may be planted in the cars, homes, and/or workplaces of selected local political targets. In each of the three examples cited above, local law enforcement officers may be called upon to gather the physical evidence and conduct a criminal investigation. To accomplish this, the investigative arms of local law enforcement agencies must be properly trained and equipped so that they may gather evidence in a safe and legally sufficient manner. It is essential that criminal investigators understand that there is little difference between the types of crime scenes described above and any other type of crime scene, with that exception that *the evidence you gather may kill you.*

PERSONNEL TRAINING

A successful criminal investigation involving the use or threatened use of a weapon of mass destruction requires the application of several different disciplines. The investigator must bring his or her basic police skills to the investigation. These skills should include interviewing and interrogation techniques and the ability to properly handle the collection and preservation of forensic evidence. In addition to the above, he or she must be trained and equipped to safely gather physical evidence at a WMD crime scene. This requires specialized training in the handling of hazardous materials and a full understanding of the appropriate statutes which may have been violated. However, this is just the beginning of the learning process for the criminal investigator. In addition to the above, he or she must be fully trained in the required sampling protocols for chemical, biological, and radiological substances. This training should include sampling techniques for aerosols, liquids, solids, surfaces, and dermal sampling.

The criminal investigator must understand his or her role and responsibilities when collecting scientific evidence at a WMD crime. While it may be acceptable for an emergency responder to violate a minor safety requirement or for an emergency responder to place a sample of the hazardous substance into an improper sampling container, it is *unacceptable* when done by criminal investigative personnel. Each action taken by criminal investigators at a weapon of mass destruction crime scene will be subject to review and cross-examination at a criminal trial. Errors such as these, although appearing minor in nature, may have a devastating effect upon the criminal prosecution. Federal OSHA laws and scientifically acceptable sampling protocols *must* be adhered to. It is important that the criminal investigator recognize that he or she *may not violate the law, to enforce the law.*

Fortunately, there are many different types of specialized training available to the criminal investigator from a variety of sources. Federal, state, and local governments offer many training programs in the areas of Hazardous Materials Incident Response, Radiological Incidents, Biohazards, Toxicology, Respiratory Protection, Confined Space Entry, Hazardous Materials Sampling, and Criminal Investigations relating to hazardous materials. In addition, many training and instructional programs are being offered in the area of Weapons of Mass Destruction. Many of these training programs are free and are offered throughout the country several times a year. The following are just a few of the suggested training programs that will assist the criminal investigator in better understanding the issues surrounding the gathering of chemical, biological and/or radiological evidence:

Occupational Safety and Health Administration (OSHA)

Emergency Response to Hazardous Substance Release

This training course will increase the criminal investigator's knowledge of emergency response procedures for facilities that must meet the requirements of either 29 CFR 1910.120(q) or 29 CFR 1926.65(q). Topics include a thorough discussion of scope, application, definitions, other related standards, elements of an emergency response plan, training requirements, the incident command system, medical surveillance, and post-emergency response.

Respiratory Protection

This training reviews the requirements for the establishment, maintenance, and monitoring of a respiratory protection program. Topics include terminology, OSHA and ANSI standards, NIOSH certifications, and medical evaluation recommendations. This training also features instruction on the use of self-contained breathing apparatus (SCBA), respirator fit testing, and supplied-air respirator systems.

Recognition, Evaluation and Control of Ionizing Radiation

This will introduce the criminal investigator to the fundamental principles of *ionizing radiation*. Topics include explanations of terminology, health effects, the OSHA ionizing radiation standard and other applicable standards, industrial sources, proper usage of *radiation* instruments, and radiation control methods. This instruction includes a field trip to Argonne National Laboratory for a hands-on exercise using radiation instrumentation to identify unknown sources.

Confined Space Entry

This training is designed to enable the criminal investigator to recognize, evaluate, prevent, and abate safety and health hazards associated with confined space entry. The training focuses on the specific requirements

of 29 CFR 1910.146 (a) through (k). These sections of the confined space standard are discussed with references to the OSHA directive, letters of interpretation, and preamble rationale. Technical topics include the recognition of confined space hazards, basic information about instrumentation used to evaluate atmospheric hazards, and confined space ventilation techniques.

Industrial Toxicology

This training addresses the principles of toxicology as they apply to industrial processes. However, some of the information may be applied to incidents involving the release of a hazardous substance at a WMD incident. Topics include an update of recent toxicological data related to OSHA standards, biological monitoring, biotransformation, an update on current methods of toxicological testing, and chemical hazards encountered in the industrial environment with emphasis on new toxicological information in support of hazard recognition.

Biohazard

This training will assist criminal investigators in evaluating biological hazards during occupational exposure. Focus is placed on work practices, personal protective equipment, control techniques, recognized pathogens, and current applicable OSHA standards.

United States Environmental Protection Agency (US EPA)

Advanced Environmental Crimes Training Program

This training will supply the criminal investigator with an understanding of advanced concepts central to the identification and collection of criminal evidence at crime scenes involving hazardous materials, hazardous substances, and hazardous wastes. In addition, instruction is offered in advanced air and underground chemical surveillance techniques. This training program also includes a practical exercise designed to teach the skills required to safely enter a facility suspected of containing numerous types of chemical hazards.

Sampling for Hazardous Materials

This training will provide the criminal investigator with basic and practical information for effectively sampling hazardous materials. The course focuses on sampling plan development, types of equipment suitable for hazardous materials sampling, and procedures for *safely collecting samples.* It is intended for personnel responsible for inspections, investigations, and remedial actions at Superfund sites. However, many of the sample collection techniques taught in this program may be applied to WMD crime scenes. Topics that are discussed include sample plan development, procedures for sampling containerized materials, surface waters, soils, soil gases, field-screening techniques, documentation, and quality assurance considerations. Instructional methods include outdoor field exercises with emphasis on the hands-on use of multimedia sampling equipment. After completing the course, the criminal investigator will be able to:

• Select the appropriate field screening method for a given contaminant and geologic environment.
• Select the appropriate sampling container and sample preservation method based on the sample media and analysis required.
• Select the appropriate sampling implements and methods for sampling various

containerized materials.
• Select the appropriate tools and methods for sampling surface water and sediments.
• Describe the basic methods of soil sampling.
• Complete the required documentation, including chain of custody and sample labels, for shipment of chemical samples to an analytical laboratory.
• Complete fundamental tasks in a sampling event from initial site investigation through field data collection.

Air Monitoring For Hazardous Materials

This training will instruct the criminal investigator in the practices and procedures for the monitoring and *sampling* of airborne hazardous materials. It is designed for personnel who evaluate releases of airborne hazardous materials at hazardous waste sites or accidental hazardous material releases. However, many of the sampling techniques may be applied to WMD incidents involving the release of an aerosol substance. Topics that are discussed include air monitoring and sampling programs, sampling techniques, sampling equipment, instrument calibration, exposure guidelines, air dispersion modeling, and safety considerations. The course will include operating procedures for specific air monitoring and sampling equipment, as well as strategies for the sampling of airborne chemical releases. Instructional methods include a combination of lectures, group discussions, problem-solving sessions, and field exercises with hands-on use of instruments. After completing this training, the criminal investigator will be able to:

• Properly use the following types of air monitoring and sampling equipment:
  • Combustible gas indicators
  • Oxygen monitors

- Detector tubes
- Toxic gas monitors
- *Photo-ionization detectors*
- *Flame ionization detectors*
- Gas chromatographs
- Sampling pumps and collection media
- Direct-reading aerosol monitors
- Identify the operational parameters, limitations, and data interpretation requirements for the instruments listed above.
- Identify the factors to be considered in the development of air monitoring and sampling plans.
- Discuss the use of air monitoring data for the establishment of personnel and operations health and safety requirements.

Hazardous Materials Incident Response Operations

This training is designed for personnel involved with the investigation and remediation of uncontrolled hazardous waste sites and, to a lesser extent, response to an accident involving hazardous materials. Many of the techniques taught in this course may be applied to incidents involving the abandonment and subsequent discovery of chemical agent precursors and related waste products. It provides basic information needed to meet the requirements of 29 CFR 1910.120 (Hazardous Waste Operations and Emergency Response).

After completing this training, the criminal investigator will be able to:

- Identify methods and procedures for recognizing, evaluating, and controlling *hazardous substances*.
- Identify concepts, principles, and guidelines to properly protect the abandonment site.
- Discuss regulations and action levels to ensure health and safety of the workers.
- Discuss fundamentals needed to develop organizational structure and standard operating procedures.
- Select and use dermal and respiratory protective equipment.
- Demonstrate the use, calibration, and limitations of direct-reading air monitoring instruments.

After completing this training, the criminal investigator will be more knowledgeable in *hazardous waste* operations, team functions, personnel safety procedures and the operation of field monitoring equipment. During some of the training exercises, participants will be required to wear chemical protective clothing and respiratory protection.

Emergency Response to Hazardous Material Incidents

This training will provide the criminal investigator with the information and skills needed to recognize, evaluate and control an incident involving the release or potential release of hazardous materials. It is intended for members of hazardous materials response teams. However, many of the techniques taught in this course may be applied to the hot zone work environment of a WMD crime scene.

The focus of the course is on recognizing and evaluating a hazardous materials incident, organizing the response team, protecting response personnel, identifying and using response resources, implementing basic control measures, refining decision-making skills, and protecting the public.

Topics that are discussed include chemical and physical properties of hazardous materials, toxicology, recognition and identification of hazardous materials, direct-reading instruments, standard operating procedures, personnel protection, and sources of information. The instructional methods used are lectures, class problem-solving sessions, and exercises. Emphasis is placed on the hands-on use of equipment to practically apply lecture information. The criminal investigator will participate in two simulations designed to apply and test the lessons learned during the training course. Participants will wear self-contained breathing apparatus (SCBA), fully encapsulating suits, and chemical splash suits. After completing this training, the criminal investigator will be able to:

• Select the appropriate personal protective equipment for responding to an incident involving hazardous materials.
• Use combustible gas detectors, oxygen meters, and detector tubes to evaluate the hazards present at a hazardous materials incident.
• Use confinement and containment techniques to control the release of a hazardous material.
• Identify the importance of an *incident command system* for effectively managing an incident involving hazardous materials.
• Develop procedures for the decontamination of investigative team personnel.
• Use size-up techniques to develop strategies and select the appropriate tactics for mitigating hazardous material incidents.

Radiation Safety at Superfund Sites

This basic radiation safety course will assist the criminal investigator should he or she encounter radioactive materials in the course of their investigative work. This training will provide the criminal investigator with an understanding of the fundamental principles of radiation safety, with emphasis placed on *radiation detection instrumentation* and contamination control work practices. Topics that are discussed include types of radiation and methods of interaction, biological effects, radiation detection and instrumentation, methods of contamination control and decontamination, transportation regulations, and available disposal options. Instructional methods include lectures, class problem-solving sessions, and exercises that emphasize the hands-on use of equipment and the practical application of lecture material. After completing this training, the criminal investigator will be able to:

• Detect the presence of radioactive materials while performing investigations at a suspected WMD crime scene.
• Implement methods of radiation exposure reduction and contamination control under the guidance of health physics personnel.
• Identify regulations concerning area posting, exposure limits, transportation requirements, and release limits.
• Propose options for remediation and disposal of radioactive materials.

THE EQUIPMENT

The well-trained criminal investigator must also be well equipped. Most successful criminal investigations, be they burglaries, arsons or homicides, usually depend upon the investigator's ability to examine and gather physical evidence. Even in situations where evidence technicians are gathering the physical evidence, it is normally done under the direct supervision of the criminal investigator. This same basic investigative principal also applies to investigations involving weapons of mass destruction. The criminal investigator must be equipped with the proper crime-scene, safety, and field monitoring equipment to allow for a safe and proper examination and collection of physical evidence found at the crime scene. The following is a listing of some of the items (non-sampling) that may be utilized by the investigator at a crime scene involving a weapon of mass destruction:

- Chemical boots
- Fully encapsulating suit
- pH Paper
- Compass

- LEL/O₂ meter
- Binoculars
- Flashlight
- Knife

- Fingerprint kit

- Bio field test kit or detector

- Crime scene tape

- Surgical gloves
- Chemical suits
- Duct tape
- Overalls

- 35mm auto focus camera
- First aid kit
- Non-sparking hand tools
- Evidence bags

- Children's bubbles

- Chemical field test kit or detector

- Evidence sealing tape

- Air-purifying respirator
- Chemical gloves
- Measuring tape
- Self-contained breathing apparatus (SCBA)

- Dosimeter
- Bold markers
- Spark-proof clipboard
- Spare 60-minute air bottle

- Communications equipment

- Geiger-Mueller detector

- Chemical dictionary

STANDARD OPERATING PROCEDURES

In addition to obtaining the proper training and equipment, there is a federal requirement to establish *standard operating procedures*.[48] These standard operating procedures must address the issues of health and safety for the criminal investigators working in areas which may contain hazardous substances,[49] hazardous materials[50] and biological hazards.[51]

These procedures should address such topics as organizational work plan, investigative team structure, site evaluation, site control, air monitoring, personnel protective equipment, communications, and decontamination procedures. In addition, it is recommended that standard evidence gathering procedures be incorporated into the standard operating procedures. Such topics as note taking, removal of fingerprints, tire track and footprint castings, the crime scene sketch, crime scene photography, and evidence chain-of-custody procedures should be addressed within the standard operating procedure (see Appendix 2). As discussed earlier, the best WMD standard operating procedures are those that incorporate the investigative function within the emergency response procedures. Whenever possible, criminal investigators should train with the emergency responders. This will help insure that each group is aware of the responsibilities and capabilities of the other.

Chapter 13

THE CRIME SCENE

When an investigative team arrives at a WMD crime scene, they may, in all likelihood, encounter a great deal of confusion. Numerous emergency responders from a variety of agencies may be actively participating in the handling of the event. These may include firefighters, uniformed police, emergency medical personnel, local heath officials, local environmental response personnel, and HazMat teams from multiple agencies. It may be difficult for these individuals to appreciate and/or comprehend the need for crime scene integrity and evidence preservation. This may be especially true when there are numerous victims still requiring some form of emergency assistance. It is essential that the safety of the public and the safety of the emergency responders take precedence over the need to identify and collect evidence. However, with proper cooperation, training, and communications, investigative team personnel and emergency responders will be able to successfully accomplish their required duties.

The criminal investigator must be cognizant of the fact that with each passing minute, valuable evidence may be lost. Massive wash downs of contaminated areas by firefighters may completely destroy any remaining physical evidence. In addition, the simple venting of an enclosed structure may remove all traces of valuable airborne evidence. It is important that the criminal investigators seek out the incident Commander immediately upon arrival and obtain as much information as possible regarding the incident. This should include the names of all witnesses, the name of the individual reporting the incident, symptoms exhibited by the victims, and the types and results of any field tests conducted by the initial emergency responders.

ARRIVAL PROCEDURES

When an investigative team arrives at a WMD crime scene, they will be confronted will a long list of tasks which may require immediate action. The need for *immediate* photography, interviews, field tests, and evidence collection must be evaluated by the

Crime Scene Coordinator. These needs must then be prioritized and the proper investigative resources allocated.

The first responders may have conducted initial field tests (i.e., pH, LEL, chemical agent, biological agent, radiological materials). If any initial field-testing has been completed prior to the arrival of the investigative team, the results and methods must be obtained. Some field testing units have an internal computer memory and their collected data may be designed for further future computer analysis (see Figure 30). The investigator must insure that this data is preserved. If a physical record of the readings exists (i.e., filmstrips, paper strips, Dräeger Tubes), they should be seized and preserved as evidence. The results of any initial field tests may help the criminal investigator determine the type(s) of analysis that will eventually be conducted on the chemical, biological, and/or radiological evidence (see Chapter 17, Analysis for Chemical, Biological, and Radiological Evidence). In addition, the criminal investigator must determine if the initial field-testing methods caused any possible cross-contamination of the physical evidence.

Photography and Videotape

Photography and videotape may serve several functions throughout the course of the WMD crime scene. When first arriving at the crime scene, the entire scene and the surrounding area should be photographed and videotaped. This is *initially* done from outside any declared hot zone. The investigation team should also make every effort to photograph any non-emergency vehicles and their license plate numbers. In addition, efforts should be made to photograph and videotape the civilians at the scene. This should include any victims, witnesses, and bystanders. The criminal investigator must be cognizant of the fact that the suspect and/or the suspect's vehicle may still be present at the crime scene. The suspect may have been overcome by the weapon or may

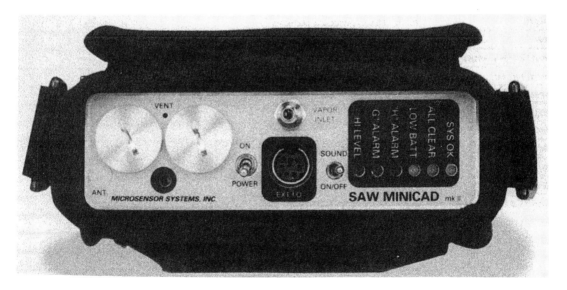

Figure 30. This Chemical Agent Detector has a built in internal memory. When criminal investigators use a field-testing device such as this, the saved internal data should be preserved. Photograph courtesy of Microsensor Systems Inc.

be present in the surrounding crowds of onlookers.

The criminal investigator should also check the surrounding area for any security cameras. Many local fast food chains, convenience stores, and banks have operating security cameras, which may assist the criminal investigator in identifying the suspect(s) or the suspects' vehicle.

Crime Scene Interviews

Witnesses, victims, and first responders should be immediately identified and interviewed at the crime scene. Their names, addresses, dates-of-birth, work addresses and telephone numbers should be recorded. When practical, a request for personal identification should be made. In addition, an interview team should be immediately dispatched to the local hospital(s) to interview any hospitalized victims. Also, other area medical facilities should be checked to determine if any victims are present. Some victims, including the suspect if he or she was contaminated, may have had only a limited exposure to the weapon and may have sought medical treatment on their own or with the aid of another. In addition, the surrounding businesses and/or homes should be checked for possible witnesses. To insure proper communications and the dissemination of vital information, the results of these interviews should be immediately reported to the crime-scene coordinator.

Victims' Personal Effects

Whenever possible, the victims' personal effects, especially when contaminated, should be collected and preserved as evidence. If the victims have gone through a decontamination process, their personal effects may have been collected by members of a decontamination team. If these personal effects are present at the crime scene, they should be immediately seized (see Chapter 16, Sampling for Chemical , Biological, and Radiological Evidence). Criminal investigators should be immediately dispatched to the local hospitals and should seize any victims' personal effects which may be present. In some jurisdictions, a search warrant may be required to seize victims' personal effects at the hospital. This issue should be discussed with the local prosecutor prior to the criminal investigator taking any action. The criminal investigator should mindful of the fact that the suspect, and his or her personal effects, may be present at the medical facility.

Chapter 14

THE INVESTIGATIVE TEAM

The successful gathering of criminal evidence at a WMD crime scene will depend on the training and experience of those individuals involved. The investigative team should be structured in a form that will insure the proper and safe gathering of all physical evidence that may exist within a hot zone. It is imperative that each member of the investigative team be properly trained and certified within their discipline (see Figure 31).

The amount of personnel and equipment needed to gather evidence inside of a hot zone will depend on the volume and types of hazardous substances involved. However, certain mandated minimum requirements for personnel and equipment must be observed.[52]

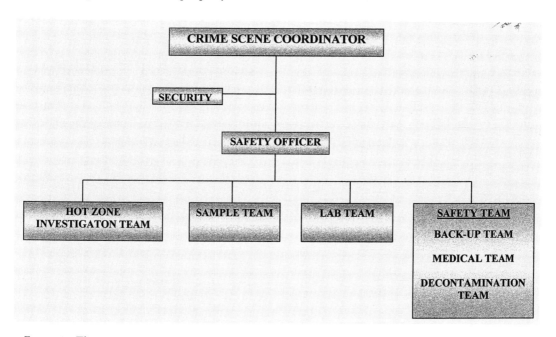

Figure 31. This is a suggested Investigative Team structure to be used at a crime scene involving the use of a weapon of mass destruction.

CRIME SCENE COORDINATOR

The primary criminal investigator assigned to the case holds the position of crime scene coordinator. He or she may be held responsible for the success or failure of the investigation. Decision-making authority must accompany this responsibility. The crime scene coordinator should remain at the Command Post (with the Incident Commander) and be in continual radio contact with other investigative team members. The crime scene coordinator should be responsible for the following duties:[53]

• Receive a full briefing from the on-scene incident commander.

• Coordinate communications with any scene security units.

• Insure that all appropriate interviews have been conducted.

• Conduct a briefing of all team personnel prior to any evidence-gathering activities being conducted in the hot zone.

• Control the paperwork at the crime scene.

• Remain in continual radio contact with any hot zone investigative entry team.

• Conduct the mandatory *post-search briefing* prior to the collection of any chemical, biological or radiological evidence.[54]

• Determine what type(s) of analysis is to be conducted on the evidence removed. (This must be established in advance due to possible sampling container requirements.)

THE SAFETY OFFICER

A safety officer *must* be present during any hot zone entry made by any investigation team members.[55] All issues regarding personnel safety are the responsibility of the safety officer. The HazMat backup team, the medical team, and the decontamination team should report directly to the safety officer. This individual will also determine the level of personal protective equipment to be worn by those individuals entering any designated hot zone. In addition, the safety officer will determine what decontamination procedures are to be followed. Entry into a hot zone should not take place without the safety officer's knowledge and approval. It is essential that the safety officer and crime-scene coordinator be in continuous communication with each other throughout all evidence-gathering activities.

THE SAFETY TEAM

The HazMat backup team acts as support and emergency rescue for the investigative team and the sample team working within the designated hot zone. If the investigative team and/or sample team consists of two individuals working within a contaminated area, there must be at least two individuals acting as their backup team. The HazMat backup team, the investigation team, crime scene coordinator, and safety officer should be in continuous radio communication with each other.

DECONTAMINATION TEAM

WMD crime scenes may involve chemical, biological, and/or radiological hazards. An evaluation of these hazards may require that a predetermined decontamination procedure be followed by those individuals exiting a designated hot zone. The specific decontamination procedure, based upon the hazards involved, will be determined by the safety officer. This procedure may include a simple removal and bagging of contaminated protective clothing. However, it may be necessary for all personnel exiting the hot zone to go through a multiple wash-down procedure. This type of decontamination procedure may produce contaminated wastewater. It is essential that this material be pumped into a recovery drum, sampled, and arrangements made for its proper disposal.

EMERGENCY MEDICAL ASSISTANCE

It is recommended that a HazMat trained medical team be present whenever a hot zone entry is made. However, if the hazard(s) present at the crime scene require the use of fully encapsulated protective suits (Level "A"), it is essential that a HazMat trained medical team be present during all evidence-gathering activities.

THE SAMPLE TEAM

The scientific sampling of the chemical, biological, and/or radiological substances is considered to be one of the most difficult and dangerous activities conducted at any WMD crime scene. The proper gathering of this type of evidence goes far beyond collecting liquid (or solid) samples and placing them into containers. These individuals must be concerned with such issues as personal safety, evidence cross-contamination, proper sampling methodologies, and maintaining the proper chain-of-custody for the scientific evidence collected. The sample team should be fully briefed by the crime-scene coordinator as to what areas are to be sampled and what types of analyses will be required for the scientific evidence collected.

THE LABORATORY TEAM

Many jurisdictions may lack the resources necessary to have a laboratory team respond to a WMD crime scene. It may be necessary for the criminal investigator to rely on the expertise of the sample team when dealing with such issues as equipment sterilization and the proper recording of sampling methodologies. However, if a laboratory team is available, it should consist of at least one person qualified in the appropriate discipline (i.e., forensic chemist, microbiologist). The laboratory team's responsibilities will begin long before they enter a WMD crime scene. Each piece of equipment that is to be used for the gathering of scientific evidence must be thoroughly inspected and sterilized prior to it being utilized at the crime scene. The laboratory team must maintain a full record of the sterilization procedure. Once at the crime scene, the laboratory team will maintain a record of the samples that have been taken, what scientific field tests have been conducted, and the results of those field tests. In addition, they will maintain a log of the sampling methodology utilized by the sample team. The laboratory team should maintain the integrity of the evidence by following procedures that will rule out any possibility of cross-contamination and/or outside contamination of the scientific evidence.

At the closure of the crime scene, this team will take custody of the chemical, biological, or radiological evidence and transport it to a laboratory or a hazardous evidence storage area. These individuals must be trained in the handling of criminal evidence and hazardous materials.

When conducting an investigation at a WMD crime scene, it is recommended that a qualified individual be appointed scene *science officer*. This individual may assist the crime scene coordinator and the safety officer in the identification of the various hazards present. He or she may also assist the crime scene coordinator in determining the proper sampling and analytical methodologies required based upon any field-test results and in the identification of a particular hazardous substance.

HOT ZONE INVESTIGATION TEAM

The duties of the hot zone investigation team will vary depending on the size and scope of the incident. Generally, it will consist of two or four (buddy system) investigators with the corresponding number of backup team members available for emergency assistance. Constant radio communication must be maintained between the hot zone investigation team, the backup team, the safety officer, and the crime scene coordinator. In addition to standard evidence gathering duties (i.e., fingerprint lifting, photography, crime scene sketch), they may have to conduct field tests, determine sampling points, and establish sampling protocols (see Chapter 15, Gathering Evidence in a Hot Zone). In situations where the suspected agent is rapidly dissipating, they may be called upon to take immediate liquid, aerosol, or soil samples. The combination of *all* of these tasks may require multiple air bottle changes, multiple decontamination procedures, and frequent rest periods. Therefore, whenever possible, the standard evidence gathering duties and the sampling duties should be conducted by separate teams of investigators.

Chapter 15

GATHERING EVIDENCE IN A HOT ZONE

EQUIPMENT AND PROCEDURES

Once all the investigative team members have been fully briefed and the safety protocols established, a minimum of two criminal investigators will enter the hot zone and commence the evidence gathering operation.[56] In order to safely and efficiently complete this task, the criminal investigators must have the proper equipment *with them* when entering the hot zone. These items may include:

- Appropriate protective clothing based upon the suspected hazard.
- Steel-toed, chemical-proof boots.
- Appropriate protective gloves based upon the suspected hazard.
- Several pairs of surgical gloves.
- A self-contained breathing apparatus with a full 60-minute air bottle.
- An aluminum (non-sparking) clipboard.
- A pen for crime-scene notes.
- A bold marker for filling in sample-point identification information on the sampling placards.
- Several preprinted placards for sample point identification.
- Duct Tape, magnetic clips, or suction cup clips for attaching sampling placards to flat

surfaces.
- An LEL/O_2 meter for atmosphere flammability readings.
- A radiological meter capable of determining the presence of alpha particles, beta particles and/or gamma rays.
- A dosimeter.
- pH paper and pH chart.
- Field test kit for chemical or biological agent.
- A waterproof auto-focus camera with sealed electronic flash.
- A waterproof auto-focus video camera.
- Evidence bags of assorted sizes.
- A knife capable of cutting tape. This item should be taped to the calf of the criminal investigator and may be used under *extreme emergency* conditions to cut away and remove a severely contaminated protective suit.
- A fingerprint kit equipped with various dusting powders, brushes, and fingerprint lifting tape.
- Communication equipment which will allow for hands-free operation and direct communication with the safety officer, HazMat backup team and the crime-scene

111

coordinator.

While inside the hot zone, the investigative team should attempt to complete the following evidence gathering tasks:

• Photograph and videotape the entire undisturbed crime scene from all angles.

• Complete a ***radiological survey*** of the entire crime scene.[57] The radiological survey should begin at the outermost perimeter, with continuous readings being made up to the surface areas of any suspected devices or to the point at which a 2mr (***Millirem***) reading is obtained.

• Complete a LEL reading to determine if any potentially flammable gases are present.[58]

• Field tests for the suspected chemical or biological substance should be conducted near or at the suspected point of detonation. These field test results (including radiological) will assist the investigator in determining the type(s) of sampling methodologies that will be needed to further the investigation. Field test results must be recorded and maintained.

• Immediate air sampling may be required if an airborne agent appears to be dissipating. In this situation, an immediate air sample may be taken through the use of a negative pressure canister (chemical agent) or through the use of various bioaerosol collection devices (see Chapter 16, Sampling for Chemical, Biological, and Radiological Evidence).

• Determine if the material has been spilled or is leaking from the device.

• Note, photograph and cast any footprints and/or tire tracks present.

• Note, photograph, and lift any fingerprints found within the hot zone. Special attention should be paid to the bottom surfaces of any containers. This is the natural gripping area used to lift various types of containers. If the suspect(s) lifted a container without gloves, the bottom surface will be the most

likely area in which fingerprints may be found. An abandoned clandestine WMD manufacturing site may be heavily contaminated and require a Level "A" entry on the part of the investigative team. Crime scenes such as these may produce fingerprints on drums, containers, laboratory glassware, and other manufacturing implements.

The ability to lift fingerprints while wearing a Level "A" chemical suit takes many hours of practice. This is primarily due to the restricted vision and loss of dexterity that is inherent in these types of suits. It is quite possible that the fingerprint(s) will become smudged during the lifting procedure. Therefore, it is recommended that all fingerprints found at the crime scene be photographed prior to being lifted (see Figures 32 &33).

• If drums and/or containers are present, photograph and record any U.S. Department of Transportation information.

• Photograph and record all markings on any containers.

Figure 32. The lifting of a fingerprint such as this would normally be an easy task. However, working in a toxic atmosphere makes this job much more difficult.

• Photograph and record all label information on the containers. If the label is legible and can be removed intact, it should be recovered and placed into an evidence bag. Many labels may have illegible, yet potentially valuable information on them. At the completion of this operation, the illegible label should be sent to the documents department of a crime lab. Information on faded labels may be raised using document enhancement techniques, such as infrared and infrared fluorescence.

• The surrounding ground area should be carefully searched for any other form of physical evidence. Any closed containers should be lifted and/or tilted so that their undersides and the ground area underneath the containers may be examined for

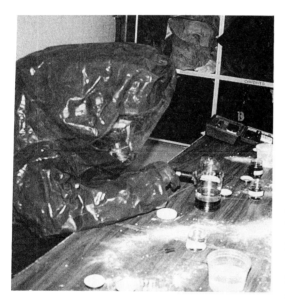

Figure 33. The lifting of this fingerprint while working in Level "A" protective clothing is extremely difficult. Limited vision and dexterity add to the difficulties.

possible physical evidence.

• A sketch should be made of the entire crime scene, including the position and location of each container and/or device. The crime scene sketch should also include the location of any other physical evidence recovered. If the hazardous substance is in a container and in *liquid form*, it should be physically examined through the use of a sterilized ***coliwasa tube*** (see Figure 34). This will supply a visual perspective of the liquid column and any possible liquid layers. This may assist the criminal investigator in determining analytical needs.

• Each area, container and/or device that has been selected for sampling should be placarded and photographed. The sampling placard should contain, at a minimum, agency information, the current date, and the field sample number (see Figure 35). If the container and/or device appears to be empty, it should be placed into an airtight container and seized as evidence.

Upon exiting the hot zone and after decontamination requirements have been met, the entire investigation team must attend a mandatory post-search briefing.[59] The briefing will be conducted by the crime scene coordinator and will address the safety and sampling protocols that are to be utilized in the collection of the chemical, biological, and/or radiological evidence. It must be emphasized that field test results *may not* produce the reliable scientific evidence needed to obtain a criminal conviction. Therefore, the collection and analysis of this type of hazardous evidence must be conducted in such a manner as to insure the scientific integrity of that evidence.

Figure 34. The white plastic stopper inside this Coliwasa tube is shown here in the closed position. To properly view the column and to obtain a proper stratified sample, it must be in the open position when inserted into the container.

DISTRICT ATTORNEY'S OFFICE

SAMPLE

1SD9-15

DATE: 9/15/99

Figure 35: Sampling placards are an essential part of the sampling process. Each sample point must be identified and photographed through the use of a placard like this.

THE CRIME SCENE NOTES

In addition to personnel lists, interview notes, crime scene sketches and the chain-of-custody notations there are, at a minimum, 20 separate pieces of information that must be recorded for *each* sample point. A WMD crime scene that produces 20 sample points may require several hundred separate notations in the crime-scene records. The following is a listing of notations that must be recorded:

• Sample Number	• Date	• Case Number	• Location
• Sample Point Description	• Device or Container Dimensions	• Volume Present	• Name of Person Taking Measurements
• Sample Time	• Lead Sampler	• Assistant Sampler	• Sample Matrix
• Analysis Requested	• Name of Photographer	• Type of Photography	• Label Information (precursors)
• Container D.O.T. Information	• Label Location (precursors)	• Equipment Decontamination	• Name of Note Taker

To better maintain and organize this amount of data, it is suggested that a preprinted form be used for each sample point at a WMD crime scene (see Figures 36 & 37).

(FRONT)
SAMPLE POINT SHEET

SAMPLE#_____DATE: ___/___/___ CASE# _____

INCIDENT LOCATION: _____

....

SAMPLE POINT
LOCATION:_____

SAMPLE POINT
DISCRITPION: (Circle) Ground   Air   Container

Device   Other:_____

....

RELATIVE MEASUREMENTS

CONTAINER/DEVICE DEMENSIONS: H:___W:___D:____

LIQUID/SOLID DEPTH: FEET_____ INCHES_____

MEASUREMENTS RECORDED BY: _____

....

SAMPLE TYPE: (Circle) Chemical   Biological   Radiological

Solid   Liquid   Wipe   Gas   Background   Other_____

....

Photographer: _____ Type: 35mm Video Digital

Above Recorded By: _____

Figure 36. The preprinted information on the front of this form will assist the criminal investigator in managing the data collected during a weapons of mass destruction sampling event.

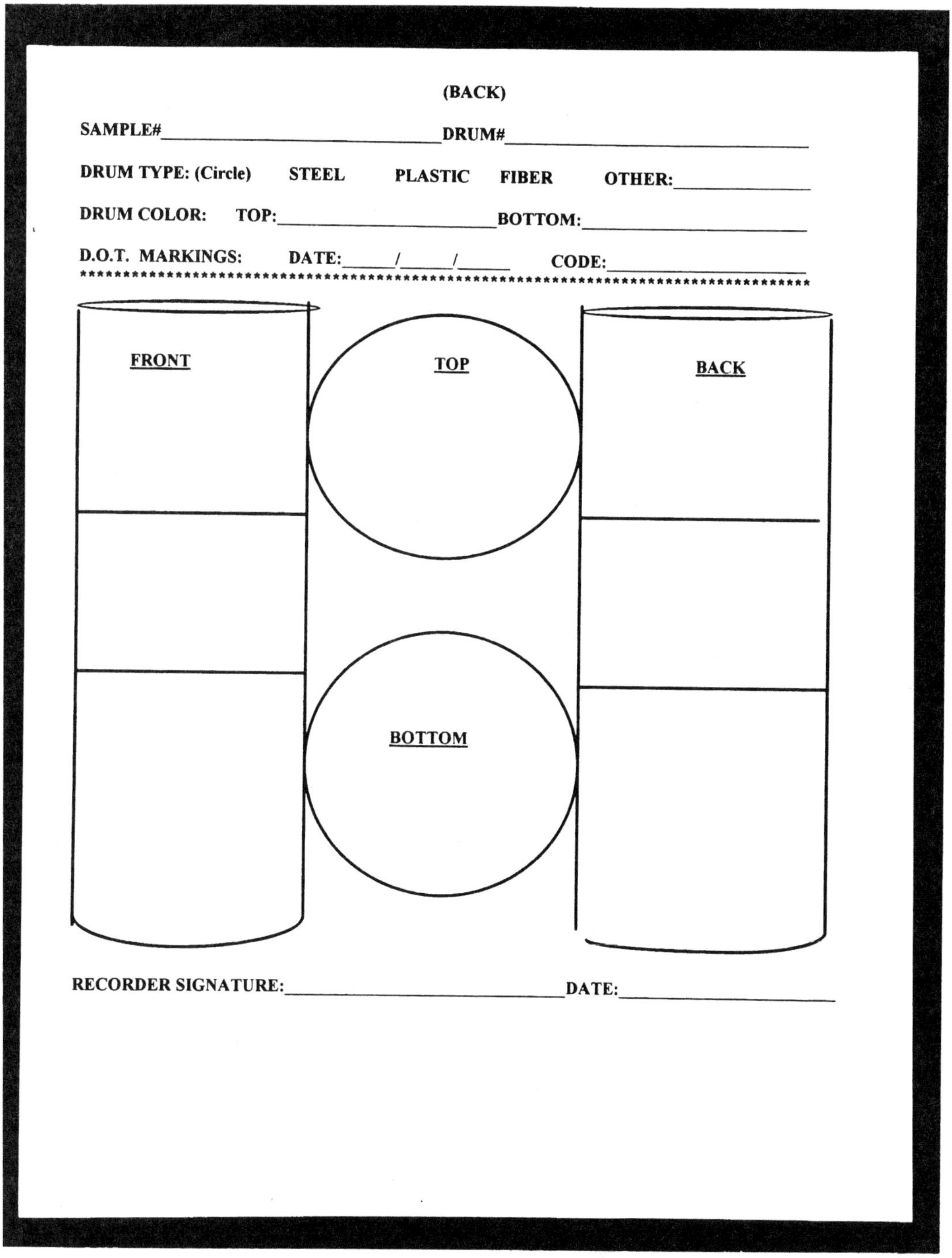

(BACK)

SAMPLE#_____DRUM#_____

DRUM TYPE: (Circle)   STEEL   PLASTIC   FIBER   OTHER:_____

DRUM COLOR: TOP:_____BOTTOM:_____

D.O.T. MARKINGS: DATE:_____/_____/_____   CODE:_____
****

FRONT   TOP   BACK

BOTTOM

RECORDER SIGNATURE:_____DATE:_____

Figure 37. The preprinted information on the rear of this form may be used to record information that appears on chemical agent precursor containers.

Chapter 16

SAMPLING FOR CHEMICAL, BIOLOGICAL, AND RADIOLOGICAL EVIDENCE

The collection of chemical, biological, and/or radiological evidence is not a new concept. Legally and scientifically sound sampling and analytical methodologies have existed for quite some time. These existing methodologies and/or protocols can be found in proven criminal cases involving the release to the environment of hazardous substances (environmental crimes). They also can be found in the current and proposed compliance *monitoring* procedures for the *Chemical Weapons Convention* and the *Biological Weapons Convention*. These seemingly different disciplines have one major commonality. That is, *the need to prove both legally and scientifically that the substance or agent in question, in fact, exists.* By examining these disciplines closely, an effective evidence gathering protocol can be designed to meet the needs of a WMD investigation and prosecution.

The proper collection of evidence samples at a WMD crime scene requires preparation and planning. The proper selection and preparation of sampling equipment, methods of sample collection, types of analysis required, cross and outside contamination control, chain-of-custody, and evidence storage are all critical to a successful investi-

gation and prosecution. The investigator has a responsibility to insure that the evidence is collected and maintained properly. The protocols utilized to gather and analyze this evidence will be required to meet a level of scientific certainty that may exceed those needs and requirements of the emergency responders. The use of chemical and biological field testing equipment (i.e., Dräeger Tubes, CAD and CAM units) may be critical to the emergency responder; however, they *may not* meet the evidence standards required by the criminal justice system. The criminal justice standard is defined as *"beyond a reasonable doubt."* Any field test kit, for any substance, which has less then a high degree of reliability and/or accuracy rating will not meet the degree of *scientific certainty* required by the criminal justice standard. To fulfill this responsibility the investigator must have adequate knowledge of these legally and scientifically acceptable sampling protocols and analytical methods.

The purpose of this chapter is to acquaint the investigator with a few of the accepted equipment-preparation and sampling protocols utilized in *hazardous* evidence collection.

THE SAMPLING PLAN

The primary objective of a sampling plan for scientific evidence is to collect samples that will allow measurements of the substance's properties that are both accurate and precise. In order to insure that this objective is met, the Crime Scene Coordinator must meet with the other members of the team and develop a sampling plan and sampling equipment protocol (see Appendix 3). This will assist in the obtaining of the criminal evidence necessary to further the investigation and, at the same time, satisfy the sample collection criteria of the approved *analytical method* used for the analysis of the evidence.

The sampling plan will generally indicate the types of analyses required (based upon prior field test results), sample point locations, sampling equipment requirements, cross-contamination and outside contamination control samples (i.e., *field blanks* and *trip blanks*), chain-of-custody procedures, personal protective equipment, and other safety issues.

A crime scene sketch should be drawn indicating the sample locations, sample numbers, and matrixes of the various sampling points. The sample matrixes may be in the form of a wipe (surface), liquids, solids, soils, and /or aerosols. The sketch should also include directional information based upon compass readings. At the conclusion of the sampling operation, the sketch should be signed and dated by the investigator.

CHEMICAL EVIDENCE

The collection of chemical evidence at crime scenes is not a new science. Many federal, state, and local law enforcement agencies have been actively collecting this type of evidence for many years. Criminal investigations that involve the release of hazardous substances (chemical, biological, and radiological), hazardous waste abandonment, hazardous waste discharges, and illegal hazardous material transportation are being conducted everyday throughout this country. A sealed trailer housing an abandoned metal refinishing operation may contain hundreds of pounds of exposed sodium cyanide and a poisonous atmosphere. Gathering the proper criminal evidence necessary to prove this type of chemical abandonment case will require a physical entry into the hot zone by qualified investigative personnel. While working in this poisonous atmosphere, investigators will be wearing Level "A" protective suits while sampling for liquids, solids, and *ambient air* (see Figure 38). The sampling of the chemical warfare agent precursor sodium cyanide (*Tabun*) may require similar chemical evidence collection protocols.

The following sampling protocols are to be used only as a *guide*. They are based upon protocols and procedures that have been successfully used in previous cases involving the misuse of hazardous substances, hazardous wastes, hazardous materials, and suspected WMD sites. It is important to note that the scientific community is continually reviewing both sampling and analytical protocols for cases involving the use, threatened use, and manufacturing of a weapon of mass destruction.

Chemical Evidence Gathering

There are several important protocols that should be utilized when sampling for liquid, solid and gaseous/aerosol chemical evidence. These protocols will assist in the furtherance of the criminal investigation and, at the same time, help insure the integrity of the chemical evidence.

Trip Blanks

A *trip blank* is a sample bottle, normally filled with distilled water, which accompanies the sample collection containers *before, during, and after* any chemical evidence collection takes place. These trip blanks are then analyzed to insure that no outside contamination or cross-contamination has occurred at *any time* during the collection, transportation, and/or storage of the chemical evidence. This technique is vital in situations involving the suspected presence of precursors. Chemical agent precursors may have many legitimate uses and may be found in numerous common products and manufacturing processes. The use of a trip blank will positively rule out any possibility of outside contamination from one of these sources. In addition, a trip blank should be kept with all sampling devices during transportation to the field. This will assist in negating any future claims that sampling device contamination occurred prior to the sampling operation (see Figure 39).

Field Blanks

A *field blank* is a sample collected from a sampling device's final rinse prior to reuse.

Figure 38. The collection of hazardous evidence is not a new science. Many lessons learned in the past may be applied to a WMD response program.

Distilled water is normally used. Shovels, spoons, *weighted samplers*, *dippers*, and *extension augers* may be used several times during the course of a suspected WMD crime scene. To insure that no outside contamination or cross-contamination (from previous samples) has occurred, a *field blank* must be utilized in-between samples. If field blanks are *not utilized*, each sample analytical result, after the first sample, may be questioned. Each field blank procedure which occurs during the course of the sampling event should be completely documented. This should include information as to the next sample number to be taken, the source and type of water used (distilled), the person's name conducting the rinse, and a description of the sampling device being decontaminated. It is also essential to document that all rinse water used to decontaminate sampling devices has been collected and disposed of properly. Clearly, the best way to avoid the need for field blanks is to utilize disposable sampling items

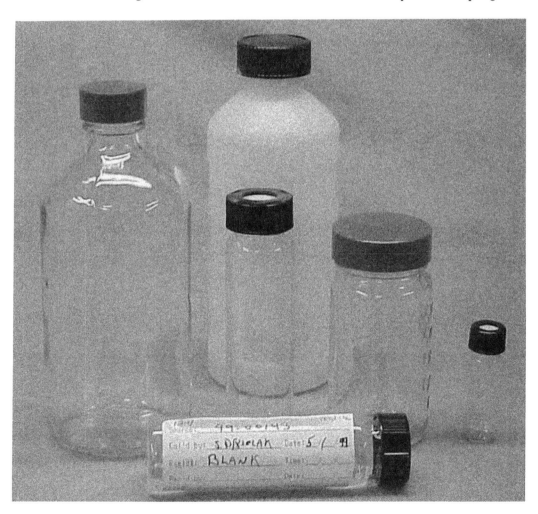

Figure 39. A Trip blank, like this one, should accompany the sample containers all throughout the sampling and analytical process.

at each sample point. However, when a piece of sampling equipment must be reused, the field blank system must be utilized.

Glove Changes

It is vital that the lead sampler and assistant sampler change their outer gloves in-between each sample, *regardless of whether any apparent glove contamination has occurred.* The chemical evidence may be volatizing. These volatized vapors may come into contact with the glove's surface thereby causing contamination. This contamination on the exterior glove surface may then be carried over to the next sample point. Due to the sensitivity of laboratory analytical equipment (parts per billion) this small amount of cross-contamination could produce a false-positive analytical result for the next sample point. This procedure insures that no cross-contamination will occur between samples (see Figure 40).

Figure 40. Failure to make a proper glove change in this situation will cause a cross-contamination of the forensic chemical evidence at the next sample point.

Representative Samples

When sampling large volumes of liquid chemical evidence, the investigator must insure that a representative or stratified sample is obtained. Each chemical constituent will have its own *specific gravity*. When dealing with liquid samples that have more than one chemical present, and are immiscible (do not mix), several separate chemical layers will often form. This effect may be found in liquid chemical samples that have been exposed to water or have been untouched for a period of time, which allowed for some form of natural chemical separation (see Figure 41)

Control Samples

Control samples should be taken from outside the hot zone area. The sample matrix of the control samples should match those samples taken from within the hot zone. If solid, liquid, or aerosol samples are taken within the hot zone, then these same types of control samples should be taken from an area believed to be uncontaminated. This will help to insure the integrity of the chemical evidence and negate any future criminal defense that the contamination found is due to some outside source or from some naturally occurring phenomenon.

Sampling Equipment and Containers for Chemical Evidence

Liquid and solid chemical evidence may be found in containers, small surface puddles and/or droplets and soil areas that may have become contaminated. The chemical evidence may represent the chemical agent, a precursor(s), or the *degradation products*. For those chemicals found in containers, one of the best and safest sampling devices to use is a sterilized *Coliwasa Tube* (see Figure 34).

This device allows the sampler to sample the chemical evidence without coming into direct contact with the substance. In addition, this device allows for the representative sample described above. A good representative or ***stratified sample*** can be taken from a chemical container or chemical device through the proper use of this sampling device. The investigator must be aware of the fact that any single chemical constituent found, at any layer of the stratum, may become a future forensic chemical link.

When sampling small puddles and/or droplets, disposable sterilized glass pipettes with rubber stoppers (see Figure 42) may be used to pickup small quantities of the chemical evidence. The chemical evidence should be expunged from the pipette into a sampling container. The pipette and/or rubber bulb *should not* be placed into the

sampling container and sealed. Any rubber parts that make up the construction of this sampling device may break down and thereby contaminate the chemical evidence. An absorbent pad or wipe may also be used to collect a chemical sample from small puddles and/or droplets. This may be accomplished by utilizing sterilized locking forceps. This will insure that the absorbent pad containing the chemical evidence does not come into contact with the sampler. The absorbent pad can then be placed directly into a sampling container. The chemical evidence can then be later extracted from the absorbent pad under laboratory conditions. For soil samples, a sterilized auger may be used to obtain a sample of the chemical which has soaked several inches into the soil. Sterilized stainless steel spoons and hand shovels can then be used to place the samples into the proper containers.

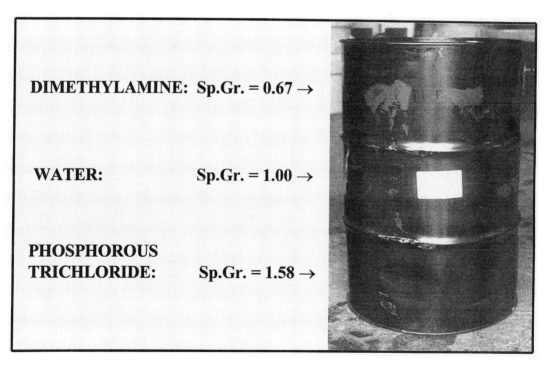

DIMETHYLAMINE: Sp.Gr. = 0.67 →

WATER: Sp.Gr. = 1.00 →

PHOSPHOROUS TRICHLORIDE: Sp.Gr. = 1.58 →

Figure 41. The two chemical agent precursors shown in this waste drum have different specific gravities. If a proper representative sample is not taken, one of the precursors will be missed.

In most situations, liquid and solid chemical evidence samples will be placed into either glass or plastic sample containers. The type of container to use will depend upon the nature of the substance being sampled as well as any sample container requirements described in a predetermined analytical methodology. The investigator should be aware of the fact that certain organic chemicals may break down the components of a plastic sample bottle. These breakdown components may then interfere with the analytical results of the chemical evidence. In most situations, an organic compound that is considered to be volatile or semi-volatile should be placed into a standard clear 10, 25, 40, 100, or 250 ml, glass, screw-cap bottle with a Teflon-lined (chemically inert) silicon septa. These wide and narrow mouthed sampling containers may be used for both liquids and solids. When sterilizing these items, the vials and septa should be washed with a detergent, rinsed with tap and distilled water and dried in an oven for 1 hour at 100°C before use.[60]

For inorganic compounds, the sampling bottle should be composed of linear polyethylene, polypropylene, borosilicate glass, or Teflon. The containers should be prepared using the following steps: detergent wash, tap water rinse, 1:1 nitric acid rinse, tap water rinse, 1:1 hydrochloric acid rinse, tap water rinse, and a metal-free water rinse.[61] The sterilization procedures described here should be fully documented and should include, at a minimum, the name of the person conducting the procedure, a detailed description of the procedure, and the date.

The investigator must be careful when choosing the types and quantities of chemical sampling equipment and containers to have available at a WMD crime scene (see Figure 43). Using the wrong type of

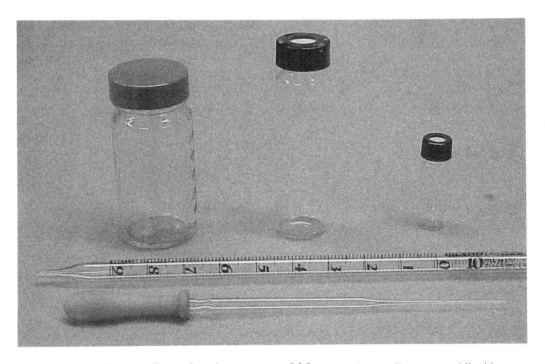

Figure 42. These small sampling devices are useful for removing small amounts of liquids.

equipment to gather chemical evidence may put an unneeded burden upon the prosecutor during a criminal trial. In addition, the use of undocumented or non-sterilized sampling equipment and/or containers *will* raise issues of prior equipment contamination and *will* raise doubt as to the validity of any analytical results.

Sampling for Chemical Agent Precursors

The precursors for chemical agents are those chemicals that are used in the manufacturing of a specific chemical weapon (see Table I). Situations may arise where investigators must determine, through analytical chemical evidence, whether or not a particular facility or building had been or is being used as a manufacturing site for a weapon(s) of mass destruction. An examination of such a site may produce numerous containers and other items that may clearly indicate the type of activity that had occurred at this site. However, the mere presence of these chemicals at a facility or crime scene is not conclusive evidence as to the manufacture or existence of a chemical weapon. Many of these chemicals may also be found in legitimate manufacturing processes and consumer products.

The investigator should be cognizant of the fact that many of these chemical precursors have their own hazardous chemical properties and some have been classified as hazardous substances.[62] They should be sampled utilizing the protocols for liquids and solids described in the next section.

The release and/or abandonment of these precursors may be classified as a crime in some jurisdictions. The investigator and prosecutor should review the chemical precursor list so that appropriate plans may be made should one or more of these

SAMPLING EQUIPMENT FOR *CHEMICAL EVIDENCE*

Stainless Steel Forceps	Glass Sample Bottles with Teflon-Lined Silicon Septa Caps	Plastic Sample Bottles Assorted sizes	Wipe Sampling Kit
Surgical Gloves	Wipe Aluminum Templates (12 x 12 in.)	Glass Coliwasa Tubes	Polyethylene Bags (½ gallon size – 0.025mm)
Children's Bubbles	Tracer Balloons	Negative Pressure Canisters	Pipettes and Rubber Bulbs
Trip Blanks	Gummed Labels	Log Book	Pens and Markers
Distilled Water	Extension Augers	Weighted Samplers	Dippers
Bailers	Measuring Tape	Wooden Measuring Sticks	Compass
Evidence Sealing Tape	PID/FID	Vegetable Dye	Stainless Steel Spoons
String	Scissors	Paper Towels	Stainless Steel Hand Trowels

Figure 43. Here are just a few of the items that will be needed to collect chemical evidence at a WMD crime scene.

chemicals be found at a crime scene.

Sampling for a
Suspected Chemical Agent

The investigator may face a variety of sampling protocols when attempting to gather evidence in order to prove the presence of a chemical agent. The sampling of liquids, soils, non-pervious surfaces, wastewater runoff, gases, and aerosols each present their own distinct sampling methodologies. Liquids may be present in large or small quantities. They may be present inside of a non-detonated device and that device may be *unitary* or *binary* in design. Soils may have to be sampled at different depths and wastewater runoff may form *hydrolysis* (degradation) products. In addition, the sampling devices for gases and aerosols, for a variety of reasons, must be chosen carefully.

In situations involving a detonated device, it is essential that the investigative team begin chemical evidence collection as soon as possible. Phosgene (CG), cyanogen chloride (CK), and hydrogen cyanide (AC) are effected by ambient air temperature and will normally be found in a gaseous state.[63] In addition, Sarin and mustard chemical agents exhibit evaporation rates that range from minutes to several hours depending upon the sample matrix, surface, and ambient temperature conditions.[64] A delayed response by the investigation team may result in the loss of this type of scientific evidence.

LIQUIDS AND SOLIDS. Chemical agents in liquid form, for the most part, are considered volatile[65] and can be collected utilizing the procedures discussed above for the precursors. Sterilized glass Coliwasa tubes and pipettes are excellent choices for this type of evidence gathering operation. The liquids should be placed into the appropriate size

glass, screw-cap bottle with Teflon-lined silicon septa. Whenever possible, the bottle should be filled completely to the top. Should the liquid(s) be contained in a unitary or binary device, the device must be rendered safe by qualified personnel prior to any attempt to sample the interior chemicals. In a binary device situation, this should include a complete separation (safe distance apart) of the chemical compounds. If the device is binary, both chemical substances must be sampled (see Figure 44). In addition, great caution must be exercised in the handling, packaging, and transporting of these samples. Should an accident occur involving the simultaneous breaking of both glass sample bottles, the originally intended chemical reaction may occur.

The sampling of solid materials, such as soils, can be accomplished through the use of a sterilized stainless steel spoon or small hand shovel. The length of time that the material has been on the ground, the soil matrix (i.e., sand, clay, etc.), and/or the introduction of water will all impact on the depth to be reached when gathering this type of evidence. The best way to handle this type of sampling event is to take several different samples, which would include the surface and various depths. The sample should be placed into an appropriate size, wide mouth, glass screw-cap bottle with a Teflon-lined silicon septa. Whenever possible, the sampling container should be filled completely to the top.

VICTIMS'/SUSPECTS' PERSONAL ITEMS. Chemical agents may be found on the clothing of victims and suspects. In situations involving a *known* release of a chemical agent (i.e., positive field test results), the proper collection and preservation of victim's and/or suspect's clothes and personal items should be considered a high priority for the criminal investigator. These items should be collected and preserved for future analysis. The collection of these items, as with *all* other criminal evidence, must be done under the *direct supervision* of law enforcement personnel. Personal items, including clothing, should be dried (if possible) and placed into sturdy plastic bags. Identifying information (i.e., name, address, date-of-birth, telephone number, physical description, etc.) should be recorded on a carbon type form with one copy being placed inside the bag and the other copy being securely mounted on the outside of the bag. The bag should then be sealed. An instant photograph of the individual's face should be taken and attached to the form. This procedure will further assist the investigator in situations where the suspect has become accidentally exposed to the chemical agent and is now seeking medical treatment as a victim.

GASES/AEROSOLS. Gas and aerosol sampling protocols will depend upon the type of suspected chemical agent present. By examining the results of previous field tests, the investigation team should have some knowledge as to the type of chemical agent suspected to be present. Most chemical agents have a vapor density which exceeds that of normal ambient air. With this information in mind, the majority of air sampling

will be conducted at or near ground level. It is at these levels that the *remaining* highest concentrations may exist. However, because compounds such as phosgene (CG), cyanogen chloride (CK), and hydrogen cyanide (AC) are temperature dependent, they may be found at varying levels. When facing compounds such as these in a contained area (i.e., building, train, car, etc.), the investigation team may wish to take samples at several different levels.

The sampling equipment used in gathering airborne evidence must be evaluated for ease of use and sample time requirements. Many battery-operated air pumps have small control panels (see Figure 45). The pumps draw samples directly through adsorbent tubes that are later analyzed using an analytical methodology such as GC/MS. The glass absorbent tube must be changed and secured with each sample. An unused absorbent tube should be maintained as a trip blank.

The small control panel may make operating the pump difficult when faced with the limitations of level "A" protective equipment. Also, the pump may have to be in operation for an extended period of time in order to obtain a proper sample.

One of the simplest and most effective

CHEMICAL AGENT	=	BINARY COMPOUND	+	BINARY COMPOUND
Sarin (GB-2)		Methylphosphoryl - difluoride		Isopropanol/Isopropyl-amine
Soman (GD-2)		Methylphosphoryl - difluoride		Pinacolylacohol
VX-2		O-ethyl O-2-diisopropylaminoethyl methylphosphonite		sulphur

Figure 44. Binary chemical devices will contain separate chemical compounds. Once separated, each binary compound should be sampled.

ways to capture airborne chemical evidence at a WMD crime scene is to utilize a stainless steel negative pressure (preevacuated) canister (see Figure 46). A fused silica lined canister maximizes recovery of ***volatile organic compounds***. When utilizing this type of sampling device, the investigator is required to open a simple valve for the sampling process to begin. When coupled with silica lined inlet restricters (i.e., 5, 10, 15 minutes), these devices can be placed in strategic sampling areas and recovered at a later time. These units can be worn in holsters, carried, or taped to the leg. Once the airborne sample has been secured, the valve should be closed. The stainless steel canister can go through decontamination

without any concern for sample integrity. The canister can be easily transported and/or shipped to a laboratory. This system interfaces with current GC/MS technology.

SURFACE AND DERMAL SAMPLING. Surface and dermal contamination may have several causes. It may be the result of a clandestine manufacturing operation or a chemical device detonation. The gathering of this type of trace chemical evidence may be vital to the success of the criminal investigation. The protocols utilized in this type of sampling are inexpensive, fast, and simple to perform.[66] However, as in other forms of chemical evidence gathering, issues involving sample point locations, equipment preparation, sampling methods, and

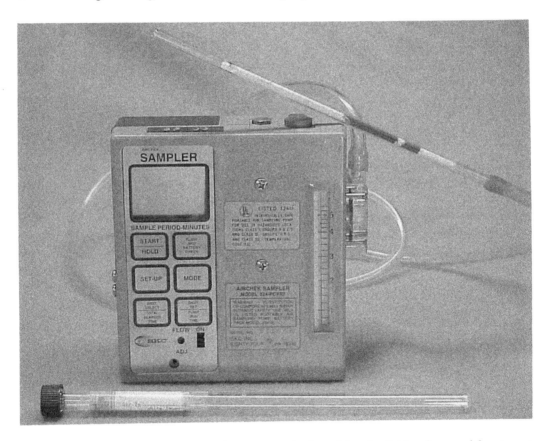

Figure 45. This type of battery operated air pump is both useful and reliable when used for air sampling. However, the control panel may be difficult to use while wearing level "A" protective clothing.

evidence preservation must all be addressed prior to the collection of any chemical evidence.

Finding the *best* locations for surface sampling may not be immediately apparent upon entrance into a hot zone. If the undisturbed remains of a detonated chemical device are present, the investigator may wish to conduct surface sampling on the device's remains and in the area of the detonation. However, in situations where a release point cannot be immediately determined, the investigator may wish to utilize field testing equipment. Chemical agent field test units may be very useful in situations such as this. However, the investigator should also consider such electronic devices as a ***Photo-Ionization Detector*** (PID) and a ***Flame Ionization Detector*** (FID). These devices (depending upon the chemical compounds present) may assist the investigator in locating contaminated areas. The PID is very sensitive to aromatic compounds, some

chlorinated compounds, and a limited amount of inorganic compounds. The FID has a wide range and is very sensitive to hydrocarbons and chlorinated hydrocarbons. This device has been called an electronic bloodhound and has the ability to backtrack certain chemical substances to their concentrated point of origin.

Interior building surfaces chosen for chemical wipe sampling may include desks, computers, overhead lights, cabinets, walls, floors, chairs, tables, benches, lunch tables, heating and ventilation ducts. In situations involving the suspected release of a chemical agent in an outside area, the investigator should obtain wipe samples from exterior walls, building intake air vents, street lamps, vehicle exteriors, mail boxes, and windows. By utilizing the PID/FID in conjunction with tracer balloons and/or children's bubbles (see Bioaerosol Sampling), the investigator may obtain the travel route of the chemical agent and thereby simplify the

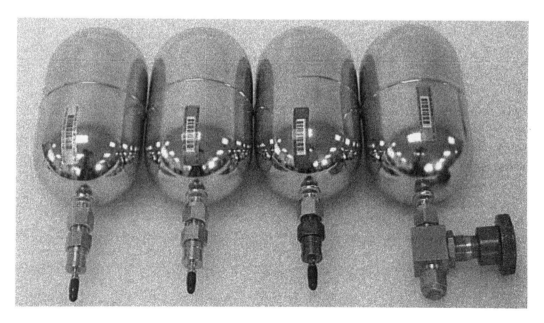

Figure 46. These negative pressure air sampling canisters are simple to use and interface well with GC/MS analysis. Photograph courtesy of Entech Instruments Inc.

surface sample point location process.

Many different forms of collection media are available for surface sampling. A great deal of research has been done in this area and is continuing today. Glass fiber filters, charcoal-impregnated pads (for volatile organic compounds), surgical gauze, smear tabs, cotton swabs, and commercially available pre-moistened wipes may all be used for surface sampling. However, some of these items may have special preparation requirements. Surgical gauze may be pre-contaminated with chemical compounds used in the manufacturing process and may require the extraction of these compounds prior to use. Commercially available pre-moistened wipes may also be pre-contaminated. The existence of any pre-contamination, from any source, may affect the analytical results. The use of "dry" or "wet" surface sampling media may depend on the area to be sampled. Generally, a moistened media will remove more of the sampled material than a dry media will. Many different solvents may be used to moisten the media. However, distilled water is one of the most common solvents used and presents the least amount of interference in both the collection and analytical process. Regardless of the type of media and solvent

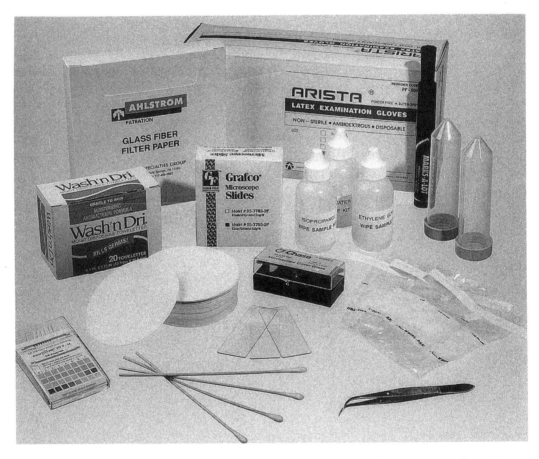

Figure 47. Surface and dermal sampling kits, such as this one, are available commercially and have a wide range of uses at a WMD crime scene. Photograph courtesy of SKC Inc.

chosen, control samples must be taken and analyzed. Samples of the media and solvent should be placed into separate sterilized glass containers, labeled, and preserved as evidence. Many of the items described above are available in "Wipe Sampling Kits"and can be purchased from a number of different sources (see Figure 47). In addition to the collection media, the investigator will need multiple pairs of surgical gloves, forceps, and *sampling templates*.[67]

There are many different methods that may be used for the collection of surface samples. Agencies such as *OSHA*,[68] *EPA*, and *NIOSH* have issued surface sampling methods guidelines for a variety of chemical hazards. In addition, surface sampling methodologies have been developed for specific chemical agents (i.e., Sarin) and certain chemical agent precursors (i.e., phosphorus pentasulfide, arsenic trichloride). However, at a crime scene involving the use of a chemical weapon, it is unlikely that the specific chemical agent or precursor will be immediately and positively identified. Therefore, the investigator should utilize the existing and scientifically acceptable surface sampling techniques for unknown substances. Once the location has been determined for a surface sample, it should be identified with a sampling placard and photographed. Its location should also be indicated on the crime scene sketch. The sample medium (i.e., gauze, smear tabs, etc.) should be removed from its storage container with a pair of sterilized locking forceps. The size of the area to be wiped may depend upon the material surface being sampled (i.e., light fixture). However, the normal surface area to be sampled should be approximately $100cm^2$. This will assist in a later determination as to the concentration of the contamination. Information regarding the concentration of the chemical agent may be of significant value to medical authorities

and the prosecution. Sampling templates may be used to insure sample area size consistency. Sterilized aluminum pans can be cut to allow for a 10cm x 10cm opening. The sterilized pan can be placed directly onto the surface to be sampled. The pan *cannot* be used for the next sample point and must be disposed of properly. The sample medium (locked into forceps) should be drawn across the surface area in the classic "S" motion.[69] An additional method is to start at the outside edge and progress toward the center of the surface area by wiping in concentric squares of decreasing size.[70] A light pressure should be applied to the sample medium while being drawn across the sample area. The sample medium should then be folded over (depending upon type of medium) with the contaminated side in, and then folded again. The forceps should be used for the folding of the sample medium and for the placing of the medium into the sample container. The container should then be sealed. The gloved hand of the sampler should not come into contact with the sample medium. This will help to insure the integrity of the collected chemical evidence. An unused sample medium *must* be placed into a sample container and sealed as a *blank*.

When obtaining dermal samples from victims and/or suspects, many of the same surface wipe procedures listed above may be used. Generally, the exposed skin areas (i.e., hands, face, and neck) are the best areas to obtain samples. The sample medium may be dry or wetted with distilled water.

Another excellent method for obtaining chemical trace evidence from the hands is to place each hand into a sturdy plastic bag containing 200mL of distilled water. Prior to utilizing this procedure, a *field blank* (equipment blank) must be created by filling each bag with distilled water. The bags should then be vigorously shaken and poured off into a sampling container with no remaining headspace. This will assist in identifying any pre-existing contaminates.

The victims' and/or suspects' hands should be placed into bags containing the distilled water and should then be sealed at the wrists. The hands should then be vigorously shaken. The bags should then be removed and their contents poured off into individual sampling containers. The sampling container should be filled to the top with no remaining headspace. The used plastic bags should be placed into a separate container and saved as evidence. The bag rinse method is considered more effective than the swab method for removing hand contamination.[71] A photograph must be taken of the sampling placard, hands, and face of the victim and/or suspect.

All surface and dermal samples should be appropriately labeled and placed into an appropriate size, sterilized, wide mouth, glass screw-cap bottle with Teflon-lined silicon septa.

Sampling for Degradation Products

The sampling for *degradation* products of chemical agents may be useful in determining suspected manufacturing sites, suspected storage facilities, and suspected areas where such an agent had been tested or used. These are the chemical compounds that may be found after the original chemical agent has been exposed to water (hydrolysis products) and other environmental media. The types and quantities of these chemicals found may vary depending upon the original chemical agent and the length of time between the original release and the time of sampling (see Figure 48).

Generally, the degradation products may be found in liquid waste streams (i.e., sanitary waste collection areas) and absorbing soils. The involatile chemical compounds can be expected to remain in soils. However,

low concentrations of these chemicals can be expected due to evaporation and degradation.[72] The soil matrix and the chemical makeup of individual compounds may impact on the depth of the chemical migration.

The investigation team should be aware of the possible existence of this type of chemical evidence. In situations involving suspected past use, manufacturing, and/or testing sites, it is essential that appropriate samples be collected and analyzed in an effort to identify these degradation products. These compounds should also be looked for whenever there has been a delayed response (i.e., several days) by the investigation team and in situations where the original chemical agent has been exposed to water.

The same chemical evidence collection protocols described above (liquids and solids) should be used in the collection of degradation product samples. It is essential that the investigation team communicate to the analytical laboratory the need to have the chemical evidence examined for these targeted chemical compounds.

Chemical Evidence Quality Control

As stated earlier, when sampling for chemical precursors, chemical agents, and chemical agent degradation products, care must be taken in selecting the proper sampling devices and sampling containers. The investigation team must insure that each item described above has been properly prepared and protected from outside contamination prior to use. When collecting suspected volatile chemical evidence, the sample containers should be filled to the top with no remaining headspace.[73] This will prevent the volatilization of minute chemical traces into the headspace of the sample containers and thereby prevent the loss of potentially valuable evidence (see Figure

49).

Control samples should be taken whenever possible. Air, water, and/or soil samples should be taken from areas outside of any suspected contaminated area. The control sample analytical results should then be compared to analytical results for any precursors, agents, or degradation products. These will offer a point of reference in establishing what chemicals may be pre-existing in the surrounding environment.

DEGRADATION PRODUCT [1]	C.A.S. #	CW AGENT
2-chlorovinylarsonous acid		Lewisite
Lewisite oxide	1306-02-01	Lewisite
Arsenic	7440-38-2	Lewisite
TDG	111-48-8	Mustard H
1,4-Thioxane	15980-15-1	Mustard H
Fluoride (as HF)	7664-39-3	Sarin GB Soman GD
2-Propanol	67-63-0	Sarin GB
Methylphosphonic acid, 1-methylethyl ester		Sarin GB
Methylphosphonic acid	993-13-15	Sarin GB VX Soman GD
Methylphosphonic acid, 1,2,2-trimethylpropyl ester		Soman GD
Pinacolyl Alcohol	464-07-3	Soman GD
Cyanide (as HCN)	74-90-8	Tabun GA
Dimethylphosphoramidic acid, monoethyl ester		Tabun GA
Dimethylphosphoramidic acid		Tabun GA
Ethanol	64-17-5	Tabun GA VX
Dimethylamine	124-40-3	Tabun GA
Phosphoric Acid	7664-38-2	Tabun GA
EA2192		VX
Methylphosphonic acid, ethyl ester		VX
Diisopropylaminoethanethiol		VX
Methylphosphonothioic acid, ethyl ester		VX
Diisopropylaminoethanol		VX

[1]Mitretek Systems: October 28, 1996

Figure 48. Chemical Agent degradation products such as these may be found at test sites and abandoned clandestine manufacturing facilities.

Labeling and Preserving Chemical Evidence

Once the liquid and/or soil samples have been seized, the sample containers should be labeled. Properly filled-out, sample-container labels will help prevent any future misidentification of the chemical evidence. Sample labels may be placed onto the sample containers prior to taking the sample. "The label should indicate the sample number, name of the collector, place of collection, and the date and time collected. Gummed labels or tags may be used."[74]

The chemical evidence containers should then be sealed. Sample seals are used to detect unauthorized tampering of the chemical evidence. The seals should contain the same information as listed on the sample

Figure 49. This volatile organic compound sample is not filled to the top as recommended by most scientifically acceptable chemical sampling standards. Small errors such as this may have an impact during the prosecution phase of the case.

label. The seal must be affixed to the containers before the samples leave the custody of the investigation team. "It must be affixed in such a way that it is necessary to break it in order to open the sample container."[75]

Another acceptable method is to place the sample containers *and the trip blanks* into see-through plastic evidence bags. The evidence bags are then heat-sealed closed. This method has several advantages. The sealed evidence envelope adds another layer of protection against possible outside contamination. In addition, the sample label information can be clearly seen through the envelope. Also, a simple inspection of the evidence envelope will determine if any unauthorized tampering has taken place (see Figure 50).

The chemical evidence should be photographed at the completion of the labeling and sealing process. These photographs may be taken with the seized sample next to the point from which it was removed. However, in order to cut down on possible personnel exposure time, the photographs of the sample containers may be taken once the evidence has been removed from the hot zone.

In order to maintain the integrity of the chemical evidence, a proper chain-of-custody must exist. The chain-of-custody should be traceable through documentation. The documentation should indicate who had custody of the chemical evidence from the time it was collected all the way through the analytical process. The signature of each individual taking custody of the evidence should appear on the documentation. The investigation team's responsibility for evidence integrity does not end with the shipping of the chemical evidence to a laboratory. The laboratory should be contacted and their chain-of-custody procedures reviewed prior to the shipment of any chemical evidence.

Storage of the Chemical Evidence

Most chemical evidence is best preserved by refrigerating it at 4°C; however, individual analytical methodologies should be consulted directly regarding holding times and preservation requirements for individual chemical compounds. The refrigeration unit should be secured in such a way as to prevent it from being damaged during transportation. The chemical evidence should be delivered to the laboratory for analysis as soon as practicable.

BIOLOGICAL EVIDENCE

The collecting of biological evidence shares many of the same challenges, protocols, and problems associated with the collection of chemical evidence. Field tests alone will not, in all likelihood, provide the biological evidence necessary to obtain a criminal conviction. With this standard in mind, the investigator must have a clear understanding of *what* is to be sampled, *where* it is to be sampled, *why* it is being sampled, and *how* it is to be analyzed. In addition, the investigator must be cognizant of the fact that some sample preparation methods can modify the analyte so that it is

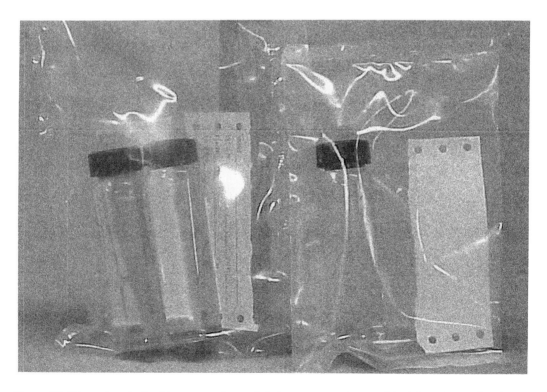

Figure 50. These chemical evidence samples and their accompanying trip blank have been placed into this see through plastic bag and then heat sealed closed.

no longer suitable for other types of analysis.[76]

The actual location of this type of crime scene may be dependent upon intelligence information, an immediate incident, or epidemiological data. Intelligence informa-

BIOLOGICAL WARFARE AGENTS[†]

AGENT	INCUBATION PERIOD	DIAGNOSTIC ASSAY
Anthrax	**1 – 5 days**	**Gram Stain** **Ag-ELISA,** **Serology: ELISA**
Brucellosis	**5 –60 days** **(occasionally months)**	**Serology: agglutination** **Culture**
Plague	**2 –3 days**	**Gram or Wright-Giemsa Stain** **Ag-ELISA** **Serology: ELISA, IFA**
Q Fever	**10-40 days**	**Serology: ELISA, IFA**
Tularemia	**2 – 10 days**	**Culture** **Serology: agglutination**
Smallpox	**7 – 17 days**	**ELISA, PCR** **Virus isolation**
Viral encephalitides	**VEE, 2 – 6 days** **EEE/WEE,** **7 – 14 days**	**Viral isolation** **Serology: ELISA or** **hemogglutination** **inhibition**
Viral hemorrhagic fevers	**4 –21 days**	**Viral isolation** **Ag-ELISA** **RT-PCR** **Serology: Ab-ELISA**
Botulinum	**1 – 5 days**	**Ag-ELISA** **Mouse neutral**
Straphylococcal enterotoxin B	**1 – 6 hours**	**Ag – ELISA** **Serology: Ab-ELISA**

*IFA, immunoflourescent assay; ELISA, enzyme-linked immunosorbent assay; PCR, polymerase chain reaction; RT-PCT, reverse transcriptase polymerase chain reaction; EEE, eastern equine encephalitis; WEE, western equine encephalitis; VEE, Venezuelan equine encephalitis: Ab, Antibody.

† Figure Source: COL. David R. Franz, et al., Clinical Recognition and Management of Patients Exposed to Biological Warfare Agents, JAMA, August 1997, Vol. 278, No. 5

Figure 51. This is a list of some of the known Biological warfare agents, their incubation periods and tests used to diagnose individuals exposed to these agents.

tion may provide a location where a biological weapon *is* being manufactured or where such a weapon *had been* manufactured in the past. There may be an immediate incident involving a suspicious package or device and, in some situations, epidemiological data may provide an incident location common to numerous victims. However, reviewing epidemiological data is a complex task. There may be numerous victims spread over a large geographical area. Information regarding possible biological agents, their incubation periods, and diagnostic data must all be evaluated and correlated (see Figure 51). The investigator must meet with the appropriate health authorities in an effort to determine the biological agent and the *means* by which the victims became exposed. In cases involving anthrax, the clinical laboratory results may determine if the outbreak is in the intestinal or pulmonary form. Intestinal anthrax may be indicative of an exposure to a food supply, while pulmonary anthrax may indicate a bioaerosol release. The one commonality among these different investigative scenarios is the need to obtain *admissible* forensic evidence in a manner that is *scientifically* sound.

Biological Evidence Gathering: Bacteria, Viruses and Toxins

Biological evidence may exist in solid, liquid, or aerosol form. This evidence may be found in a device, a body of water, a liquid waste stream, flat surfaces, soils, air filters, heating and ventilation systems, and/or culture media. Each form that the biological evidence is found in may require a different evidence collection protocol. As with chemical evidence, these protocols will assist in the furtherance of the criminal investigation and, at the same time, help insure the integrity of the biological evidence collected.

In situations involving an aerosol release of a suspected biological agent, it is essential that the investigative team begin sampling operations as soon as possible. Interior and/or exterior air currents may carry the biological agent away from the point of release, making sampling more difficult.

Equipment Preparation

Every piece of sampling equipment must be cleaned and sterilized prior to utilization. Items such as glass impingers, pipettes, vacuum hoses, battery-operated air pump, spoons, and shovels must all be properly prepared prior to use. Sample containers should be washed with soapy water, rinsed with tap water, rinsed with distilled water, and baked in an oven for two hours at a temperature between 160°C and 170°C. Any method chosen for the sterilization procedure must be scientifically sound, *fully documented*, and must include, at a minimum, the actual procedure, date of the procedure, and the name of the individual conducting the procedure. This is of particular importance with biological evidence. Even such a primary sterilization procedure as autoclaving may not destroy DNA.[77] This may raise a question of pre-existing contamination when such analytical procedures as *DNA PCR* are utilized.

Individual sealed packets containing sterilized forceps, wipes, and 40ml bottles and/or test tubes can be prepared in advance or commercial surface sampling kits can be utilized. Preparation procedures for these items should also be recorded (see Figure 52).

Sterilization is just one aspect of equipment preparation. Certain bioaerosol collection devices may use a *nutrient media* (agar). These items may have special storage requirements (i.e., temperature, sterile wrapping, etc.) and may carry expiration dates. *Gravitational* (depositional) and *filter* devices should be sealed and stored in such way as to negate any future claim of possible pre-contamination.

Glove Changes

The outer gloves of the sampler *must* be changed in-between sample points. The gloves should be *carefully* replaced with a new pair of pre-sterilized gloves from a sealed packet. Although the *alcohol-glovewash* method has been the accepted practice in biological sampling for many years, a complete glove change will avoid the possible criminal trial issue surrounding the alcohol's effectiveness for sterilization. Nearly every sample collection will require the sampler to come into direct glove contact with either a sampling device, collection media (i.e., agar strips), and/or the sample container. Biological contamination on the exterior glove surface can easily be carried over to the next sample point. One tiny biological organism is enough to cross-contaminate a subsequent sample. Due to

the sensitivity of the analytical equipment and analytical procedures which reproduce the biological organism, absolute sample integrity must be maintained at all times.

Control Samples

Control samples should be taken from outside the hot zone area. The *sample matrix* of the control samples should match those samples taken from within the hot zone. If aerosol, wipe, and soil samples are taken within the hot zone, then aerosol, wipe, and soil control samples should be taken from an area believed to be uncontaminated. It is the responsibility of the investigator to insure that every measure is taken to negate any future criminal defense that the contamination found is due to some outside source or from some naturally occurring phenomenon.

Sampling for a Suspected Biological Agent

When sampling for a biological agent, the

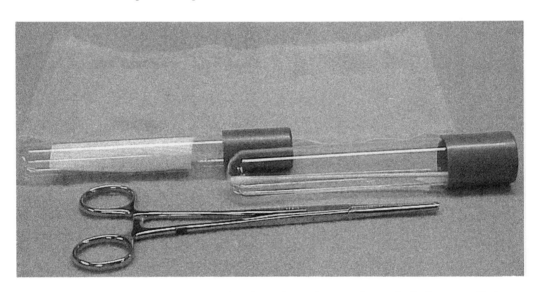

Figure 52. Small kits for surface or dermal biological sampling can be made for low cost. Each item must be sterilized and a record of the sterilization procedure maintained.

investigator must first determine the type(s) of sampling to be conducted. Samples from suspected devices, soil, water, and/or a bioaerosol (airborne biological agent) each requires specialized sampling equipment (see Figure 53). When making sampling equipment choices, the investigator must consider reliability and ease of use. Every piece of sampling equipment must be tested to insure that it will function properly under tough field conditions (i.e., freezing temperatures and/or extreme heat). In addition, sampling devices that require a great deal of dexterity may be difficult to operate when wearing Level "A" or Level "B" protective equipment. The best sampling devices are those that are capable of collecting the biological evidence in a scientifically acceptable manner, are structurally and/or mechanically sound under extreme field conditions, and are easy to operate.

LIQUIDS AND SOLIDS. Biological agents in liquid form may be found in devices, bodies of water, water runoff areas, clandestine manufacturing facilities, clandestine manufacturing facilities' waste streams, and water runoff from contaminated areas. For the above described areas, and for devices that have been rendered safe before detonation, sterilized pipettes and Coliwasa tubes may be used to collect liquid samples. These collection devices *should not* be reused at the crime scene. The liquid sample(s) should then be placed into sterilized 100ml glass bottle(s) with Teflon-lined (chemically inert) silicon septa. Whenever practical, the bottle(s) should be filled to approximately 90 per cent of their capacity. During storage of the sample, some of the organisms may settle to the bottom of the container. The remaining 10 per cent headspace allows for a proper mixing of the liquid sample prior to analysis. If only a small amount of liquid is available for sampling, a 40ml glass bottle may be used.

The investigator should be cognizant of the fact that additional analysis may be required and must insure that enough

SAMPLING EQUIPMENT
FOR
BIOLOGICAL EVIDENCE

Stainless Steel Locking Forceps	Glass Sample Bottles with Teflon-Lined Silicon Septa Caps	Glass Coliwasa Tubes	Wipe Sampling Kit
Surgical Gloves	Wipe Aluminum Templates (12 x 12 in.)	Agar Collection Slides (flexible)	Polyethylene Bags (½ gallon size – 0.025mm)
Children's Bubbles	Tracer Balloons	Liquid impinger with Air pump	Pipettes and Rubber Bulbs
Trip Blanks	Gummed Labels	Log Book	Pens and Markers
Distilled Water	Extension Augers	Weighted Samplers	Dippers
Bailers	Measuring Tape	Impaction Sampler	Compass
Evidence Sealing Tape	Scissors	Stainless Steel Hand Trowels	Stainless Steel Spoons

Figure 53. Here are just a few of the items that may be needed when collecting biological evidence at a WMD crime scene.

sample material is available for that analysis. It is important to note that an *organic chemical compound* found within a liquid biological sample may provide an important future forensic chemical link and must be protected from volatilization. To protect this type of evidence, separate samples (using separate sampling protocols) should be taken. This is especially true for clandestine manufacturing facilities that have attempted to remove biological evidence through the use of cleaning agents and solvents.

VICTIMS'/SUSPECTS' PERSONAL ITEMS. Biological agents may be found on the clothing of victims and suspects. In situations involving a *known* release of a biological agent (i.e., positive field test results), the collection and preservation of victims' and/or suspects' clothes and personal items is vital to the investigation. These items should be collected and preserved for future analysis. The collection of these items must be done under the *direct supervision* of law enforcement personnel. Personal items, including clothing, should be dried (if possible) and placed into sturdy plastic bags. Identifying information (i.e., name, address, date-of-birth, telephone number, physical description, etc.) should be recorded on a carbon-type form with one copy being placed inside the bag and the other copy being securely mounted on the outside of the bag. The bag should then be sealed. An instant photograph of the individual's face should be taken and attached to the form. This procedure will further assist the investigator in situations where the suspect has become accidentally exposed to the biological agent and is now seeking medical treatment as a victim.

SOILS. When determining sample point locations for surface soil, several factors must be considered. The suspected point of release must be identified and used as a starting point. This area and downwind areas should be selected for sampling. The wind direction at the time of release should be determined (i.e., National Weather Service). If it is determined that the wind direction has changed since the time of the original release, a compass reading should be taken to determine the original dispersal direction. There may have been a *fall-out* of larger particles (onto soil surface) along this directional route which would make this area a prime surface soil sampling location. If the wind direction has remained unchanged since the time of the original release, the bubble and/or tracer balloon technique described in bioaerosol sampling should be used.

Surface soil samples may be collected with sterilized stainless steel spoons and/or hand trowels. If the suspected release of the biological agent is relatively recent (hours) the sample should be taken from the surface of the soil. If the suspected release time is historic in nature (days, weeks, months), the surface and subsurface should be sampled. Natural environmental conditions (heavy rain) may cause the suspected biological organism to migrate down into the soil. For subsurface soil samples, a sterilized stainless steel auger may be used. However, the auger must not be reused at subsequent sample points unless it has be thoroughly cleaned and sterilized. If this device is to be reused, a field blank must be taken (see Chemical Evidence Gathering). The soil samples should be placed into large mouth, 100 ml, sterilized glass bottles with Teflon-lined silicon septa and, when practical, the sample bottle should be filled to the top with no remaining headspace.

SURFACE AND DERMAL. When sampling flat surfaces such as floors, counters, and/or walls, a swab or wipe may be used. "Swabbing methods work in one of two ways. A cotton Q-tip or sterile pad or puff is used to wipe a surface and is then either wiped directly across an agar surface or immersed in a solution to remove the collected microorganisms."[78] If a sterile gauze pad is used, it should be locked into a pair of sterilized stainless steel forceps. The flat surface area should then be wiped in the classic "S" pattern. The wipe should then be released into a 40ml sterilized glass bottle or sterilized test tube. The stainless steel forceps should not be reused. For air filters found in buildings and common carriers, the filter itself may be seized (depending on size), a portion may be removed and placed into a large mouth, sample bottle or a wipe sample may be taken. If a portion of the filter is to be removed, a sterilized scalpel (or other sterilized instrument) should be used for cutting the sample. Sterilized forceps should

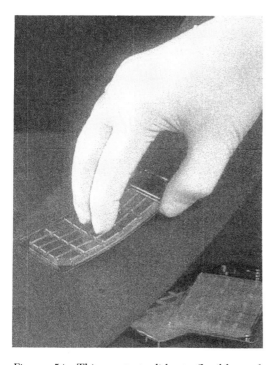

Figure 54. This contact slide is flexible and contains a built-in culture media. It is also an excellent sampling device for areas containing irregular surfaces. Photograph courtesy of Biotest Diagnostics Corporation.

be used to place the sample into the sampling container.

Another method that may be utilized for surface sampling is the agar contact collection plate or slide (see Figure 54). These items are pre-wrapped for sterilization and can be used in place of the wipe. The flexible slide is placed into direct contact with the suspected contaminated surface area. The plastic side of the plate is held in one gloved hand and the agar medium is gently pressed into the surface. This method is extremely effective on rough and uneven surfaces. Each agar plate or slide should be held in place for approximately 5 seconds.[79] Any existing surface biological organisms will be picked up by the agar medium. The agar medium may then be placed into a container, sealed, and labeled. By properly utilizing the above-described sampling devices, the investigator can avoid coming into direct glove contact with the suspected biological agent and therefore decrease the possibility of sample cross-contamination. Sample blanks for all collection mediums, including agar, should be collected, placed into sampling containers, properly labeled, and preserved as evidence.

BIOAEROSOLS. "The term *bioaerosol* refers to airborne particles containing (1) intact living or dead microorganisms (as single units, in homogeneous or heterogeneous groups, or attached to other particles), (2) microbial spores (resistant reproductive structures produced by many fungi and some bacteria), (3) fragments of microorganisms and larger organisms (body parts of arthropods, skin scales from mammals, and pollen and plant debris), and (4) other particles from living or dead organisms (excreta from arthropods, such as dust mites and cockroaches and allergens)."[80]

Situations may arise requiring the investigator to take an air sample to determine the presence of an airborne biological agent.

The circumstances surrounding the release of the biological agent will determine the optimum bioaerosol sample point location(s). Generally, interior bioaerosol samples should be taken at varying heights and locations. This is required due to biological decay in aerosols. "Aerosol decay occurs through both physical decay (the fall-out of large particles) and biological decay (death of the biological agent)."[81] Based upon this, the optimum sampling height may be unknown to the investigator. Therefore, various sampling heights should be considered at the suspect location. These locations may include interior open areas (i.e., shopping malls, passenger terminals) air-inlets, vents, pipes, and heating and ventilation systems. If outside bioaerosol samples are to be taken, wind direction and velocity should first be determined. In addition, every effort should be made to determine the exact wind direction that existed at the *time of the release*. If it is determined that the wind direction has remained *unchanged*, the investigator may determine the airflow patterns through the use of children's bubbles or tracer balloons. By releasing these items at the suspected point of the original release, a visual perspective is given of the airflow patterns and drafts. This is especially useful in areas containing large structures that may divert airflow patterns. By examining the traveled routes of the bubbles and/or balloons, the investigator will be able to determine optimum surface sampling locations for short and long distances.

"Bioaerosol collection needs to be coupled with a compatible analytical method what will allow an investigator to detect, quantify, or identify particular bioaerosols as needed."[82] Based upon this, the selection of the proper sampling equipment becomes vital. Bioaerosol sampling devices include liquid-filled impingers, filtration, gravitational, and impaction devices. Each of these collection devices is scientifically acceptable for bioaerosol sampling. However, as stated above, it is essential that the investigator examine each device to determine its functional ability under field conditions and its compatibility with the intended analytical method or methods.

Liquid filled impingers are considered one of the best devices for collecting bioaerosol samples. There are many different kinds of impingers and this type of aerosol collection technology is continually changing and improving. Impingers must be used in conjunction with a battery-operated air pump and each air pump must be calibrated prior to use. Impingers are normally constructed of glass and must be sterilized prior to use. After sterilization, the entire unit should be placed into a sealed package. Impingers and their air pumps should *not* be reused at a crime scene. If additional bioaerosol sampling is required, a new sterilized impinger and air pump should be removed from its sealed package and used. The impinger can be mounted directly to the pump through the use of a small metal bracket (see Figure 55). The sampler's inlet allows for airborne particles to be drawn in. The collection liquid inside the impinger traps the particles as they are drawn into the impinger. This collection liquid is normally a dilute buffer solution. However, a sterile 0.1% (v/v) peptone water solution is a suitable alternative.[83] The solution should be loaded into the impinger just prior to use and outside of any hot zone area. During this loading procedure, a sample of this solution *must* be taken and used as a field blank. The field blank must be analyzed to prove that the solution was not contaminated prior to use. It is recommended that samples not be taken at temperatures below 5°C (41°F) to avoid crystallization of the medium.[84]

The air pump can be set with a timer or it can be manually turned on. Presetting the timer is useful when Level "A" sampling is required. The reduction of dexterity and visibility may make the operation of the pump's controls difficult while operating in the hot zone area. By presetting the timer, the entire unit will automatically begin sampling without the need to set small and difficult to read buttons and switches. The volume flow rate, time, temperature, and relative humidity should be recorded in the sample log. This information will assist laboratory personnel in determining airborne concentrations of the biological agent. The impinger can be left in a stationary location or it may be carried to various areas by utilizing a holster. The sample duration is normally approximately 30 minutes.[85] However, under most conditions, the longer the pump is running, the better the chances are for capturing an airborne organism.

After the sampling event has concluded, the collection fluid should be placed into a sterilized glass bottle with screw cap, labeled, and secured as evidence. This collection liquid can later be placed onto nutrient media (i.e., agar) and then incubated. Colonies of the organism may form and these can be counted and identified through the analytical method of **Growth Culture Analysis**. Other analytical methodologies, such as DNA/ PCR, Microscopic Analysis, Biochemical Assay, and **Immunoassay** can also be used. Also, due to its all glass construction (fragile) and air pump requirements (calibration), ease of operation under extreme field conditions must be considered.

Filtration devices are also used for bioaerosol sampling. As with the impinger system, an air pump is required. The air pump draws an airflow through some form of porous collection filter. These collection filters can be made of mixed cellulose ester, polyvinyl chloride, or polycarbonate. After

the collection process, the filters should be placed into sterilized containers and labeled.

Gravitational devices are simply collection plates. When placed in an area, the agar medium on the surface of the plate will catch any airborne microorganisms that fall to the ground. This type of collection device may be ineffective whenever there is air movement.

Impaction devices collect bioaerosol samples by drawing air over a collection surface. Biological organisms are separated directly onto an agar strip by centrifugal force. These surfaces may be made of a nutrient agar or an adhesive coated surface, which will allow for microscopic analysis. These are hand-held battery operated devices that allow the sampler to preset air volumes (see Figure 56).

The agar strips can be preloaded into several rotor assemblies. The device is lightweight and easy to carry. These units come with small tripods for stationary sampling or they can be carried to several locations for continuous sampling. After the required sample has been taken, the contaminated rotor assembly (containing the agar strip) may be removed, placed into a sterilized container, and labeled. A new rotor assembly can then be placed onto the unit for additional sampling. Sterile sleeves can be used to protect the instrument from cross-contamination during the sampling operation. These units have available remote control (limited distance) and may be attached to a robot for automated sampling.

Several of the devices described above utilize the *culture-based* method for future analysis. Although this method has been used for many years in the field of microbiology, the time required for the biological agent to multiply to detectable levels may take several days, or in some situations, several weeks.[86] This type of method and the resulting analytical availability time may not meet the needs of a criminal investigation. The investigator should be aware of the fact that new and improved bioaerosol sampling devices are continually being

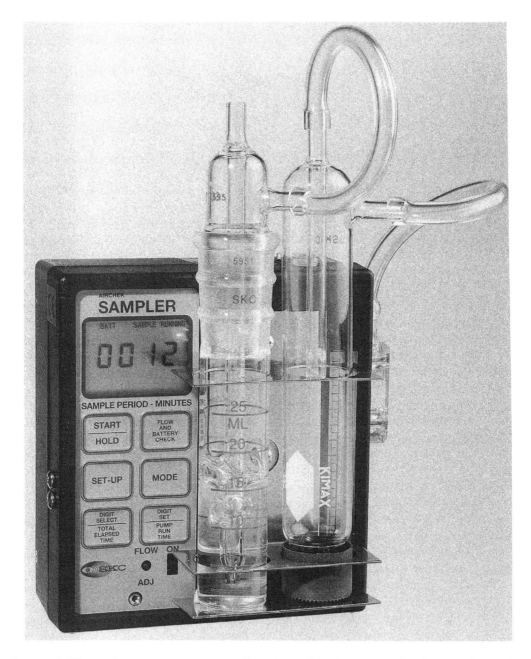

Figure 55. This midget impinger is an excellent device for obtaining quality bioaerosol samples. However, the low visibility and lack of dexterity associated with a level "A" protective suit may make this unit difficult to operate under extreme conditions. Photograph courtesy of SKC Inc.

developed and marketed. Whenever possible, the investigator should determine in advance, the best type of bioaerosol sampling device that will produce a sample from which qualitative, quantitative and expedient analytical results may be obtained.

Labeling and Preserving Biological Evidence

Once a sample has been collected, the sample containers should be properly labeled. Properly filled-out sample-container labels will help prevent any future misidentification of the biological evidence. Sample labels may be placed onto the sample containers prior to taking the sample. The label should indicate the sample number, name of the collector, place of collection, and the date and time collected. A gummed label should be used. The biological evidence containers should then be sealed. The sample seals are used to detect unauthorized tampering of the evidence. The seals should contain the same information as listed on the sample label. The seal must be affixed to the containers before the samples leave the custody of the investigation team.

Another acceptable method is to place the sample containers (and their respective trip and field blanks) into see-through plastic evidence bags. The evidence bags are then heat-sealed closed. This method has several advantages. The sealed evidence envelope adds another layer of protection against possible outside biological contamination. In addition, the sample label information can be clearly seen through the envelope. Also, a simple inspection of the evidence envelope will determine if any unauthorized tampering has taken place (see Figure 50).

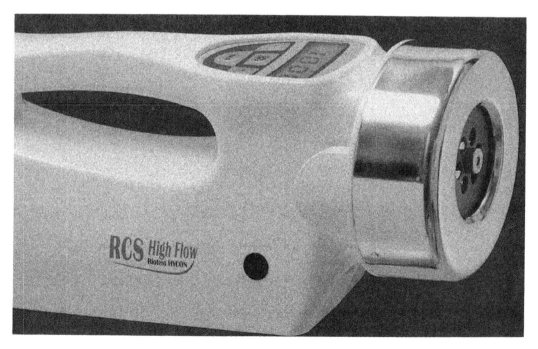

Figure 56. This bioaerosol impaction-sampling device has several key advantages. It is easy to carry, its collection media can be changed quickly and it can be run by remote control if necessary. Photograph courtesy of Biotest Diagnostics Corporation.

The biological evidence should be photographed at the completion of the labeling and sealing process. These photographs may be taken with the seized biological sample(s) next to the point from which it was removed. However, in order to cut down on possible personnel exposure time, the photographs of the sample containers may be taken once the evidence has been removed from the hot zone.

In order to maintain the integrity of the biological evidence, a proper chain-of-custody must exist. The chain-of-custody should be traceable through documentation. The documentation should indicate who had custody of the biological evidence from the time it was collected all the way through the analytical process. The signature of each individual taking custody of the evidence should appear on the documentation. The investigation team's responsibility for evidence integrity does not end with the shipping of the biological evidence to a laboratory. The laboratory should be contacted and their chain-of-custody procedures reviewed prior to the shipment of any biological evidence.

Biological Evidence Storage

Once the biological evidence (including blanks) has been placed into the proper sampling containers, it should be protected from ultraviolet light and temporarily (prior to packaging and shipping) stored in a refrigeration unit. The temperature inside the unit should be approximately 5°C (41°F). The refrigeration unit should be secured in such a way as to prevent it from being damaged during transportation (see Packaging and Shipping). A complete inventory of all samples should be made and the information noted in the sampling logbook. Whenever possible, the biological evidence should be delivered to the analytical laboratory within six hours.[87]

RADIOLOGICAL EVIDENCE

Crime scenes involving the use of radiological substances share many of the same evidence collection issues associated with chemical and biological weapons crime scenes. One such issue is the fact that evidence must be collected and preserved in a safe and scientifically acceptable manner. Radiological evidence may be found in the form of liquids, solids, soils, **airborne radioactive material**, surface contamination (including dermal), or in a device. The radiation found at a crime scene may be from a single source, multiple sources, or as the result of a detonation from a *radiation dispersion device* (RDD) or *improvised nuclear device* (IND). In addition, the radiation may be in the form of **alpha particles**, **beta particles**, **neutrons** or **gamma rays**.

Results from field testing equipment, such as the **Geiger-Mueller Detector**, *will not* be sufficient evidence to prove the existence of a particular radiological substance. As is the case with chemical and biological substances, proper sampling and analysis of the radiological evidence must be performed. In addition, the investigator *must* insure that the source of radiation being detected is not due to a naturally occurring phenomenon or from some other outside source (i.e., research facility or nuclear power plant).

Radiological Evidence Gathering

Gathering radiological evidence is not a new science. Many different techniques and scientific methodologies have been developed to sample and identify the various types of man-made and naturally occurring radiological substances. Extensive scientific research done in the areas of international treaty verification, detonation fallout data, and accidental release data (i.e., Three Mile Island, Chernobyl) have produced evidence gathering techniques which may be utilized by the criminal investigator. These techniques will help to further the investigation and, at the same time, insure the integrity of the radiological evidence.

Trip Blanks

A radiological trip blank is a small volume of non-irradiated soil that accompanies the sample collection containers and sampling equipment *before*, *during*, and *after* and radiological evidence collection takes place. Soil blanks may be obtained from the National Institute of Standards and Technology (NIST). These soils, collected in 1943, contain no artificial radionuclides and have served as quality control blank samples for a number of radiation monitoring programs.[88] The soil should be kept in a sealed and sturdy polyethylene bag (s) and *must* be analyzed to prove that no outside contamination or cross-contamination occurred at any time during the collection, transportation, and /or storage of the radiological evidence. This technique is vital due to the fact that there are many forms of pre-existing **background radiation**. Background radiation may be in the form of naturally occurring radioactive materials used in the construction of buildings (granite), cosmic and natural terrestrial radiation, global fallout and certain consumer products (smoke detectors).[89] The use of a trip blank will help to negate any future claims that the evidence collected was irradiated by some *other* source during the evidence collection, transporta-

tion. and/or storage process.

Glove Changes

When taking liquid, solid, soil or surface (including dermal) radiological samples, it is essential that the lead sampler and assistant sampler change their outer gloves inbetween each sample, *regardless of whether any apparent glove contamination has occurred.* Any contamination on the gloves may be carried over to the next sample point and may jeopardize any future analytical results. New outer gloves should remain sealed in their original package until their use is required.

Control Samples

In a case involving the release of a radiological substance (i.e., air, ground or water contamination), control samples should be taken from outside the contaminated area. The *sample matrix* of the control samples should match those samples taken from within the hot zone or any other contaminated area. If solid, liquid, surface, or air samples are taken within the hot zone, then these same types of control samples should be taken from an area believed to be uncontaminated. This will help to insure the integrity of the radiological evidence and will also assist in negating any future criminal defense that the contamination found is due to some outside source or from some naturally occurring phenomenon.

Sampling Equipment and Containers for Radiological Evidence

Radiological evidence may be found in various forms and matrixes. These can include exposed radiological sources and sources from detonated and non-detonated devices. In addition, radiological evidence (including *daughter*/degradation products) may be found in soils, liquids, vegetation, surfaces, human skin, and in the form of gases and airborne particles. Each form or matrix may require specialized sampling equipment. The investigator must insure that this equipment has been properly prepared and is free of any contamination.

Radiological sources may require a telescoping grappling device for collection and various size *pigs* for the storage of a seized source. Soil samples will require the use of sterilized stainless steel topsoil cutters, augers, and polyethylene sample bags. Liquid samples will require sterilized pipettes, coliwasa tubes, and plastic bottles. Surface samples (smears) will require wipes and forceps and air sampling will require a *high volume air sampler* and appropriate filter media (see Figure 57). When attempting to trace localized interior or exterior airflow patterns, the investigator may wish to utilize tracer balloons and/or children's bubbles. In addition, the investigator will be required to utilize the appropriate radiological *survey meter* to help locate specific sampling locations.

The equipment used for evidence collection and containment (i.e., polyethylene sample bags and plastic sample bottles) should be *frisked* prior to use. This is accomplished by using the appropriate survey meter to insure that the equipment is free of *contamination*.

Sampling for a Suspected Radiological Substance

A crime scene involving the release or potential release of a radiological substance *will* require radiological sampling. The sampling methodology will be dependent upon a variety of factors. These may include the type of radiation present, the source from which it is radiating, and/or the sample matrix. In most cases, emergency response personnel will have identified the location of the radiological material. The investigators should verify this information and locate other potential sample points through the use of an appropriate survey meter. The

SAMPLING EQUIPMENT
FOR
RADIOLOGICAL EVIDENCE

Stainless Steel Locking Forceps	Plastic Sample Bottles	Glass Coliwasa Tubes	Wipe Sampling Kit
Surgical Gloves	High Volume Air Mover	Air Sampling Filter Media	Polyethylene Bags (½ gallon size)
Children's Bubbles	Tracer Balloons	Telescoping Grappler	Pipettes and Rubber Bulbs
Trip Blanks	Gummed Labels	Log Book	Pens and Markers
Pigs	Extension Augers	Top Soil Cutter	Rubber Mallet
Survey Meters (alpha, beta, gamma)	Measuring Tape	Stainless Steel Spoons	Compass
Evidence Sealing Tape	Scissors	Dosimeters	Appropriate Safety Equipment

Figure 57. Here are some of the items that will be needed when sampling at a WMD crime scene involving radiological materials.

results of these surveys should be recorded.

AIRBORNE RADIOACTIVE MATERIAL. At crime scenes involving the release of airborne radioactive material (i.e., radiation dispersion device), investigative personnel will want to begin air sampling as soon as practical. If there appears to be a large amount of air movement (i.e., wind and/or drafts), the sample team may wish to utilize *tracer balloons* and or children's bubbles in an effort to determine localized airflow direction and fallout patterns. This technique is effective in urban areas and/or industrial settings that contain multiple structures, side streets, and/or alley ways which may impact on the air flow pattern. If the radiological release is recent, the airflow direction may also assist in determining air-sampling locations. If survey instruments are used in an area containing airborne contamination, the investigator must insure that the survey instrument probe does not become contaminated. This may produce false positive readings and the misidentification of sample points.

While utilizing the appropriate safety protocols, the sample team will gather airborne radiological evidence through the use of a high volume air sampler (see Figure 58). This is a vacuum device that draws air through a collection filter media at approximately 5 cfm. The filter media may be made of a Teflon membrane, glass fiber, or cellulose and is designed to trap airborne radioactive particles that are drawn into the filter. Air sample flow rates should be as high as possible to minimize the sample team's stay time within the contaminated area while not sacrificing sampling efficiency.[90] However, caution must be exercised so that a high flow rate does not damage the filter. The sampling event must be timed and recorded. The sampling device should be held at least 1 meter above the ground's surface. Under no circumstances should the

sampling device be placed on the ground while operating. This may result in surface contamination being drawn into the filter media. The filter media should be changed in-between sample points. This should be accomplished by removing the contaminated filter medium with a gloved hand. The filter can then be frisked to determine if any airborne radiological particles have been captured. If radiation is found to be present on the filter media, it should then be placed into a plastic evidence bag. The bag should be labeled, sealed, and secured as evidence. The label should indicate the name of the sampler, sample point number, sample point location, date, time, and duration of the sample (i.e., minutes and seconds). A permanent marker may be used to label the evidence bags. A glove change should be made before any new filter mediums are removed from their containers. All sample areas should be placarded, marked on the crime scene sketch, and photographed. The sample placards should include, at a minimum, the sample numbers and date.

A background air sample must be taken upwind and outside of any contaminated area. The background sample should be taken utilizing the same procedures listed above. At the conclusion of the background sample, the filter should be placed into a plastic bag, labeled, sealed, and secured as evidence.

SOLID SOURCES. Radiological sampling of solid material may include actual radiological sources (see Figure 59), a radiological source that is part of a radiological device or contaminated clothing obtained from victims and/or suspects. Devices containing radiological substances normally come in two forms. The radiation dispersion device (RDD) is normally comprised of a timing device, radiological source, and an explosive charge (see Figure 60). The *improvised nuclear device* (IND) must contain *special nuclear materials*, such as µ-235, µ-233 and Pµ-239. In addition to these special nuclear materials, the IND will also contain a conventional high explosive and the necessary triggering device to detonate the weapon.[91] Normally, an IND will produce neutrons that can be detected by properly trained and equipped emergency response personnel. Qualified individuals (i.e., DOE personnel and/or explosives specialists) must render these types of devices safe, before any radiological sampling takes place. Suspected IND devices should not be approached and should be left for qualified US Department of Energy personnel.

Once a RDD has been declared safe from detonation and the explosive material has been removed, the source material may be collected as evidence. If it is in a solid form (or a liquid in a sealed container), a telescoping grappling device may be used to transfer the radioactive material from the RDD to a containment pig. In situations involving low-level sources, forceps may be used for the source removal. Whenever possible, a *gamma spectroscopy* should be made of the source material prior to being sealed as evidence in a containment pig. The shielded walls of the containment pig will interfere with this analytical procedure. The pig should then be labeled, sealed, and secured as evidence. Photographs should be taken of the device, source, sample placard, and containment pig.

In situations involving a *known* release of a radiological substance (i.e., positive survey meter results), the collection and preservation of victims' and/or suspects' clothes and personal items are vital to the investigation. These items should be collected and preserved as evidence for future analysis. Contamination of clothing and personal items may be determined by a simple frisk. The survey meter probe should be held less

Figure 58. This high volume air sampler is an excellent device for sampling airborne radioactive particles. The power for this unit can be supplied by a 12 volt battery or generator.

than 0.5 inches from the surface being surveyed for beta and gamma contamination and at approximately 0.25 inches away from the surface for alpha contamination. The survey meter probe should be moved slowly over the surface at a rate of approximately 2 inches per second. The frisk should be performed in the following order: head (pausing at the mouth and nose for approximately 5 seconds); neck and shoulders; arms (pause at each elbow; chest and abdomen; back, hips, and seat of pants; legs (pause at each knee); shoe tops and shoe bottoms (pause at sole and heel).[92]

The collection of clothing and personal items must be done under the *direct supervision* of law enforcement personnel. Seized contaminated clothing and personal items should be placed into sturdy plastic bags.

Identifying information (i.e., name, address, date-of-birth, telephone number, physical description, etc.) should be recorded on a carbon type form with one copy being placed inside the bag and the other copy being securely mounted on the outside of the bag. The bag should then be sealed. An instant photograph of the subject's face should be taken and attached to the exterior copy of the form. This procedure may further assist the investigator in situations where the suspect has become accidentally exposed to the radiological substance and is now seeking emergency medical assistance as a victim.

SOILS. In cases involving the release of a radiological substance over a large outdoor area, the sample team may be required to obtain soil samples. Multiple personnel, with

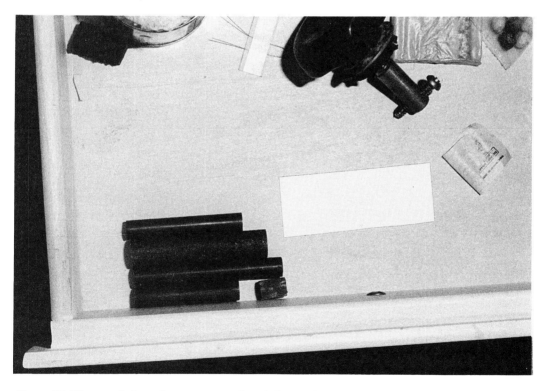

Figure 59. These radiological sources were found during the search of a suspect's dwelling. Firearms and explosives were also found.

multiple survey meters, should be used to assist in locating sample points. Investigative personnel should survey the area slowly and establish (or confirm) the 2mr (milliroentgen/hour) line. Appropriate soil samples may be taken at the 2mr line. However, caution must be exhibited when attempting to locate surface samples. Airborne contamination produces surface contamination and, conversely, surface contamination produces airborne contamination.[93] In other words, the simple act of walking through a contaminated area may disturb surface contamination and thereby making it airborne. When searching for surface soil sample points, the detection probe should be held several inches from the ground (by its wire) during the survey. Under no circumstances should the detection probe come into contact with the ground's surface. If contact is made, the probe may become contaminated and give continual false positive readings. Once a sample point has been located, the area should be placarded, marked on the crime scene sketch, and photographed. Any existing surface vegetation should be cut at the surface level and placed into a sturdy polyethylene sample bag. Approximately 1 kilogram of vegetation should be collected from an area approximately 1 m^2.[94] A template or measuring device should be used when determining sample area size. Any cutting instruments (i.e., clippers or scissors) should be removed from their sealed storage bags and frisked prior to use.

When removing surface soil samples, a 5-cm topsoil cutter should be used. If there is a

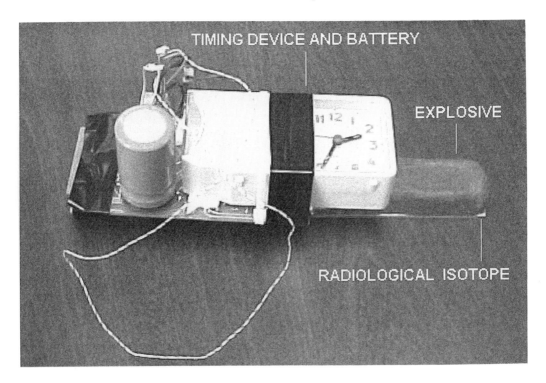

Figure 60. This Radiological Dispersion Device is designed to spread radioactive material over a large area. Devices such as these must be rendered safe before a proper identification of the radiological material can be made.

thick root mat, a 10-cm or 15-cm cutter can be used. The handle should be twisted gently to cleanly remove the topsoil plug. The soil plug should then be placed into a sturdy polyethylene sample bag. A minimum of 10 soil samples should be taken to provide a representative sample of the contaminated area.[95] For deeper soil samples, a stainless steel barrel auger may be used. The auger, handle, and soil removal device (i.e., small flat blade knife) should be removed from their sealed storage bags and frisked before use. The handle is twisted into the ground's surface until the auger is approximately three-quarters full. When the auger is removed, a small flat blade knife may be used to remove the soil from the auger.[96] The soil should then be placed into a sturdy polyethylene sample bag. The auger should not be reused at any additional sample points until it has been completely decontaminated and frisked. This decontamination procedure, the name of the individual conducting the procedure, and sample point numbers (i.e., numbers before and after decontamination) must be recorded in the sample log. All vegetation and soil samples must be sealed in their sample bags, labeled and secured as evidence. The label should indicate the name of the sampler, sample point number, sample point location, date, and time.

In an effort to determine the total amount of an initial airborne contaminate that has fallen out in a given area, all analytical values must be related to the surface area sampled. The surface *area* and *depth* define the volume; the *weight* of the volume of dry soil defines the field bulk density. This data is necessary in that, during the analytical stage, it may be converted to radioactivity concentrations per unit surface area.[97] This data is obtained by simply measuring the length, width, and depth of the sample point. The physical weight of the sample can be determined during the analytical procedure.

These measurements and the individual's name that obtained the measurements must be recorded in the sample log.

Background soil samples (control samples) must be taken utilizing the procedures indicated above. These samples must also be labeled, sealed, and secured as evidence. A sampling placard must be used and photographed at the sample point location. The locations of all background samples must be noted on the crime scene sketch.

SURFACE AND DERMAL. During the investigation of the crime scene, it may become necessary to obtain surface and/or dermal samples. Survey instrument readings may be necessary in determining contaminated surface areas; however, actual samples of the radioactive materials should be taken so that a positive identification of the radiological isotope can be made. Interior building surfaces chosen for radiological wipe (smear) sampling may include desks, computers, overhead lights, cabinets, walls, floors, chairs, tables, benches, lunch tables, heating and ventilation ducts. In situations involving the suspected release of a radiological agent in an outside area, the investigator should obtain ***wipe samples*** from exterior walls, building intake air vents, street lamps, vehicle exteriors, mail boxes, and windows. By utilizing the field survey instruments in conjunction with tracer balloons and/or children's bubbles (see Bioaerosol Sampling), the investigator may obtain the localized travel route of the radioactive particles and thereby simplify the surface sample point location process.

Surface and dermal sampling for radiological materials is not a new science. Both the EPA[98] and DOE[99] have established sampling protocols for radioactive materials. Therefore, the investigator should utilize the general existing and scientifically acceptable surface sampling techniques for these substances. Once the location has been determined for a surface sample it should be identified with a sampling placard, marked on the crime scene sketch and photographed. Any sampling equipment or media that is to be used should be removed from its sealed container and frisked prior to use. The sample medium should be removed from its storage container with a pair of locking forceps. A 2.4-cm diameter filter paper disk or a 5-cm Whatman No. 1 filter may be used.[100] The size of the area to be wiped may depend upon the material surface being sampled. However, a 100-cm^2 (10-cm x 10-cm) area should be chosen whenever possible. The sample medium (locked into forceps) should be drawn across the sample area in the classic "S" or "Z" motion.[101] An additional method is to use the "S' or "Z" motion making each wipe approximately 12 inches high. A light pressure should be applied to the sample medium while being drawn across the sample area. The forceps should be used for the placing of the medium into the sample container. A plastic sample bottle or a sturdy polyethylene sample bag may be used. The container should then be sealed. The gloved hand of the sampler should not come into contact with the sample medium. This will help to insure the integrity of the collected radiological evidence. An unused sample medium *must* be frisked, placed into a sample container and sealed as a *blank*. A gummed label containing sample information may be attached to the outside of the sample container. If a polyethylene sample bag is used, it may be labeled with a permanent marker.

Dermal sampling may be required in cases involving skin contamination of victims and/or suspects. This can be accomplished at the same time as the clothing and personal item surveys as described above. Careful attention should be paid to any exposed skin areas including the hands, face, and neck areas. The survey meter probe should be held approximately 0.5 inches from the surface being surveyed for beta and gamma contamination and at approximately 0.25 inches away from the surface for alpha contamination. The survey meter probe should be moved slowly over the surface at a rate of approximately 2 inches per second.[102] When a contaminated area is located through the use of the survey meter, the radiological material should be recovered as evidence. Wipe samples are not recommended. Surface pressure caused by the wiping process may force any contamination that is present deeper into the skin surface. When recovering dermal radiological evidence, a sticky tape should be applied gently to the surface of the skin and then removed. The removed tape should then be frisked to insure that the evidence has been recovered. A sample of unused tape should be frisked, placed into a sample container, and maintained as a blank. The radiological evidence should then be placed into a small plastic sample bottle, labeled, and sealed as described above. A sample placard should be held next to the sampled contaminated dermal area (i.e., hands, face, etc.) and photographed. The subject's face should also be photographed. The contaminated dermal areas should be noted in the sample log.

LIQUIDS. Radiological substances in liquid form may be found in devices (RDD), bodies of water, water runoff areas, clandestine manufacturing facilities, clandestine manufacturing facilities' waste streams, and water runoff from contaminated areas. For the above described areas, and for *radiological dispersion devices* that have been rendered safe before detonation, sterilized and frisked pipettes and Coliwasa tubes may be used to collect liquid samples. These collection devices *should not* be reused at the crime scene. Radiological samples taken from puddles, ponds, or other types of still water should be removed from the *surface* area of the water. The liquid sample(s) should then be placed into a (frisked) plastic-sampling bottle. An additional sample should also be taken utilizing a sterilized 40-ml glass bottle(s) with Teflon-lined (chemically inert) silicon septa. Whenever practical, the bottle(s) should be filled to their capacity. The investigator should be cognizant of the fact that additional analysis (i.e., chemical) may be required and must insure that enough sample material is available for that analysis. It is important to note that an *organic chemical compound* found within a radiological substance sample may provide an important future forensic chemical link and must be protected from volatilization. To protect this type of evidence, separate samples (using separate sampling protocols) should be taken. This type of dual analysis may be critical when examining the liquid waste stream of a clandestine manufacturing facility.

All liquid sample points should be placarded, marked on the crime scene sketch, and photographed. Sample bottles should be labeled properly, sealed, and secured as evidence.

Radiological Evidence Preservation and Storage

Once the radiological evidence has been placed into the proper sampling containers, it should be stored (prior to packaging and shipping) in such a way as to avoid any *cross-contamination*. A complete inventory of all samples should be made and the informa-

tion noted in the sampling logbook. Radiological evidence containers must be sealed. Sample seals should be used to detect unauthorized tampering of the radiological evidence. The seals should contain the same information as listed on the sample label. The seal must be affixed to the containers before the samples leave the custody of the investigation team.

Another acceptable method for sample sealing is to place the sample containers *and the trip blanks* into see-through plastic evidence bags. The evidence bags are then heat-sealed closed. The sealed evidence envelope will add another layer of protection against possible outside contamination. In addition, the sample label information can be clearly seen through the envelope. Also, a simple inspection of the evidence envelope will determine if any unauthorized tampering has taken place (see Figure 50).

In order to maintain the integrity of the radiological evidence, a proper chain-of-custody must exist. The chain-of-custody should be traceable through documentation. The documentation should indicate who had custody of the radiological evidence from the time it was collected all the way through the analytical process. The signature of each individual taking custody of the evidence should appear on the documentation. The investigation team's responsibility for evidence integrity does not end with the shipping of the radiological evidence to an appropriate US Department of Energy laboratory. The laboratory should be contacted and their chain-of-custody procedures reviewed prior to the shipment of any radiological evidence.

PACKAGING AND SHIPPING OF HAZARDOUS EVIDENCE

Chemical, biological, and/or radiological evidence collected at a WMD crime scene will, under most circumstances, be considered a **hazardous material** for labeling, packaging, and shipping purposes. A hazardous material is a substance or material, which has been determined by the Secretary of Transportation to be capable of posing an unreasonable risk to health, safety, and property when transported in commerce. The term hazardous material also includes hazardous substances and hazardous wastes.[103] When preparing hazardous evidence for shipping, the investigator must insure that the evidence is preserved (i.e., temperature), described (i.e., shipping papers), packaged, marked, labeled, and shipped properly.

Evidence samples for chemical agents, their precursors, and/or their degradation products will normally be preserved for shipping at a temperature of approximately 4°C. Biological evidence samples will normally be preserved at a temperature of approximately 5°C. However, analytical methodologies for known and/or suspected chemicals and biological substances should be consulted directly for individual **holding times** and preservation requirements.

The labeling and packaging of hazardous evidence is strictly regulated by the United States Department of Transportation (US DOT). The US Code of Federal Regulations, Title 49, Parts 171 through 177 governs the ground and air shipments of hazardous materials within the United States. Publication 49 CFR 172.101 supplies an alphabetical table of individual hazardous materials and their description, packaging, marking, labeling, and shipping requirements. International air shipments of hazardous evidence are regulated by either the International Civil Aviation Organization's (ICAO) *Technical Instructions for the Safe Transportation of Dangerous Goods by Air* or the International Air Transport Association (IATA). Maritime shipment of hazardous evidence is regulated by the International Maritime Organization's International Maritime Dangerous Goods (IMDG) code. The United States Department of Transportation regulations allows for the use of the ICAO Technical Instructions and the IMDG code under certain circumstances.[104]

In most instances, the investigator will be utilizing the US DOT regulations for the shipping of "Non-Bulk" packages. The "Non-Bulk" packages may contain several samples. Packages such as these are considered "Combination Packages" which usually contain one or more small sample containers inside of a larger container. A "Packaging Group" number is assigned to the hazardous material based upon how dangerous the material is suspected to be. A hazardous material with a Packaging Group I requirement is considered very dangerous. A Packaging Group II classification would indicate that the hazardous material is of a moderate danger, while Packaging Group III is considered to be a minor danger. Generally, *unidentified* hazardous evidence obtained from a suspected WMD crime scene would require a Package Group I classification. In addition to the packaging classification, the hazardous material is further identified with a hazard classification. These include Class 1 (Explosives), Class 2 (Gases), Class 3 (Flammable Liquids), Class 4 (Flammable Solids), Class 5 (Oxidizers: Organic Peroxides), Class 6 (Poisons), Class 7 (Radioactive Materials), Class 8 (Corrosive Materials), Class 9 (Miscellaneous Hazardous Materials). There are also subdivisions for each class (i.e., Class 2, Division

2.3: Phosgene – Class 6, Division 6.2: Infectious Substances) These classifications are also used to determine how the material must be labeled, packaged, and shipped.

Many of the chemical evidence samples taken from a WMD crime scene may fall within the Division 6.1 category (i.e., Poisons: cyanide). Evidence samples such as these are considered to be toxic to humans and are also considered a health hazard for transportation purposes. When chemical evidence samples such as these are offered for transportation to an analytical laboratory, certain general packaging requirements must be met. A combination package containing several evidence samples must be packed so that the closures on the inner packages are in the upright position. The inner packagings of combination packages must be packed, secured, and cushioned so as to control any movement of the chemical evidence and be constructed as to prevent breakage and/or leakage. If the chemical evidence samples are suspected to be reactive (with each other) they should be packaged separately. Both liquid and solid chemical evidence samples may be packaged and shipped in their original glass sample containers when all other transportation requirements are met.[105]

Biological evidence samples collected at a suspected WMD crime scene may fall into the Division 6.2 category (i.e., **Infectious Substance**: bacillus anthracis). An infectious substance (or etiologic agent) is considered to be a viable microorganism, or its toxin, that causes or may cause disease in humans or animals.[106] When offered for transportation, this type of biological evidence must meet certain general packaging requirements. The inner or primary container must be a watertight primary receptacle. The secondary container must also be watertight. An absorbent material must be placed between the primary container and the

secondary container. If multiple primary containers are placed into a single secondary container, they must be wrapped individually. The absorbent material must be sufficient to absorb the entire contents of all primary receptacles. An itemized list of the package contents must be enclosed between the secondary container and the outer container. When infectious substances require refrigeration, the refrigeration material (i.e., pre-frozen packs, dry ice) must be placed outside of the secondary container. In addition, interior supports must be provided to secure the secondary container in the original position after the refrigeration material dissipates (see Figures 61 & 62).

Radiological evidence will normally be turned over to qualified US Department of Energy personnel present at the crime scene. These individuals will normally handle radiological evidence transportation (and analysis). In addition, U.S. Department of Energy Personnel are exempt from hazardous material transportation regulations when dealing with matters affecting national security.[107] However, the criminal investigator should be aware of the packaging and shipping requirements for this type of hazardous evidence. There are three types of containers used for the shipping of radiological materials. These are *Type A Packaging*, *Type B Packaging*, and *Transport Containers*. The *Type A Packaging* is designed to meet the general requirements for most low-level shipments. These types of packages may be in the form of fiberboard boxes, wooden boxes, or metal drums (see Figure 63). Materials shipped in *Type A Packages* are normally labeled with a *Radioactive White I* or *Radioactive Yellow II* label. A *Radioactive White I* label indicates that the maximum radiation level at any point of the packages' external surface must read less than or equal to 0.5 milli-roentgen/hour.[108] This type of packaging will normally contain one small sample bottle located in the center of the package. It must be packaged in such a way as to avoid breakage and /or leakage of the sample bottle. A *Radioactive Yellow II* label indicates that the maximum radiation level at any point of the package's external surface reads greater than 0.5 milliroentgen/hour but less than or equal to 50 milliroentgen/hr.[109]

Type B Packages are designed to survive serious transportation accidents and fires. These types of containers may be in the form of a lead pig or concrete cask and normally contain radiological substances that would require a *Radioactive Yellow III* label (see Figure 64). A *Radioactive III* indicates that the

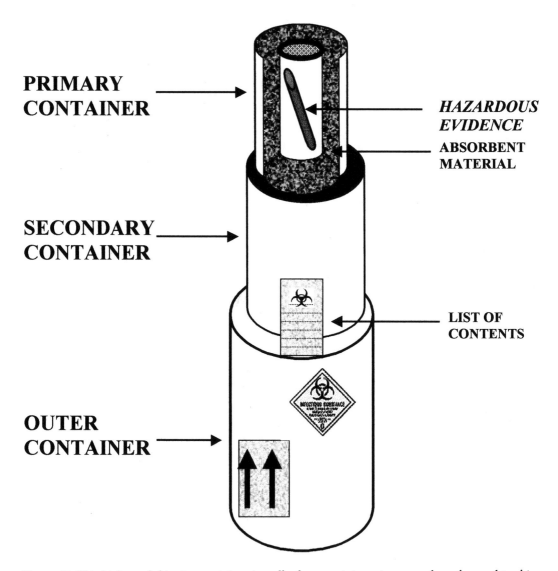

PRIMARY CONTAINER

HAZARDOUS EVIDENCE

ABSORBENT MATERIAL

SECONDARY CONTAINER

LIST OF CONTENTS

OUTER CONTAINER

Figure 61. This biohazard-shipping container is really three containers in one and can be used to ship biological evidence samples. However, Federal Department of Transportation regulations should be reviewed prior to the shipment of any hazardous evidence.

maximum radiation level at any point of the package's external surface reads greater than 50 milliroentgen/hour but less than or equal to 200 milliroentgen/hour.[110] *Transportation Containers* are designed to carry fissile materials, nuclear fuel, and other highly radioactive materials and would not normally be used for the shipping of radiological evidence. There are many additional transportation regulations regarding the packaging and shipping of radiological material. The criminal investigator must insure that *all* packaging and labeling requirements are met prior to the shipment of this type of hazardous evidence.

The U.S. Department of Transportation regulations are continually updated and must be reviewed for changes immediately prior to the shipment of *any* hazardous evidence. When reviewing these regulations,

the investigator will find that certain types of hazardous evidence (i.e., phosphorus trichloride, phosgene) may be barred from both passenger aircraft and cargo aircraft.[111] Other chemicals may have maximum quantity limitations for shipping purposes. Therefore, the investigator should create a packaging and shipping protocol that will address the transportation requirements for all possible chemical, biological, and/or radiological evidence. When creating this protocol, the investigator must also consider that the hazardous evidence may be in the form of liquids, solids, and/or aerosols. A supply of appropriate labels and packages should be maintained at all times. In addition, the laboratory that is to be utilized for hazardous evidence analysis should be contacted in advance to determine if it has any special requirements for the receiving of hazardous

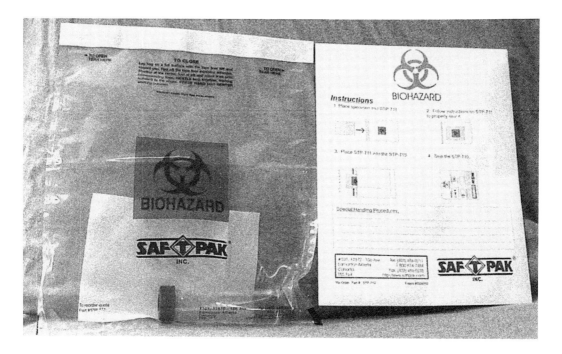

Figure 62. This secondary container system is a combination of an outer Tyvek envelope and an inner leakproof bag. Should the primary sample container break, sample integrity can still be maintained. Packaging courtesy of Saf-T-Pak.

evidence packages. The various types of hazardous materials labels and shipping packages are available from a wide range of commercial vendors.

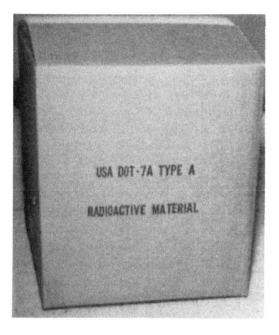

Figure 63. This "Type A" fiberboard package is designed for shipping low level radiological evidence.

Figure 64. This "Type B" package is designed for high level radiological materials and is designed to survive a serious transportation accident.

Chapter 18

ANALYSIS FOR CHEMICAL, BIOLOGICAL, AND RADIOLOGICAL EVIDENCE

The analysis for chemical and biological evidence will normally be done in special governmental laboratories that are equipped to handle these types of substances in a safe manner. However, the use of a governmental laboratory does not guarantee a perfect qualitative and quantitative analysis. The laboratory protocols used and any analytical findings may be subjected to challenge during the trial phase of the case. While the majority of the analytical laboratory's activities will be outside of the criminal investigator's control, there as several steps that the investigator can take to help preserve the integrity of the scientific evidence.

The laboratory's chain-of-custody protocols should be reviewed by the criminal investigator prior to the transportation or shipment of any evidence. Information regarding evidence access and storage should be fully documented by the laboratory. This should include detailed information regarding which individual(s) handle the scientific evidence during the analysis phase and information as to which individuals have access to the evidence during storage.

Every effort should be made to limit the number of individuals involved in the analytical process. It may be the practice of the laboratory to have one individual do the *digestion procedure* on a particular chemical sample, another may calibrate the analytical instrument, another may load the sample onto the instrument, while a different individual may read the data and complete the laboratory report. Each one of these individuals may be subject to direct testimony and cross-examination during a criminal trial. This type of scientific evidence handling may place an unneeded burden upon the prosecutor. By discussing these issues with the laboratory director prior to the transportation or shipment of the hazardous evidence, the investigator may be able to limit the number of individuals who may be called to testify at a later date.

HAZARDOUS EVIDENCE ANALYSIS:
INSTRUMENTATION AND METHODOLOGIES

There are many instruments and analytical methodologies that may be used for the analysis of chemical, biological and radiological evidence collected at a WMD crime scene. The investigator should be aware of the different types of analysis that will be made available during the course of the investigation. This should include a general understanding of the analytical procedure, as well as its capabilities and limitations. The different types of analytical instruments and methodologies available today are too numerous to include here. However, several established analytical procedures for the examination of hazardous evidence do exist. A general understanding of these procedures will assist the investigator during the course of an investigation involving the analysis of chemical, biological, or radiological evidence.

Chemical Evidence Analysis

The analysis of chemical agents, their precursors, and their degradation products will normally be conducted through the use of chromatography and mass spectrometry. Most chemical warfare agents and their precursors are volatile and relatively non-polar. Evidence samples of these precursors may appear in a variety of matrixes (i.e., liquids, soils, and aerosols). They can be detected and identified unequivocally by *gas chromatography-mass spectrometry* (GC-MS).[112] However, for certain environmental samples (i.e., those found at an abandoned manufacturing or test site), the hydrolysis products (degradation) are considerably less volatile and more polar than the chemical agent and its precursors. For chemical evidence samples such as these, a *liquid chromatography-mass spectrometry* (LC-MS)

analysis may be superior to current GS-MS methods.[113]

Gas Chromatography/ Mass Spectrometry

A gas chromatograph/mass spectrometer (GC/MS) is an instrument used to detect the presence and concentration of numerous volatile and semi-volatile organic chemical compounds in a sample (see Figure 65). Although the use of the GC/MS is common to the analysis of both volatile and semi-volatile compounds, it is the preparation of the sample that decides which group is actually being determined. This instrument has the capability to positively identify and measure the concentration of organic chemical compounds in the parts-per-billion (ppb) range. It is an essential tool in identifying the presence of various chemical compounds that may constitute a chemical warfare agent or one of its many precursors.

In the volatile and semi-volatile analysis, the GC/MS must be calibrated using standards of known purity and concentrations. These standards are analyzed in the same manner as the chemical evidence. Once analyzed, the results for the calibration standards are reviewed by the analyst to verify that the GC/MS correctly identified all of the compounds in the standard and produced an accurate result for each. Once this has been accomplished, a measured amount of a sample is injected into the instrument to determine if any organic compound(s) of interest are present, and if so, at what concentration(s). In a volatile organic compound analysis, this would be accomplished by placing a measured portion of the sample (liquid or solid) into a glass impinger. The impinger is part of a sample concentrating device that purges (strips) the volatile organic compounds (VOCs) from the sample matrix via a stream of helium gas. For the VOC analysis of a solid sample, the impinger must be heated to 40°C. The helium gas stream is then passed through a trap containing adsorbents that recapture the VOCs. The trap is then heated and the flow of the helium is reversed through the trap. This causes the release of the VOCs. They are then transferred and cryogenically trapped using liquid nitrogen (-150°C) at the head of the capillary column. The cryogenic trap is then rapidly heated to 200°C, causing the frozen VOCs to liquefy, vaporize, and pass into the capillary column. The capillary column is located in the oven chamber of the gas chromatograph and is purged with a constant flow of helium gas. The time at which this transfer takes place is called the "injection time." The capillary column is normally constructed of fused silica and its interior surface has the capability to separate organic compounds from the sample as they pass through. At the "injection time," the gas chromatograph is programmed to increase the temperature of the oven in order to facilitate the separation of the organic compounds. In general, compounds with lower boiling points pass through and exit (*elute*) the column first. The end of the capillary column is interfaced with a detector (mass spectrometer). The "retention time" of a compound is the time it takes from the "injection time" until the compound reaches the mass spectrometer. As the chemical compounds exit the column, they enter the ion source of the mass spectrometer. Here they are exposed to an electron beam, which imparts enough energy into the molecule of the organic compound to rupture some of the chemical bonds holding the molecule together. This process of fragmentation is called "electron ionization." Electron ionization produces positively,

negatively, or neutrally charged fragments. In this method, the positively charged fragments are accelerated into a mass filter. The mass filter then separates the fragments based upon their mass. It is these fragments and retention times that are measured by the mass spectrometer. The fragment ions are then compared to the fragment ions of the previously run standards. It is this comparison that supplies the final identification and quantification of the organic compound(s) present in the sample.

If the result for a particular compound exceeds the linear range of the calibration curve, the sample must be diluted and re-analyzed. This is accomplished by diluting a measured amount of the sample with "organic-free" distilled water or high purity methanol. Once diluted, a measured volume of the diluted sample is re-analyzed. The result of this analysis is corrected for the initial sample dilution to calculate the actual concentrations in the sample.

Biological Evidence Analysis

There are numerous methods that may be utilized to analyze biological evidence that has been collected at a WMD crime scene. Three of the most common and scientifically acceptable methods utilized today are *Growth Culture Analysis*, *Immunoassay*, and *Deoxyribonucleic Acid/Polymerase Chain Reaction* (DNA/PCR). Many factors will influence the type of analysis to be chosen. These factors may include analytical time requirements, the amount of material available for analysis, the sampling methodology and/or the condition of the sample (i.e., dead vs. live microorganisms). As with the chemical analysis (see above), the criminal investigator should have a general understanding of these biological analytical procedures. This general knowledge will assist the investigator in understanding the sample collection requirements, as well as, the capabilities and limitations of the various analytical methodologies. The investigator should also understand that clinical analysis methodologies conducted during an epidemiological investigation (i.e., blood samples) may differ from those conducted on samples removed from a WMD crime scene.

Growth Culture Analysis

Growth culture analysis is a cell-culture method. Cell-culture methods are preferred by many analysts and are routinely used in both industry and science. In this analytical procedure, the sample microorganism (biological agent) is placed into a solid or liquid nutrient media (i.e., agar). The microorganism begins to feed on the nutrient media which, in turn, causes growth. The microorganism multiplies to a point in which there is a sufficient amount available for further biological analysis. Although the analytical results of this test are considered accurate and reliable, the investigator should be aware of the fact that this type of analytical methodology may take a relatively long period of time to complete (i.e., days or weeks). When immediate identification is required, other forms of biological agent identification should be considered.

Figure 65. This gas chromatograph/mass spectrometer (GC/MS) is used to detect and quantify volatile and semi-volatile chemical compounds. Note the glass impingers on the upper right side of the photograph.

Immunoassay

Immunoassay is an efficient and inexpensive way of identifying and measuring different types of biological entities. Immunoassay technology may be found in many commercial products including at-home pregnancy tests and drug screening kits. One of the most commonly used immunoassay tests is the ***enzyme-linked immunosorbent assay*** (ELISA). ELISA is used to detect the presence of a specific *antigen* (biological agent). In this type of analytical methodology, a known antibody is normally attached to the walls of a microtiter plate. The antigen is then introduced. When the known antibodies bind to the antigen, identification can be made. A secondary antibody is also introduced, creating a "sandwich" effect. A color substrate (i.e., biotin) is added so that this antibody/antigen binding process can be seen. Positive identification and quantification of specific biological agents can be made through the use of a microtiter analyzer. Radioactive isotope-labeled antibodies may also be used to identify and quantify this binding process. Several of the key advantages to this type of analysis is that the procedure can be performed rapidly (approximately 6 hours), they are portable, and have the capability of recognizing dead microorganisms.[114]

Deoxyribonucleic Acid/Polymerase Chain Reaction – DNA/PCR

DNA probes utilizing polymerase chain reaction amplification have been successfully used in the biological warfare compliance regime. One of the chief reasons for this is the fact that each species of biological warfare microorganism has several DNA sequences unique to it.[115] If these DNA sequences can be detected and identified, then a positive identification of the biological agent can be made.

In its simplest form, this analytical procedure utilizes polymerase enzymes extracted from hot spring bacteria. The polymerase enzyme is a DNA duplicating protein. These enzymes have the ability to copy any single strand DNA they encounter. They are mixed with an ample supply of A, C, T, G bases (building blocks of DNA) and the DNA from the suspected biological agent. Also added to the mix is a pair of short, single-stranded DNA sequences (primers) of about 20 bases, complementary to the DNA of interest.

The first step in this process is called *denaturing.* The test tube is heated close to boiling for a short period of time. The double-stranded DNA then separates into two single strands. The primers bind to the exposed single strands at places where the sequence of primer bases is complementary to that of the DNA.

The second step of the process is called *annealing.* The temperature of the test tube is lowered to approximately 55 degrees centigrade for a few seconds, causing the primers to bind permanently to their sites on the single-strand DNA. The DNA of interest is now single-stranded along most of its length, with a few small double-stranded areas where primers have aligned themselves.

The third step of the process is called *extending.* The temperature is raised to approximately 72 degrees centigrade for approximately one minute, which causes the polymerase protein to go to work. It moves along the single-stranded portion of the DNA, beginning at a primer, and creates a second strand of new DNA to match the first. After extension, the DNA of interest is double-stranded again, and the number of strands bearing the sequence of interest has been doubled. The three steps are repeated about 30 times, resulting in an exponential increase of up to a billion-fold of the DNA of interest (biological agent).[116]

This DNA copying procedure is straightforward and easily automated; the ingredients are mixed together, then heated and cooled cyclically until they produce as many copies of the genes as needed.[117]

The DNA/PCR amplification procedure, and others like it, has such a high sensitivity that they are capable in theory of detecting a single microorganism. In addition, this analytical method has the capability of identifying dead microorganisms. New versions of DNA probe methods are rapid (less than an hour to complete an identification) and are portable.[118] However, when taking into consideration sample preparation time, PCR reaction time and the time required for the analysis, a more realistic sample turn-around time would be, at a minimum, one day.

This type of method has the additional advantage that the target DNA (DNA within the biological agent) is difficult to destroy, so there is a greater probability that the DNA would remain intact *after autoclaving* and after a cleanup of a facility.[119] In fact, this analytical procedure has detected Mycobacterium in *autoclaved* samples.[120] This type of analytical advantage will be useful to the investigator in cases involving suspected abandoned manufacturing sites and testing areas.

Radiological Evidence Analysis

There are several methods that may be used to analyze radiological evidence. In most situations involving the use or threatened use of a radiological material as a weapon of mass destruction, U.S. Department of Energy personnel will be conducting scientific analysis at the crime scene. Specially trained and equipped US DOE radiological response teams have the ability to positively identify radiological materials through the use of mobile laboratories. These mobile laboratories can identify radiological material collected via a smear sample (*Alpha Beta Smear Counter*), beta samples (*Liquid Scintillator*), and gamma sources (*Gamma Spectroscopy*). Radiological evidence collected at a WMD crime scene, including airborne particles, soils, liquids, surface and dermal samples may all be analyzed using one of these methodologies.

In addition, **daughter products** (degradation products) can be analyzed, identified, and traced back to their original form. This will assist the investigator in the identification of the original radiological source material. This type of analytical advantage is useful to the investigator in cases involving suspected abandoned manufacturing sites and testing areas for radiation dispersion devices (RDD) and/or improvised nuclear devices (IND).

THE LABORATORY: *POST ANALYSIS*

A laboratory's post-analysis activities may become critical to the prosecution's criminal case. The saving of all notes and computer records may be a legal requirement in some jurisdictions. The investigator should meet with the prosecutor and determine if any legal requirements exist in this area. Should there be a requirement that *the laboratory maintain all notes and computer records*, the investigator must relay this information to the laboratory director. In addition, the investigator should determine what procedures the laboratory will utilize for the storage of the scientific evidence *after* analysis. The stored evidence must be maintained properly until such time that the prosecutor indicates, in writing, that the evidence may be disposed of or released.

Chapter 18

INTERDICTION TECHNIQUES

This book has primarily focused on those law enforcement activities that are expected to take place after the detonation of a weapon of mass destruction. The following investigative techniques are designed to assist the criminal investigator in locating and entering a suspected WMD manufacturing facility. Through the identification of specialized manufacturing equipment, raw materials, and/or waste products, suspect manufacturing sites may, at times, be located prior to the actual use of a weapon of mass destruction.

CHEMICAL AGENTS: *MANUFACTURING*

The manufacture of a chemical agent requires the use of specific types of raw materials and equipment. The raw materials for this type of weapon normally come in the form of chemical precursors (see Table I). However, many of these precursors have a dual use and are commonly found in general industrial manufacturing. The investigator should establish contact with all local industrial chemical suppliers. The WMD chemical precursor list should be reviewed with each chemical supplier. The investigator should emphasize the need for strict inventory controls for any chemical deemed a chemical agent precursor. A notification system should be created which will alert the investigator whenever materials from the chemical precursor list are stolen or purchased by individuals who are not associated with any known and/or legitimate manufacturing company.

The manufacturing of a chemical agent will require specific types of equipment and facilities. However, as with the chemical precursors, much of this equipment may also be used by legitimate businesses. It is the combination of the chemical agent precursors and specific manufacturing equipment that will alert the investigator to the possibility of a WMD manufacturing facility. Equipment utilized in the manufacture of a chemical agent may include the following:

High alloy, corrosive resistant equipment	Welded pipelines	Canned pumps	Special pumps and seals
Air locks	Large-capacity ventilation systems	Air treatment systems (i.e., charcoal filters)	Air monitoring systems
Ventilation hoods	Chemical clothing	Self-contained breathing apparatus	Respirators
Decontamination equipment	Empty storage drums	Drum dollies	Laboratory glassware

Other warning signs which may indicate the presence of a clandestine manufacturing facility are the presence of lookouts, late night activity, intrusion detection devices, excessive restrictions of access during local governmental inspections of raw product storage and waste treatment areas, empty chemical precursor containers, and workers wearing protective clothing.

Precursor Container Tracing

A unique aspect to most forms of manufacturing is that some type of waste product is normally formed. When the manufacturing process uses hazardous materials within the manufacturing process, some form of hazardous waste is normally created. This is true for circuit board manufactures, auto body shops, clandestine drug labs, and facilities manufacturing weapons of mass destruction. In many instances, this waste product is placed into used drums and eventually abandoned. Many of these drums will have, at one time, contained a raw hazardous chemical product or chemical agent precursor. By identifying the waste product and tracing the containers, the investigator may be able to pinpoint the original point of generation.

The key to this investigative technique is to secure the abandonment waste scene and have it treated as a crime scene. Valuable forensic evidence may be lost if the area is trampled upon by well-meaning, but ill-informed emergency responders and civilians from various environmental agencies. Fingerprints, footprints, and tire tracks must be preserved, examined, and photographed.

One of the first investigative tasks that should be accomplished is the interview of any possible witnesses. Once this has been completed, the investigator should examine and photograph the crime scene from a distance. It is these observations which may help in determining the type of vehicle which was used to dispose of the material. If the waste material has been placed into 55-gallon drums and abandoned, a list of vehicle types may be established based upon the amount of material found at the crime scene. This is accomplished through the use of simple mathematics.

Depending on the actual density of the waste, one 55-gallon drum may weigh anywhere between 300 and 650 pounds (i.e., chemical density of 1.4 = 11.676 lb. per gallon x 55 gallons = 642.18 lb. per drum). Ten full drums of waste material may weigh between 3,000 and 6,420 pounds. The laboratory utilized for the scientific analysis will be able to provide the various densities for the chemical samples removed during the chemical evidence-gathering operation. In addition, ten upright drums of waste will take up approximately 35 square feet of space (i.e., drum diameter = 1.875 ft.; 1.875^2 = 3.51 sq. ft. x 10 drums = 35.1 sq. ft.). In this case, the investigator will know that based upon a chemical density of 1.4, with a total of ten 55-gallon drums, he or she will be searching for a vehicle that has a minimum load capacity of 6,420 pounds and a storage capacity of at least 35 square feet. These drum weights and drum volumes may assist the investigator in narrowing the list of possible vehicle models used in the crime.

In addition to the above, a careful examination of the crime scene may determine whether or not a vehicle lift gate was used to unload the waste drums. Many trucks come equipped with a lift that will allow the drums to be slowly lowered to the ground. Marks and/or indentations on the surface of the ground made by the weight of the drums and marks left behind by a lift gate resting on the ground may indicate the use of such a device. If it is suspected that the vehicle was equipped with such a lift gate device, it will further narrow the list of possible vehicle models used to transport the waste to the crime scene. If a lift gate was not used and the waste drums were dumped off the back of a vehicle, some waste spillage may have occurred. This may have been caused by loose bunghole plugs and/or loose drum lids. It may also be caused if the drums rupture upon hitting the ground. When this type of spillage occurs, some interior and/or exterior vehicle contamination may result. If this is the case and the suspect vehicle is eventually located, trace chemical samples from the suspect vehicle can be compared with the sample analysis conducted on the waste found at the crime scene.

In addition to the chemical analysis comparisons, the investigator should note that waste contamination, due to spillage, may leave behind a distinctive odor. Many of the

Figure 66. This rental truck was used to transport and illegally dispose of pesticides. Chemical samples removed from the floor were later matched with the original chemical containers.

chemical agent precursors have a distinctive odor and will seep into the walls and floor of the vehicle. This distinctive odor may last for several days or weeks (see Figure 66). When a suspected vehicle has been located and spillage is suspected, the vehicle should be checked for chemical odors and samples removed for trace chemical analysis.

As with any other type of crime, the person or persons abandoning this waste material may have left behind other physical evidence that may assist the investigator in making their eventual identification. Clearly, the most valuable identifier is a fingerprint left behind by the suspect(s). Particular attention should be paid to the edges and bottoms of containers. These are the areas where hands are naturally placed when moving or lifting heavy containers such as these. However, on many occasions, finger-prints will not be found on the waste containers. They may, however, be found on

discarded empty cans, bottles, tools, cellophane wrappers, and the interior of chemical gloves utilized by the suspect(s). In addition, any footprints left behind by the suspect(s) will assist the investigator in the identification process. Shoe size and type of shoe worn by the suspect(s) may assist the investigator at some future point in the investigation.

When waste containers are abandoned, perpetrators have a tendency to abandon other items along with the waste. Items such as cash register receipts, shopping bags, computer printouts, invoices, and hand tools may also be found at the scene. Any of these items may supply information useful in identifying the suspect(s). It should also be noted that many of these items may be found in the interior of the containers (see Figure 67). Any containers with removable tops should have their interiors' inspected for other physical evidence. Any documents

Figure 67. This document was found floating on top of the chemical product inside of an abandoned chemical container. The document was used to track down the suspects.

found inside these containers should be carefully packaged for future examination. These packages should also be clearly marked so that document examiners are aware of the possibility of hazardous chemical contamination.

Any labels found on the containers should be recorded, photographed, and removed whenever possible. For labels that have been painted over, a *carburetor cleaner spray* may be used to remove the paint. The carburetor cleaner should not be sprayed directly onto the label. It should be applied to a clean cloth and the cloth should then be used to carefully remove the paint. It is essential that this type of label identification operation be conducted *after* all chemical sampling has been completed. Otherwise, the chemical constituents contained in the carburetor cleaner may interfere with the chemical analysis.

When attempting to remove a label from a container, the investigator may wish to use a small scraper. The glue backing on the label should first be loosened. This can be accomplished by applying heat from a small hand-held hair dryer. However, a great deal of caution must be exhibited when utilizing any electrical device near a volatile chemical agent precursor. The investigator must obtain the Safety Officer's approval before attempting any operation of this type.

Information regarding the original manufacturer, lot numbers, and the type of chemical product may be listed on the label. If this information is present, the chemical manufacturer should be contacted and a list of customers obtained. By limiting the inquiry to a specific geographical area, the investigator will be able to obtain a list of the product users within his or her area. These product users can then be further investigated to determine if they are the source of the abandoned chemical agent precursor waste and/or containers.

If the only information remaining on the label is the product name, the criminal investigator can begin checking with chemical manufacturers to determine to whom products such as these had been sold. One such source for this type of information is the *OPD Chemical Buyers Directory*. This publication and database may supply the investigator with a list of companies that manufacture that particular chemical agent precursor. Each of these chemical manufacturers will likely use different types of labels. By supplying these companies with photographs of the labels recovered at the crime scene, the actual chemical supplier may be identified and a local customer list obtained.

The U.S. Department of Transportation lists many chemical agent precursors as hazardous materials (for transportation purposes). The investigator will frequently find U.S. Department of Transportation information stenciled on the sides of hazardous material containers (see Figure 68). It is also common to find this information on small labels. The U.S. Department of Transportation requires the manufacturers of chemical containers to place certain data on the containers prior to them being filled with a hazardous chemical.[121]

The information in Figure 68 is interpreted as follows:
• UN = UNITED NATIONS.
• 1A2 = 1 (DRUM), A (STEEL), 2 (OPEN HEAD).
• Y = PACKAGING FOR GROUP II & III TESTS.
• 1.2 = SPECIFIC GRAVITY OR MASS FOR PACKAGE DESIGN.
• 100 = PRESSURE TEST IN KILO PACALS (HYDROSTATIC TEST).
• 5/96 = MONTH & YEAR OF DRUM MANUFACTURE.
• US = COUNTRY OF ORIGIN.
• M4709 = CODE FOR NAME AND

ADDRESS OR SYMBOL OF DRUM
MANUFACTURER.

The two most important pieces of information listed above are the month/year of the container's manufacture and the code that lists the name and address of the container manufacturer. These two items alone may assist the investigator in determining the point of generation for the chemical agent precursor waste and/or the container.

The month and year of the container's manufacture, or "*DOT date*," is vital for the simple fact that it will provide a time period as to when the chemical precursor was originally sold. Most chemical supply companies will fill newly purchased and tested drums within 30 to 60 days. By adding this time period to the DOT date on the container, the investigator will have determined an approximate time period for the sale of the original chemical (i.e., 30–60 days after DOT date to date of discovery).

The code listing the container manufacturer's name and address can also assist the criminal investigator. Many containers are manufactured with particular color schemes (i.e., blue drums with yellow tops). A chemical manufacturer may utilize and order only one drum color scheme from the container manufacturer. Once the container manufacturer has been located, they should be shown a photograph of the suspect containers. If there are any distinguishing features on the container (i.e., color scheme and DOT date), the container manufacturer may be able to identify the raw chemical product manufacturer that purchased the drum.

The names and addresses of container manufacturers are listed by their code numbers in a DOT database in Washington, D.C. A copy of this database can be obtained by contacting the U.S. Department of Transportation, Hazardous Material Administrator, Washington, D.C.

In addition to the investigative techniques listed above, the investigator should thoroughly review the laboratory analysis of any chemical agent waste found at a waste

Figure 68. The Department of Transportation information stenciled on this chemical container can be used to track down the original chemical supplier.

abandonment crime scene. As a general rule, the more unique the chemical is, the greater the possibility of locating the suspect. Unique chemicals and unique chemical combinations may only be produced by a handful of chemical manufacturers. This fact, combined with any information obtained regarding the containers' manufacturer sales records, may greatly reduce the list of possible chemical manufacturers.

BIOLOGICAL AGENTS: *MANUFACTURING*

The criminal investigator should be cognizant of the fact that many biological organisms that are hazardous to humans, plants, and animals are readily available through biological research supply houses. Other, more dangerous microorganisms are available on the black market. Many of these microorganisms are routinely stored in academic and government research laboratories and may be subject to theft. The theft or unauthorized possession of any of the biological materials listed in Figure 69 should be thoroughly reviewed by the investigator.

AGENTS AND TOXINS†

HUMAN PATHOGENS	TOXINS	BACTERIA	ANIMAL PATHOGENS	PLANT PATHOGENS	RICKETTSIAE	PROTOZA
Crimean-Congo Haemorrhagic fever virus	Abrin	Bacillus anthracis	African swine fever virus	Colletotrichum coffeanum var. virulans	Coxiella burnetti	Naegleria fowleri
Eastern equine Encephalitis virus	Anatoxin A	Brucella abortus	Avian influenza virus	Dothistroma pini	Rickettsia prowazekii	Naegleria australiensis
Ebola virus	Botulinum Toxins	Brucella melitensis	Camel pox virus	Erwinia amylovora	Riskettsia rickettsii	
Sin Nombre virus	Bungarotoxins	Brucella suis	Classic swine fever virus	Ralstonia solanacearum		
Hantaan virus	Centruroides toxins	Burkholderia mallei	Contagious bovine	Puccinia graminis		
Junin virus	Ciguatoxin	Burkholderia pseudomallei	Contagious caprine	Puccinia striiformiis		
Lassa fever virus	Cyanginosins	Chlamydia psittaci	Foot and mouth disease virus	Pyricularia oryzae		
Machupo virus	Staphylococcal enterotoxins	Francisella tularensis tularensis	Newcastle disease virus	Sugar cane Fiji disease virus		
Marburg virus	Modeccin	Yersinia pestis	Peste des petits ruminants virus	Tilletia indica		
Rift Valley virus	Ricin		Rinderpest virus	Ustilago maydis		
Tick-borne encephalitis virus	Saxitoxins		Teschen disease virus	Xanthomonas campestris pv citri		
Smallpox virus	Shigatoxin		Vesicular stomatitis virus	Xanthomonas albilineans		
Venezuelan equine encephalitis virus	Tetanus toxin		African horse sickness virus	Xanthomonas campestris pv oryzae		
Western equine encephalitis virus	Tetrodotoxin		Lumpy skin disease virus	Sclerotinia sclerotiorum		
Yellow fever virus	Toxins of Clostridium perfringens			Claviceps purpurea		
Monkeypox virus	Toxins of Corynebacterium diphtheriae					
	Trichothecene mycotoxins					
	Viscumin					
	Volkensin					

†Table Source: The Biological and Toxin Weapons convention Database/AD HOC Group 44, 13th Session, January 1999

Figure 69. Many of these biological agents and toxins are stored in research laboratories and are subject to theft.

The manufacture of a biological weapon, and the means for dispersing the organisms, requires the use of specific types of raw materials and equipment. Raw materials that produce anthrax, the plague, brucellosis, tularemia, and smallpox can be isolated from natural sources; tricothecene myco-toxins may be derived from corn; aflatoxin from peanuts; and ricin from castor beans.[122] The investigator should create and con-tinually update a target list itemizing the various types of raw materials and equip-ment needed to manufacture and disperse a biological weapon. Purchases and/or use of these types of items by persons not affiliated with any legitimate research program should be thoroughly reviewed by the investigator. The equipment target list should include such items as the following:

Self-contained aerosol dispensers	Aerosol generators	Aerosol analytical equipment or particle size
Fermenters	Bioreactors	High throughput self-sterilized centrifuges
Cross flow or tangential filtration equipment	Freeze-drying equipment	Drum-drying equipment
Cell disruption equipment	Spray-drying equipment	Biological safety cabinets
Test animals	Automatic DNA sequencing equipment	Automatic DNA synthesizer
Biosafety hoods	Ultra deep freezers	Vaccines
Automatic peptide sequencing equipment	Automatic peptide synthesizer	Liquid nitrogen containers

RADIOLOGICAL DEVICES: *MANUFACTURING*

The most common radiological threat to be faced by law enforcement personnel will be the dispersal of radioactive materials. This type of release has the potential to contaminate large numbers of civilians. The dispersal may be caused by an explosive charge (RDD) or through the introduction of a radiological source into a heating and ventilation system. Regardless of the type of dispersal method used, the one commonality amongst these types of releases is the need for a radiological source material. Although *special nuclear materials* (i.e., µ-235, µ-233 and Pµ-239) are highly regulated, they are still subject to theft and availability on the black market. The investigator should make every effort to identify the locations of these types of radiological sources within his or her jurisdiction. A notification system should be established which would alert the investi-gator to *any* loss of this type of material.

Low level radiological sources are common in most communities today. They have many legitimate uses and are commonly found in industry and medical institutions. The investigator should make every effort to determine what types of low level radiological sources are available in his or her jurisdiction. As with the *special nuclear materials*, a system of notification should be established should any of this material become lost or stolen.

When attempting to manufacture this type of weapon, other materials may be required in order to handle the radiological materials safely. These items may include lead shielding, radiation pigs, lead-lined aprons, and/or radiation monitoring instruments (see Figure 70). Possession and/or purchases of items such as these by persons not associated with a legitimate industrial or medical facility should be thoroughly reviewed by the investigator.

Figure 70. This crate was found at a suspect's home. The crate is filled with lead shielding.

SURREPTITIOUS SAMPLING TECHNIQUES

Once a suspect WMD manufacturing facility has been located, there are several investigative techniques that can be utilized to surreptitiously gather additional evidence. In addition to the standard techniques of surveillance, trash examination, ground photography, and aerial photography, the criminal investigator can attempt to surreptitiously sample the air and liquid waste streams exiting the suspect facility.

Remote Air Sampling

Remote air sampling is one of the best methods available today in determining if certain types of chemical agent precursors are being used at a facility. In some instances, a small amount of volatile and semi-volatile organic compounds may be released into the air during the chemical weapon manufacturing process. Because many of these substances are lighter than air, they will exit any vent, window, or doorway and enter the outside air. From here, these substances will be carried from the facility by any prevailing winds or drafts. Today's air sampling devices will allow the investigator to set a timer, leave the area, and return at a later time to retrieve the samples (see Figure 45). A chemical analysis of the sample may reveal the presence of chemical agent precursors in minute concentrations.

However, using this investigative technique for the gathering of scientific evidence must be well planned. Many variables may bring into question the validity of the sample results. Other nearby manufacturing facilities, vehicle traffic, and/or low flying aircraft may contaminate the air sample to such an extent that it is no longer reliable.

The best investigative technique to use in a remote air sampling operation is to place air sampling devices on all four sides of a suspect facility (see Figure 71). The investigator should then determine and document the wind velocity and direction. Each

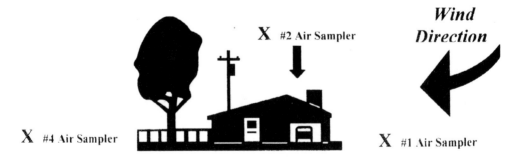

Figure 71. The surreptitious placing of air sampling devices around a clandestine WMD manufacturing facility may provide the evidence needed to obtain a search warrant.

remote air sampler should have its timer set so that all of the units begin sampling simultaneously. This will enable one to determine what air contaminates originated *up* wind of the facility and which contaminates came directly *from* the suspected facility.

This technique has been used successfully in cases involving clandestine narcotics manufacturing laboratories. In several cases, remote air sampling has been used to show that trace amounts of tetrachloroethylene (i.e., **parts per billion**) were coming from a particular building. By surrounding a suspect building or dwelling with air monitoring devices, it was easily determined that the building in question was the only possible source of the tetrachloroethylene. The presence of this compound, along with its known use as a precursor in the manufacturing of cocaine, helped supply the necessary probable cause to obtain a search warrant. This same technique can be used to identify airborne trace amounts of chemical agent precursors.

Remote Liquid Waste Stream Sampling

As stated earlier, whenever a manufacturing process utilizes a hazardous material (chemical, biological, or radiological), trace amounts of the materials may be found in the waste stream. If the waste stream can be surreptitiously accessed and sampled, valuable evidence may be produced. **Portable liquid samplers** can be placed into an existing sewer system and retrieved at a later time (see Figure 72). This equipment can be set to automatically sample the waste stream based upon time, flow rates, and/or waste stream characteristics (i.e., pH). The samples can then be retrieved and analyzed for trace amounts of chemical agent precursors, biological organisms, or radiological materials. The results of the analysis may be used to further the investigation or for the obtaining of a search warrant.

However, as in the air sampling technique discussed above, the investigator must be certain that the suspect facility is the originating source of the contamination. There may be several businesses or dwellings discharging into the same sewer system. By thoroughly reviewing all available sewer system piping plans, the investigator will be able to determine the proper positioning of the portable liquid sampler. For the best results, two portable liquid samplers should be used to bracket the suspect facility (see Figure 73). When utilizing two portable liquid samplers, the investigator must insure that sample-timing

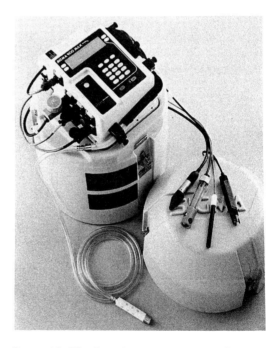

Figure 72. This liquid waste stream sampler can take numerous liquid samples over long periods of time. The sample containers can then be retrieved and analyzed. Photograph courtesy of the American Sigma.

devices have been synchronized for both units. These samplers also have the ability to transmit data via cell phone technology. If a facility is in the act of discharging a waste stream, the portable liquid sampler will send a message to a nearby receiving unit. The investigator monitoring this unit will know that the discharge is occurring at that point in time.

Raman Light Detection and Ranging (Raman LIDAR)

One of the newest and potentially effective standoff-surveillance techniques is based upon Raman LIDAR. This system operates by transmitting through the atmosphere a short duration, high-energy pulse of ultraviolet laser light. As the light spreads out through the atmosphere, it is scattered with a frequency shift which is characteristic of the molecules in its path. This effect is known as *Raman Scattering.*[123] The LIDAR is the optical equivalent of radar in which a laser is used as a transmitter.

Because the very short wavelengths of laser radiation are efficiently scattered by the substances in the atmosphere, a LIDAR can measure the concentrations of these atmospheric substances. This system also has the capability of detecting and identifying specific molecular species.

The Raman spectra of numerous chemical agent precursors has already been determined and placed into research databases. When the instrument is used, the spectra from the suspected chemical agent or chemical agent precursor is compared to the existing spectra within the database.

One such Raman Scattering system has been developed by Brookhaven National Laboratory. This mobile system has successfully detected and identified chemicals in the atmosphere from several miles away. This technology, when fully developed, will provide the investigator with *real time* qualitative and quantitative analytical results that may be used to determine the chemical agent and/or precursors being used at a suspected WMD manufacturing facility.

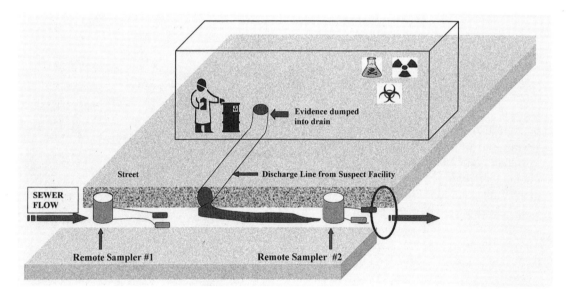

Figure 73. The surreptitious sampling of a clandestine WMD manufacturing facility's liquid waste stream may provide the evidence needed to obtain a search warrant.

Chapter 19

SEARCHING THE SUSPECT FACILITY

The search of an operating or abandoned WMD manufacturing facility will require an extraordinary amount of planning and preparation on the part of the criminal investigator. In some instances, a search warrant may have to be obtained before any entry into the facility can take place. When searching a facility such as this, it is essential that every effort be made to safeguard the health and safety of all members of the search team. In addition, *the facility must be declared safe from armed suspects and/or booby traps prior to any entry being made by an investigative team.* The planning stage for a WMD facility search operation will require many steps. Each of these steps is designed to meet the many problems and obstacles that may arise during a law enforcement action of this type.

DETERMINING GOALS

The clandestine manufacturing of a weapon of mass destruction may violate a wide range of state and federal statues. Each of these statutes must be reviewed and their elements examined. The requirements of the statutes may serve as a guide as to the types and amount of scientific evidence gathering that must be conducted at the suspect facility. As stated earlier, a positive reading on a field-testing instrument (chemical, biological, or radiological) will, in all likelihood, be deemed insufficient to obtain a criminal conviction. A more detailed and scientific evidence collection regime will be required.

Once the type of evidence (as defined by the statute) has been identified, the investigator will be required to research the sampling and analytical protocols needed to meet the requirements of that particular statute. The sampling protocols may be designed for specific organic chemicals, biological organisms, or radiological materials. Each sample type may require unique sampling procedures and sample containers. The analysis protocols may include the use of gas chromatography/mass spectrometry (*chemical*), deoxyribonucleic acid/polymerase chain reaction (*biological*) or gamma spectroscopy (*radiological*). Armed with this knowledge, the investigator will be able to gather the scientific evidence in a legally and scientifically acceptable manner.

EQUIPMENT REQUIREMENTS

Due to the unique nature of the evidence being gathered (*hazardous*) and the locations where it may be found (i.e., pipes, drums, tanks, vats, ***leaching pools***, waste streams), it is essential that the investigator determine his or her equipment needs carefully. The search of an *abandoned* WMD manufacturing facility may require the exposing and sampling of a liquid waste system which may contain chemical, biological, or radiological evidence, while the sampling of drums and small containers of chemical agent precursors found at an *operating* WMD manufacturing facility will require a completely different equipment protocol. In addition to the proper sampling equipment, the investigator must also be equipped with the necessary safety equipment. The following is a listing of many of the equipment items (non-sampling) that may be needed during the search of a facility suspected of manufacturing a weapon of mass destruction:

- Chemical boots
- Fully encapsulating suit
- pH paper
- Compass

- Surgical gloves
- Chemical suits
- Duct tape
- Coveralls

- Air purifying respirator
- Chemical gloves
- Measuring tape
- Self-contained breathing apparatus

- LEL/O$_2$ meter
- Binoculars
- Flashlight
- Knife
- Fingerprint kit

- 35mm Auto focus camera
- First aid kit
- Non-sparking hand tools
- Evidence bags
- Children's bubbles

- Dosimeter
- Bold markers
- Spark-proof clipboard
- Spare 60-minute air bottle
- Communications equipment

- Bio field test kit
- Confined space safety equipment
- Back hoe
- Lights
- Metal detector
- Video camera
- Crime scene tape

- Chemical field test kit
- Decontamination line
- Picks and shovels
- Ground penetrating radar
- Remote drum opener
- Evidence sealing tape
- Vegetable dye

- Geiger counter
- Emergency medical equipment
- Ladders
- Compressed air supply
- Jackhammers
- Chemical dictionary
- Tracer balloons

PERSONNEL REQUIREMENTS

Personnel planning is one of the most important elements in preparing for the execution of a search at a facility of this type. Each member of the search team has a specific role to play. Having *too many* individuals at an operation of this type may be more damaging than not having enough. In addition, the presence of untrained and unqualified personnel at a search of a suspected WMD manufacturing facility may be dangerous to all involved. A simple rule should apply in these situations. *Only those persons who are properly trained, properly equipped, and have a specific assignment should enter the facility.*

The Search Team

The successful execution of *any* criminal search warrant depends on those assigned to the operation. A WMD facility search warrant is no different. Each team member must be properly trained and qualified within his or her own discipline. Severe damage to the prosecution's case may result if it is later determined that the personnel at the scene were not properly trained in the handling of hazardous materials or that the Sample Teams were not properly trained in the taking of chemical, biological, or radiological evidence samples.

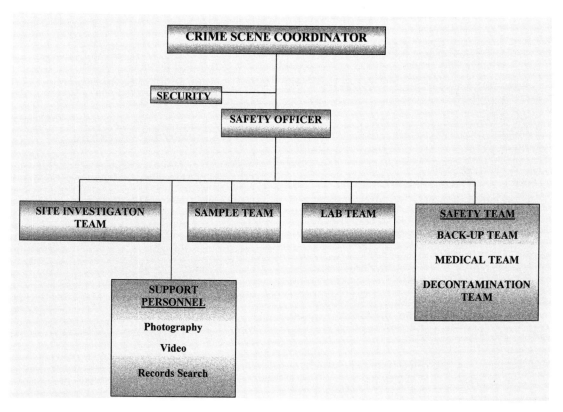

Figure 74. This is a suggested structure for a search team entering an operating or abandoned WMD manufacturing facility.

In addition to having qualified personnel present, a clear chain-of-command must exist. However, this command structure must have a built-in flexibility to change at a moment's notice. Due to the hazardous nature of the evidence being gathered, the simplest evidence gathering operation may turn disastrous at any moment. With this command flexibility, each team member will be aware of *"who's in charge"* at any given moment during an emergency.

The search team structure is similar to the team structure utilized at a crime scene involving the use or threatened use of a weapon of mass destruction (see Chapter 14, The Investigative Team). The key differences is the addition of a Site Investigation Team and the assignment of additional hazardous material trained law enforcement personnel for photography, video taping, and record searches (see Figure 74).

Once inside the suspect facility, a systematic search for scientific evidence must be completed. In order to accomplish this, a Site Investigation Team should be established. This team should consist of a criminal investigator, a member of the laboratory team (i.e., forensic chemist, microbiologist or nuclear physicist), a member of the Sample Team and a member of the Safety Team. This type of team structure will bring four distinct disciplines into one working group. Each sample point can then be evaluated from the prospective of the investigative needs, scientific requirements, sampling protocols, and potential safety issues.

THE BRIEFING

The pre-search briefing is a critical part of the operation's execution process. Many individuals from different agencies may be brought together in an effort to collect evidence in a safe, efficient, and legally acceptable manner. It is essential that each person on the team be made aware of what his or her role is and by what manner the assigned tasks are to be accomplished. It is at this juncture that input is received from all members of the search team and based upon this, the final operations plan is developed.

Federal law requires that a written emergency response plan be developed and implemented to handle anticipated emergencies prior to beginning any hazardous material operations.[125] The briefing may be utilized to satisfy this requirement. It is recommended that the briefing be held by the crime scene coordinator at least 24 hours prior the to commencement of the operation. This will allow ample time for the preparation of any required equipment. The following topics should be addressed during this pre-search briefing.

Chain-of-Command

The crime scene coordinator and his or her executive officer are to be identified at the briefing. Each team member shall be made aware that the crime scene coordinator will have absolute authority over the operation. If the crime scene coordinator should become incapacitated during the course of the operation, the executive officer will assume command.

Safety Officer

The site *safety officer* must be selected and identified at the briefing. The role of the safety officer is to be fully explained to all present. It must be made clear that this individual shall assume command of the operation in the event of a hazardous material emergency. In addition, it must be made clear to all search team members that any area containing possible hazardous materials is *not* to be entered without the knowledge and approval of the safety officer.

Site Investigation Team

This group of individuals will systematically search the facility's interior and exterior for scientific evidence. Each site investigation team is to be made up of four individuals. Each of these individuals shall have been trained in a different discipline. The site investigation team should consist of a criminal investigator, a member of the sample team, a member of the laboratory team, and a member of the safety team.

The criminal investigator shall be an individual who is well versed in the applicable statute(s) and will determine what evidence must be gathered to further the investigation. In addition, this individual will make the final determination as to whether or not a particular area or item will be sampled for scientific evidence. The criminal investigator will also decide, based upon the needs of the investigation, the types of analyses that are to be conducted as they relate to each sample point.

The sample team member will evaluate each sample point in an effort to ascertain his or her sampling equipment needs. It is important to note that each sampling event, depending upon type, size, and area, may require a different sampling protocol in order to properly obtain the needed scientific evidence.

The forensic chemist, microbiologist, or nuclear physicist will act as scientific advisor throughout the search process. He or she will consult with the criminal investigator as to the different types of analytical methodologies needed for each individual sample point.

The function of the Safety Team member is to evaluate each sample point for any possible safety hazards. The sampling of vats, piping, storage tanks, and containers each represents different types of hazards that may be faced by the sampling team. This individual will address such safety concerns as levels of protection, fire and explosion hazards, contamination hazards, and confined space entry requirements for each individual sample point.

The Sample Team

The sample team(s) will be established at the briefing. It is here that the lead sampler(s) will be named. These individuals, along with an assistant sampler(s), will conduct all scientific evidence gathering activities during the course of the operation.[126] The lead sampler for each sample team should be the individual who has the most experience in gathering hazardous evidence for *criminal prosecution purposes*. In all likelihood, this individual will be required to testify at the criminal trial regarding the protocols and methods used to gather the scientific evidence.

Type of Facility

The search team should be thoroughly briefed as to the type of manufacturing (i.e., chemical agents, biological agents, radiological devices) being done at the suspect facility. Each type of manufacturing facility will have its own unique equipment and system of operation. Each type of facility will also utilize different hazardous materials within its process. Every effort should be made to thoroughly brief the entire search team as to the suspected manufacturing process. Having some basic knowledge as to how the suspect facility's system operates will greatly assist the entire search team in locating and seizing the needed scientific evidence.

Suspected Hazards

Based upon the information developed during the initial investigation and having a basic knowledge as to the type of facility about to be searched, a listing of suspected hazardous materials should be established. Once this list has been created, the proper *Material Safety Data Sheets* (MSDS) and/or other written materials should be obtained for each individual hazard expected to be present. Each member of the search team should be supplied with copies of the relevant Material Safety Data Sheets and other supporting safety documentation.

Expected Protection Levels

Personal Protective Equipment (PPE) levels should be established based upon the type of facility and the suspected hazards. It is always a good policy to plan for the unexpected by bringing equipment of at least one level of greater protection than is indicated by the information developed during the initial investigation. Therefore, if the suspected hazards at the site require *Level "C" protection equipment*, then Level "B" protection equipment should be brought to the site. Likewise, if the suspected hazards at the site require *Level "B" protection equipment*, then *Level "A" protection equipment* should be brought to the site.

A great deal of planning and preparation is needed when the scientific evidence to be gathered requires the use of Level "A" safety equipment. This type of evidence gathering operation is both difficult and dangerous. The inherent properties of Level "A" protection equipment (total encapsulation) makes evidence gathering a difficult task (see Figure 38). Limited sight distances, limited mobility, high interior suit temperatures, and allowable working time all impact the individual's ability to gather evidence. In addition, the very nature of the evidence being gathered (hazardous) makes this operation a dangerous one. *Whenever possible, Level "A" evidence gathering operations should be avoided.* However, if it should become necessary to utilize this level of protection to gather the scientific evidence, it is essential that well-trained and experienced personnel conduct the operation.

Decontamination Requirements

Decontamination requirements must be established at the briefing. The types of hazardous materials involved, as well as any MSDS information, will help to determine the decontamination requirements. These may range from a simple stripping and bagging of contaminated clothing, to a full decontamination line equipped with scrubbing areas, rinsing areas, and waste water containment.

Emergency Medical Requirements

Each search team member will be advised as to the location of the first-aid station. The first-aid station should be utilized for minor injuries only. The location of the nearest medical facility should also be established during the briefing. In the event of a Level "A" evidence gathering operation, it is recommended that an ambulance, staffed by hazardous material trained medical technicians, be standing by during the course of the operation.

The Sampling Operation

Each suspected sample point should be evaluated during the pre-search briefing. It is during this evaluation that the various types of scientific evidence to be seized will be established. In addition, the required sampling equipment necessary to gather the scientific evidence will be discussed.

Various analytical tests may be required depending upon the types of scientific evidence being seized. Each of these analytical tests may require special scientific evidence gathering protocols and evidence containers.

In many instances, the number of samples planned for may be far exceeded by the number of samples actually taken during the course of the operation. Therefore, it is essential that extra scientific evidence gathering equipment and containers be brought to the site.

Site History

A complete review of the site's history should be made at the briefing. It is common to have numerous types of industries occupying the same physical location over a period of months or years. Knowing what types of industry formerly occupied the site may help the search team in determining what equipment and/or hazardous materials were left behind by a former occupant.

Photographs

Each member of the search team should review all ground and aerial surveillance photographs. These photographs will assist in the pinpointing of sample points and in determining where to locate the command post, first-aid station, and decontamination areas.

Facility Diagram

A diagram of the facility, based upon surveillance and intelligence information,

should be drawn and reproduced for each member of the search team. The diagram should indicate all buildings on the site and all suspected manufacturing areas. It should also include all suspected sample point areas. The diagram should contain a map legend indicating points of direction.

Weather

Proper weather conditions are a critical component for the successful execution of an operation of this type. Projected outside temperatures, wind direction, and wind velocity should be determined in advance. The weather forecast for the operation date should be distributed to each member of the search team.

Adjustments in the operation's execution date and/or time should be considered if the weather conditions are expected to have a negative impact on the health and safety of the search team members or on the collection of the scientific evidence. Very cold temperatures may freeze certain hazardous materials, making it difficult to obtain a proper sample. These same cold temperatures may affect electronic sensing equipment such as LEL/O_2 meters and freeze water lines in the decontamination system. Snow covered ground may hide discharge pipes and waste collection systems that would normally be visible. Extreme heat may have a devastating effect upon sampling team and backup team personnel. On hot days, the individuals wearing chemical suits may be faced with extremely hot in-suit temperatures. This may lead to medical problems for these individuals, which may then jeopardize the entire operation.

Many of these problems may be overcome with careful planning. If extremely cold conditions exist, a heated area can be established in a bus or truck to protect personnel and equipment from the elements. In extremely hot conditions, a large air-conditioned vehicle may be utilized. In high heat situations, the sample team and backup team members can be equipped with a simple flag-man's vest with disposable chemical ice packs in the interior pockets. The vest may be worn under a chemical suit and will assist in maintaining a cooler in-suit temperature.

Communications

As with any major law enforcement operation, a good communications system is essential. The crime-scene coordinator, safety officer, science personnel, and the site investigation teams must have the ability to communicate effectively with each other. The best way to accomplish this is with an intrinsically safe radio system set to a dedicated channel. The system should have the capability for "hands-free" operation. Many such radio systems exist which utilize bone microphones or throat activated transmitters. A communication protocol should be established and distributed to the entire search team.

Search Warrant Review

In situations involving the use of a criminal search warrant it is important to make certain that the plan meets *all* of the criteria set forth in the warrant. The search warrant's itemized list of areas to be searched and evidence to be seized should be compared with each team's assignment. This is especially important to the records team and sample team. Each member of the search team must be made aware of *where* they are allowed to search and *what* evidence they are allowed to seize as dictated by the parameters listed in the warrant. This is best accomplished by having each team member review the search and seizure sections of the search warrant.

THE STAGING AREA

On the day of the search execution, all those who are assigned to the search team should meet at a pre-designated time and place. This *staging area* should be located relatively close to the facility that is about to be searched. By utilizing a staging area, the investigator will be able to accomplish several important last-minute tasks.

Personnel and Equipment Check

The use of a staging area provides an opportunity for the crime scene coordinator to insure that all required personnel and equipment are present and in operating order. If an individual member of the search team is not present, this will afford an opportunity to have that individual replaced prior to the execution of the search.

Operation's Plan Review

It is possible that new information may have been received during the time period between the search briefing and the staging event. The operation's plan review provides an opportunity to address the entire search team as to any new data and/or change in plans.

THE SEARCH

An orderly progression of events is essential when executing a search at an operating or abandoned WMD manufacturing facility. Without this orderly progression, the criminal investigator will find the search personnel and their equipment scattered throughout the facility in an unorganized state. By following the search operation's plan, each individual will know exactly where to go and what duties to perform upon his or her immediate arrival.

The search team should enter the facility only after it has been declared safe. The safety officer shall determine the exact positioning of vehicles and equipment for all search team members. These decisions may be based upon wind direction, availability of a fresh water supply, and suspected sample points. Every effort should be made to avoid having the search team members inadvertently park their vehicles over waste discharge systems, leaching pools, and/or underground piping. Once the positioning of vehicles and equipment is completed, the site investigation team and any records search team may be deployed.

Interior Search

The site investigation team should search the entire interior of any suspected buildings on the site. This search should be completed in a systematic fashion (i.e., grid search) and should include all basement and attic areas. As stated earlier, each type of WMD device will require a different type of manufacturing equipment (see Chapter 18, Interdiction Techniques). When conducting a search of this type, fielding testing instruments (chemical, biological or radiological) may be useful in determining areas that require sampling. Manufacturing equipment, on-site safety equipment, test animals, laboratory equip-

ment, raw products (i.e., chemical agent precursors, radiological sources), waste storage, and waste systems should all be located, photographed, inventoried, sampled, and seized when appropriate (see Figures 75, 76 & 77).

In addition to the items listed above, the criminal investigator should insure that all ventilation systems, sink elbows, and piping systems are located and marked for sampling. When a ventilation system contains filters, they should be removed and sealed as evidence. If no filter is present, a surface wipe sample should be taken from the interior of the system. Sink elbows should be removed and their contents poured off into a sample container. If no fluid is present in the elbow, the elbow should be rinsed and the rinse collected as evidence. For chemical evidence, distilled water may be used. For biological evidence, a dilute buffer solution may be used. When attempting to locate radiological evidence, a survey meter may be used to "frisk" the *interior* of the elbow. The elbow should then be sealed as evidence (see Figure 78).

All piping to and from any suspected manufacturing area should be traced. If the suspected piping system runs above ground level (i.e., attached to the walls or ceiling), any low-pitch-point should be identified for sampling. These low-points may accumulate small amounts of hazardous evidence. A sample may be obtained by drilling a small hole into the pipe and collecting the sample as it drains.

Any suspected pumps and hoses should be identified for seizure. Small pumps may be used to transfer raw products to mixing areas during the manufacturing process. These pumps should be seized, marked for sampling, and photographed. Any interior fluid in the pump should be drained into a sample container. If no fluid is present in the pump, distilled water should be introduced as a rinse. The rinse should then be collected for future analysis (see Figure 79).

All interior waste receptacles should also

be searched. Items such as clothes and broken laboratory glassware should be marked as evidence, photographed, inventoried, and seized when appropriate. The interiors of these receptacles should be

Figure 75. This chemical mixing vat is available commercially and is commonly used in the chemical mixing and repackaging industry. It can also be used in the manufacturing of chemical agents.

Figure 76. During the search of a suspected WMD manufacturing facility, it may become necessary to sample raw chemical products.

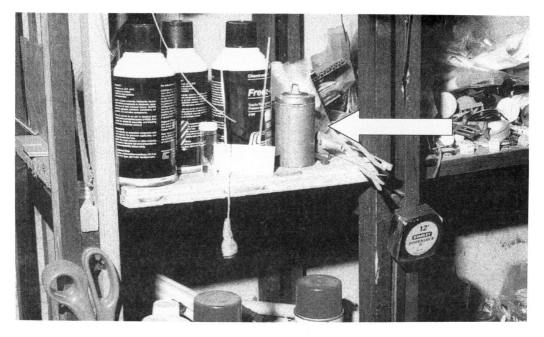

Figure 77. The search of this facility produced a radiological source hidden in plain sight on a cluttered equipment shelf. The arrow is pointing at the radiological source's containment pig.

Figure 78. Sink elbows are natural evidence collection pits. Chemical, biological and radiological evidence may be found in its interior.

rinsed (see above) and the rinse collected as evidence. If laboratory coats or aprons are located, the pockets of these items should be marked for sampling. These pocket areas are natural collection points for trace amounts of evidence.

Exterior Search

The Site Investigation Team should conduct the exterior search in the same systematic way as their interior search. The exterior should be searched for manufacturing products and equipment storage. The ground should be searched for underground storage areas and waste system discharge areas. Paved areas that have new asphalt or concrete patches should be thoroughly investigated. All depression areas should be examined for possible recent excavation. The investigator can locate ground surface depressed areas by simply lying flat on the ground and looking across its surface. Any depressed areas can clearly be seen from this position. Any liquid waste discharge systems (i.e., leaching pool or storm drain) should be exposed, marked for sampling, and photographed.

The roof should be examined for the presence of any vents and/or aerosol testing equipment. Any vents should be marked for an *interior* surface wipe or scrape sample. The area surrounding the roof vent should also be examined for any signs of staining.

Figure 79. Small pumps such as this may be used to move chemical agent precursors from one containment to another during the manufacturing process. Valuable trace evidence may be found in its interior.

All stained areas should be marked for sampling. Any aerosol testing equipment should be photographed, inventoried, and seized (see Figures 80 & 81).

Post-Search Briefing

A post-search briefing is required under federal regulations.[127] This briefing should be attended by the crime-scene coordinator, safety officer, science personnel, all safety team members, and sample team members.

During this briefing, the site investigation team will make a full report as to their findings.

It is during this post-search briefing that each sample point will be decided upon and the sample plan established. The types of analyses needed for each sample point will also be determined. Sampling and safety protocols must be set on a sample-by-sample basis. The site safety officer and the crime-scene coordinator must approve each sample point prior to the commencement of

Figure 80. Another natural evidence collection pit is the sanitary system. The system should be exposed and sampled for evidence.

the sampling operation. It is recommended that the safety officer and the crime-scene coordinator, when practical, personally view each sample point prior to the commencement of the sampling operation.

Sample Point Identification

Each sample point should be clearly identified with a field sample point number placed on a ***sampling placard*** (see Figure 35). The first digit on the placard refers to the number for that particular sample point. The next two letters are the initials of the lead sampler. The last numbers are the date. The placards should be placed at each sample point prior to sampling. This will assist the sample team in clearly identifying the sample point at which they are collecting

scientific evidence. In addition, each sample point and placard should be photographed. The location of the sample points and the field sample point number should be noted on the crime-scene sketch. The field sample point number will be the control number utilized for hazardous evidence identification and chain-of-custody purposes.

The Sampling Order

When deciding the sampling order, the crime-scene coordinator and the safety officer should attempt to have the most difficult samples taken first. Certain sample points may require Level "A" protective equipment. Other samples points may require a confined-space entry. Weather conditions and available lighting conditions may

Figure 81. This roof vent is designed to exhaust chemical fumes created during a chemical mixing process. The interior of the vent and the white chemical stains of the roof should be sampled for trace evidence.

also play a role in determining the sampling order. It would be unwise to have a *tired* sample team, in Level "A" protective equipment, removing chemical or biological agent samples under *poor* lighting conditions. It is these types of considerations that must be addressed when determining the appropriate sampling order.

Chain-of-Custody

During the course of the search, the sample team may take dozens of scientific evidence samples. The sampling process may take many hours to complete. These facts, combined with meal periods, and frequent rest periods may add to the potential for a break in the chain-of-custody. It is vital that the chain-of-custody be maintained throughout the evidence gathering operation.

Pipe Tracing

The criminal investigator may find it necessary to trace certain pipes that are suspected of being part of the manufacturing process. To accomplish this, it is recommended that a vegetable dye be used. *Dye testing* should commence at the *conclusion* of the sampling operation. This will avoid any future legal defense relating to sample

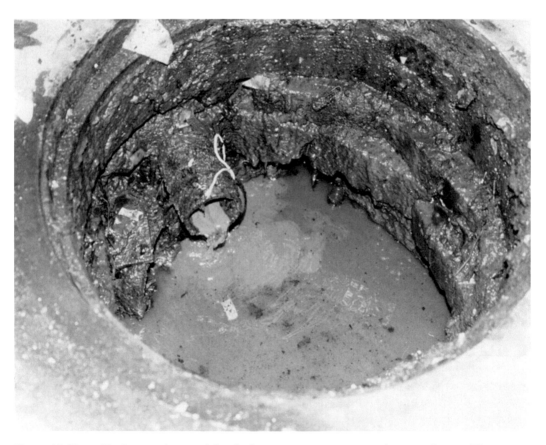

Figure 82. Vegetable dyes can be a useful tool when attempting to trace underground pipes. These pipes can lead to natural evidence collection pits such as leaching pools and leaching fields.

contamination due to the introduction of the dye into the manufacturing system. Each suspected pipe, sink, and floor drain should be dye tested. It is recommended that a different color of vegetable dye be used for each suspected area. A written record should be maintained indicating the time, dye color, and location of the test area. The names of the individuals conducting the dye test procedure must also be recorded. All dye testing points should be photographed and noted on the crime-scene sketch (see Figure 82).

The Prosecutor

When practical and safe to do so, the prosecutor should visit the crime scene prior to its closing. This will afford the prosecutor an opportunity to obtain a better under-standing of the case he or she is about to prosecute. Crime-scene photographs and videotapes, although informative, do not offer the same perspective as a personal viewing. The prosecutor should receive a full briefing from the crime-scene coordinator. The prosecutor should arrive at the facility *after all evidence gathering activities have ceased.* This avoids the possibility of the prosecutor becoming a witness in his or her own case.

The Receipt

Some jurisdictions may require that a general receipt be left at the facility for any items seized in cases involving the execution of a search warrant. If such a requirement exists, the amount of samples removed and any other items seized during the execution of the warrant should be recorded on the receipt. It is recommended that carbon paper be used when filling out the receipt. This will provide the crime-scene coordinator with an exact copy of the receipt left at the facility.

Closing the Scene

When the crime-scene coordinator has determined that all evidence has been gathered, he or she and the safety officer should inspect the interior and exterior of the facility one last time. They should remove any material and/or equipment inadvertently left behind by members of the search team (i.e., contaminated clothing, sampling equipment). The interior and exterior should also be inspected for any hazards left behind by the search team. Any uncovered hazardous material containers, tanks, storm drains, or leaching pools must be made safe prior to the search-team exiting the facility.

APPENDICES

Appendix 1

RECOMMENDED RESPONSE GUIDE
FOR RESPONSE TO A WMD INCIDENT

Communications:

- Determine whether the incident has occurred, is ongoing, or is a threat.
- Obtain as much information about the situation as possible, including the following:
  - What types of materials(s) are involved?
  - How many people are effected?
  - What are the signs and symptoms of the injured people?
  - Has there been a fire or explosion?
  - What is the exact location of the incident?
- Assign sufficient personnel, including supervision, to the initial response.
- Make other notifications as requested by response personnel.

First Responders:

- Approach the scene from an upwind and uphill direction.
- Park vehicles a safe distance from the scene and keep access routes open for other emergency traffic.
- Be alert for the possibility of secondary or additional devices.
- Do not touch or otherwise handle any suspect devices or materials.

- Restrict access to the scene by unauthorized personnel.
- Identify and record those leaving the scene.
- Avoid contact with contaminated victims.
- Request additional assistance, including specialized resources such as bomb squads and hazardous materials teams as soon as possible.
- Assist in evacuation of the danger area.
- If the material is identified, refer to the appropriate guide in the *North American Emergency Response Guidebook.*
- Isolate the affected areas and victims.
- Assist in directing victims to decontamination or triage areas.
- Provide security for the scene.

Supervisors:

- Establish a command post in conjunction with other agencies.
- Notify appropriate investigative personnel.
- Request sufficient manpower and resources to secure the perimeter.
- Maintain strict accountability of law enforcement personnel at the scene.
- Designate a staging area for law enforcement resources.

- Begin assigning positions within the Incident Command System.
- Designate a media area.
- Establish an incident log to document all actions taken.
- Ensure that appropriate notifications have been made.

Appendix 2

STANDARD OPERATING PROCEDURES

WEAPONS OF MASS DESTRUCTION

CRIME SCENES

ARRIVAL

Immediately upon arrival the investigator will meet with the incident commander. He or she shall receive a full briefing as to the events that have occurred. The investigator is to ascertain the following information and conduct the following procedures:

1. Ascertain names and current location of all witnesses and victims.
2. Ascertain types of all field tests conducted and the results of those tests.
3. Ascertain the location of all victims' personal effects and secure those items as evidence.
4. Conduct a briefing for all investigative team personnel.
5. Dispatch an interview team to interview all available witnesses and victims.
6. Secure the area as a crime scene. Uniformed police personnel should man outer perimeter areas (safe areas). Radio communications should be established

with these units.

7. If personal effects have not been collected, the crime scene coordinator must dispatch an an investigative team to supervise the collection processes utilizing the following procedures. Whenever possible, this should be completed *before* any decontamination process begins.
   a. Place all victims' personal effects into a large plastic bag. One bag should be used per victim.
   b. Complete duplicate hazardous evidence recovery sheet and place one copy into evidence bag.
   c. Seal evidence bag.
   d. Take instant photograph of victim's face and staple to second copy of hazardous evidence recovery sheet.
   e. Attach second copy of hazardous evidence recovery sheet to outside of evidence bag.

8. Whenever possible, the crime scene coordinator should order an immediate dermal sampling operation for a selected amount of victims.

9. Safety protocols for the hot zone investigation team must be established by the safety officer.

10. Radio communications between the crime scene coordinator, hot zone investigation team, safety officer, and emergency backup team is to be established.

11. A minimum of two investigators will enter the hot zone. A corresponding number of emergency backup personnel shall be standing by. The hot zone investigation team shall have the following equipment with them:

   a. Appropriate protective clothing based upon the suspected hazard.
   b. Steel-toed, chemical-proof boots.
   c. Appropriate protective gloves based upon the suspected hazard.
   d. Several pairs of surgical gloves.
   e. A self-contained breathing apparatus with a full 60-minute air bottle.
   f. An aluminum (non-sparking) clipboard.
   g. A pen for crime-scene notes.
   h. A bold marker for filling in sample-point identification information on the sampling placards.
   i. Several preprinted placards for sample-point identification.
   j. Duct tape, magnetic clips, or suction cup clips for attaching sampling placards to flat surfaces.
   k. An LEL/O₂ meter.
   l. Radiological instruments.
   m. A dosimeter.
   n. pH paper and pH chart.
   o. Appropriate field testing unit for chemical or biological agents.
   p. A waterproof auto-focus camera with sealed electronic flash.
   q. A waterproof auto-focus video camera.
   r. Evidence bags of assorted sizes.
   s. A knife capable of cutting tape.
   t. A fingerprint kit.
   u. Communication equipment.
   v. Children's bubbles.
   w. Measuring tape.

While inside the hot zone, the investigative team should attempt to complete the following evidence gathering tasks:

   a. Photograph and videotape the entire undisturbed crime scene from all angles.
   b. Complete a radiological survey of the entire crime scene. The radiological survey should begin at the outermost perimeter, with continuous readings being made up to the surface areas of any suspected devices or to the point at which a 2mr (millirem) reading is obtained.
   c. Complete a LEL reading to determine if any potentially flammable gases are present.
   d. Field tests for the suspected chemical or biological substances should be conducted near or at the suspected point of detonation. Field test results must be recorded and maintained.
   e. Determine if the material has been spilled or is leaking from the device.
   f. If required, conduct an immediate air sampling operation utilizing the appropriate air sampling equipment.
   g. Note, photograph, and cast any footprints and/or tire tracks present.
   h. Note, photograph, and lift any fingerprints found within the hot zone. Special attention should be paid to bottom surfaces of any containers.
   i. If drums and/or containers are present, photograph, and record any U.S. Department of Transportation information.
   j. Photograph and record all markings

on any containers.

k. Photograph and record all label information on the containers. If the label is legible and can be removed intact, it should be recovered and placed into an evidence bag.

l. The surrounding ground area is to be searched for any other form of physical evidence. Any closed containers should be lifted and/or tilted so that their undersides and the ground area underneath the containers may be examined for possible physical evidence.

m. A sketch should be made of the entire crime scene, including the position and location of each container and/or device. The crime scene sketch should also include the location of any other physical evidence recovered.

n. If the hazardous substance is in a container and in *liquid form*, it should be physically examined through the use of a sterilized coliwasa tube. Any material stratification should be noted and reported to the sample team.

o. Each area, container, and/or device that has been selected for sampling should be placarded and photographed. Binary devices must be placarded for two samples. The sampling placard should contain, at a minimum, the current date and the field sample number. If the container and/or device appears to be empty, it should be placed into an airtight container and seized as evidence.

12. Upon exiting the hot zone and after decontamination requirements have been met, the entire investigation team must attend the post-search briefing. The briefing will be conducted by the crime scene coordinator and will address the safety and sampling protocols that are to be utilized in the collection of the scientific evidence.

13. Radio communications should be established between the sample team, safety officer, crime scene coordinator, and emergency backup team.

14. A two-person sample team shall enter the hot zone to collect the scientific evidence. A two-person emergency backup team must support the sample team.

15. Scientific evidence shall be collected using the appropriate sampling protocol. Sampling protocols shall be determined based upon the type of material present and its matrix.

16. After the sample team has exited the hot zone and decontamination procedures have been completed, all scientific evidence containers are to be sealed and photographed.

17. Radiological evidence is to be inventoried and held for U.S. Department of Energy Personnel.

18. Chemical or biological evidence is to be inventoried, placed into a cooler, and stored at the appropriate required temperature.

   Chemical Agents: 4°C
   Biological Agents: 5°C

19. Biological evidence samples must be delivered to the appropriate laboratory within six hours.

20. All other physical evidence collected at the crime scene should be inventoried, photographed, and sealed.

21. Chain-of-custody paperwork must be completed for *all* evidence collected at the crime scene.

Appendix 3

SAMPLING EQUIPMENT PROTOCOL

Chemical Evidence

1. Chemical Evidence Gathering Equipment

A. Trip Blanks

One 40 ml glass sample container filled to top (no headspace) with distilled water. Trip blanks must be used in all cases.

B. Field Blanks

Distilled water shall be used to rinse decontaminated sampling equipment. Field blanks/equipment rinses shall be conducted on each sampling device that is to be reused at the crime scene. Procedure must be documented.

C. Glove Changes

Sample team members must change outer gloves in between every sample point.

D. Representative Samples

Whenever practical, a representative sample of the existing chemical strata should be taken.

E. Control Samples

Control samples of all sampling materials (i.e., wipes, swabs, absorbent tubes) should be maintained. Background samples for the appropriate sample matrix must be taken (i.e., soil, air, and/or surface water).

F. Field Test Equipment

The following field testing equipment shall be utilized for locating appropriate sampling points:

1. Chemical agent test kit.
2. Flame ionization detector.
3. Photo-ionization detector.
4. Children's bubbles.
5. Tracer balloons.

2. Chemical Sampling Devices

A. Liquids:

1. Sterilized glass pipettes with rubber stoppers.
2. Sterilized locking forceps with absorbent wipe.
3. Sterilized coliwasa tube.
4. Sterilized dipper.
5. Sterilized weighted sampler.
6. Sterilized bailer.
7. Sigma remote liquid sampler.

B. Solids:

1. Sterilized auger.
2. Sterilized stainless steel spoon.
3. Sterilized stainless steel hand shovel.

C. Aerosols/Gases:

1. Battery operated air pump with absorbent tube.
2. Fused silica lined stainless steel negative pressure canister with silica-lined restricter.

D. Surface and Dermal:
1. Surface wipe-sampling kit with stainless steel forceps.
2. Sample templates.
3. $1/2$ gallon/0.025mm polyethylene bags (hand sampling).
4. Distilled water.

3. Chemical Sample Containers

A. Glass Containers:
1. Sterilized 10, 25, 40, 100, or 250 ml glass, screw-cap bottle with Teflon-lined silicon septa. To be used for organic chemical compounds.

B. Plastic Containers:
1. Sterilized linear polyethylene or polypropylene bottles (assorted sizes). To be used for inorganic compounds (i.e., trace metals).

Biological Evidence

1. Biological Evidence Gathering Equipment

A. Trip Blanks

One 40 ml glass sample container filled to 90% of capacity with a dilute buffer solution. Trip blanks must be used in all cases.

B. Field Blanks

Distilled water shall be used to rinse decontaminated sampling equipment. Field blanks/equipment rinses shall be conducted on each sampling device that is to be reused at the crime scene. Procedure must be documented.

C. Glove Changes

Sample team members must change outer gloves in between every sample point.

D. Control Samples

Control samples of all sampling materials (i.e., wipes, swabs, dilute buffer solution, and agar medium) should be maintained. Background samples for the appropriate sample matrix must be taken (i.e., soil, air, and/or surface water).

E. Field Test Equipment

The following field testing equipment shall be utilized for locating appropriate sampling points:
1. Biological agent test kit.
2. Children's bubbles.
3. Tracer balloons.

2. Biological Sampling Devices

A. Liquids:
1. Sterilized glass pipettes with rubber stoppers.
2. Sterilized locking forceps with absorbent wipe.
3. Sterilized coliwasa tube.
4. Sterilized dipper.
5. Sterilized weighted sampler.
6. Sterilized bailer.
7. Sigma remote liquid sampler.

B. Solids:
1. Sterilized auger.
2. Sterilized stainless steel spoon.
3. Sterilized stainless steel hand shovel.

C. Bioaerosols:
1. Liquid filled impinger with battery operated air pump.
2. Filtration device.
3. Gravitational device.
4. Impaction device with multiple preloaded rotor assemblies.

D. Surface and Dermal:
1. Surface wipe-sampling kit with stainless steel forceps.
2. Sample templates.
3. $1/2$ gallon/0.025mm polyethylene bags (hand sampling).
4. Dilute buffer solution.

3. Biological Sample Containers
A. Glass Containers:
1. Sterilized 10, 25, 40, 100, or 250 ml glass, screw-cap bottle with Teflon-lined silicon septa. To be filled to 90% of their capacity during sampling.

Radiological Evidence

2. Radiological Evidence Gathering Equipment
A. Trip Blanks
One Polyethylene Bag containing non-irradiated soil. Trip blanks must be used in all cases.
B. Field Blanks
If additional contaminates are suspected (i.e., chemical) distilled water shall be used to rinse decontaminated sampling equipment. Field blanks/equipment rinses shall be conducted on each sampling device that is to be reused at the crime scene. Equipment should be frisked with radiological instrument prior to reuse. Procedure must be documented.
C. Glove Changes
Sample team members must change outer gloves in between every sample point.
D. Control Samples
Control samples of all sampling materials (i.e., wipes, swabs, and filter media) should be maintained. Background samples for the appropriate sample matrix must be taken (i.e., soil, air, and/or surface water).
E. Field Test Equipment
The following field testing equipment shall be utilized for locating appropriate sampling points:
1. Radiological instruments capable

of detecting and measuring alpha, beta, and gamma radiation.
2. Children's bubbles.
3. Tracer balloons.

2. Radiological Sampling Devices
A. Liquids:
1. Sterilized glass pipettes with rubber stoppers.
2. Sterilized locking forceps with absorbent wipe.
3. Sterilized coliwasa tube.
4. Sterilized dipper.
5. Sterilized weighted sampler.
6. Sterilized bailer.
7. Sigma remote liquid sampler.
B. Solids:
1. Sterilized auger.
2. Sterilized topsoil cutter.
3. Rubber mallet.
4. Telescoping grappler.
5. Sterilized stainless steel spoon.
6. Sterilized stainless steel hand shovel.
C. Airborne Radioactive Material
1. High volume air sampler with appropriate filter media (i.e., Teflon membrane, glass fiber, or cellulose).
D. Surface and Dermal:
1. Surface smear-sampling kit with stainless steel forceps.
2. Sample templates.
3. Sticky tape.

3. Radiological Sample Containers
A. Plastic Containers:
1. Sterilized linear polyethylene or polypropylene bottles (assorted sizes).
B. Polyethylene Bags:
1. Bags must be capable of being sealed. To be used for radiological soil, grass, and leaf samples.

NOTES

1. *Emergency Response to Terrorism: Basic Concepts, Student Manual.* US Department of Justice, Federal Emergency Management Agency. p. SM 0–2. 1998.
2. Powell, William. *The Anarchist Cookbook.* Barricade Books, Inc.: p. 105. 1989.
3. Powell, William. *The Anarchist Cookbook.* Barricade Books, Inc.: pp. 108–110. 1989.
4. U.S. Army Medical Research Institute of Infectious Diseases. *Medical Management of Biological Casualties Handbook,* Second Edition. p. 4. 1996.
5. Webster, William. *Can We Stop The Super-Terrorists?* Reader's Digest, January, 1997. pp. 94–95.
6. U.S. Army Medical Research Institute of Infectious Diseases. *Medical Management of Biological Casualties,* Second Edition. p. 47.
7. United States Department of Transportation. *1996 North American Emergency Response Guidebook.*
8. Association for Professionals in Infection Control and Epidemiology, Inc., Center for Disease Control. *Bioterrorism Readiness Plan: A Template for Healthcare Facilities.* p. 5.
9. Sidell, Frederick R., et al. *Janes Chem-Bio Handbook.* pp. 158–161. 1998.
10. U.S. Army Medical Research Institute of Infectious Diseases, *Medical Management of Biological Casualties,* Second Edition. Summaries. 1996.
11. United States Department of Transportation. *1996 North American Emergency Response Guidebook.* p. 326.
12. *Hazardous Materials for First Responders.* Fire Protection Publications. pp. 191–193. 1998.
13. *Hazardous Materials for First Responders.* Fire Protection Publications. pp. 240–243. 1998.
14. US Department of Transportation. *1996 North American Emergency Response Guidebook.* pp. 298–299.
15. US Department of Transportation. *1996 North American Emergency Response Guidebook.* p. 327.
16. US Department of Transportation. *1996 North American Emergency Response Guidebook.* p. 340.
17. US Department of Transportation. *1996 North American Emergency Response Guidebook.* p. 297.
18. *Emergency Response to Terrorism: Basic Concepts, Student Manual,* US Department of Justice, Federal Emergency Management Agency. pp. SM 2–3. 1998.
19. Bowen, John E. *Emergency Management of Hazardous Materials Incidents.* National Fire Protection Association. p. 235–237. 1995.
20. OSHA Respiratory Protection Standard, 29 CFR 1910.134.
21. Noll, Hildebrand, & Yvorra. *Hazardous Materials: Managing the Incident.* Fire Protection Publications. p. 301. 1995.
22. Franz, David. Biological Terrorism: Some Thoughts on Protecting Our Citizens. Lecture, 11/17/99, US Department of Justice, Center for Domestic Preparedness, Office of Justice Programs, Weapons of Mass Destruction Training Program.
23. Franz, David. Biological Terrorism: Some Thoughts on Protecting Our Citizens.

Lecture, 11/17/99, US Department of Justice, Center for Domestic Preparedness, Office of Justice Programs, Weapons of Mass Destruction Training Program.

24. *Bomb and Physical Security Planning.* Department of the Treasury, Bureau of Alcohol, Tobacco and Firearms. p. 7. 1987.

25. *Bomb and Physical Security Planning.* Department of the Treasury, Bureau of Alcohol, Tobacco and Firearms. pp. 8–9. 1987.

26. Miller, Ken. Chemical Agents as Weapons: Medical Implications. Fire Engineering. pp. 62–63. February, 1999.

27. Decontamination Decision Matrix. *Decontamination for Weapons of Mass Destruction, Nuclear, Biological and Chemical Environments.* National Terrorism Preparedness Institute. 1999.

28. Conner, T.W. Incident Command Systems for Law Enforcement. *FBI Law Enforcement Bulletin.* p. 14. September, 1997.

29. OSHA Hazardous Waste Operations and Emergency Response, 29 CFR 1910.120.

30. Iannone, Nathan F. *Supervision of Police Personnel.* Prentice-Hall, Inc. pp. 24–25. 1987.

31. Noll, Hildebrand, & Yvorra. *Hazardous Materials: Managing the Incident.* Fire Protection Publications p. 98. 1995.

32. Presidential Decision Directive 39, Terrorism Incident Annex to the Federal Response Plan.

33. Urban Search and Rescue Teams were employed in response to the bombing of the federal building in Oklahoma City in 1995. They were staged in the Atlanta area prior to and during the 1996 Summer Olympics.

34. Public Law 104–201, Sections 1413–1414.

35. Hillman, Michael R. *Biological/Chemical Terrorism and SWAT Response.* The Tactical Edge. p.12. Spring, 1999.

36. Superfund Amendments & Reauthorization Act of 1986 (Emergency Planning and Community Right-to-Know Act of 1986, 42 U.S.C. 11003).

37. Presidential Decision Directive 39, Terrorism Incident Annex to the Federal Response Plan, Sect. II: Policy, Amended February 7, 1997.

38. Superfund Amendments & Reauthorization Act of 1986 (Emergency Planning and Community Right-to-Know Act of 1986, 42 U.S.C. 11003).

39. OSHA Hazardous Waste Operations and Emergency Response, 29 CFR 1910.120(q)(6)(i).

40. OSHA Hazardous Waste Operations and Emergency Response, 29 CFR 1910.120(q)(6)(ii).

41. OSHA Hazardous Waste Operations and Emergency Response, 29 CFR 1910.120(q)(6)(iii).

42. OSHA Hazardous Waste Operations and Emergency Response, 29 CFR 1910.120(q)(2).

43. OSHA Hazardous Waste Operations and Emergency Response, 29 CFR 1910.120(q)(8).

44. Noll, Hildebrand, & Yvorra. *Hazardous Materials: Managing the Incident.* Fire Protection Publications. p. 187–8. 1995.

45. Reese, James T., et al. *Critical Incidents in Policing,* Revised. Law Enforcement Applications for Critical Incident Stress Teams. US Department of Justice. pp. 201–211. 1991.

46. OSHA Hazardous Waste Operations and Emergency Response, 29 CFR 1910.120(q)(9)(i).

47. Presidential Decision Directive 39, Terrorism Incident Annex to the Federal Response Plan, Sect. II: Policy, Amended February 7, 1997.

48. OSHA Hazardous Waste Operations and Emergency Response, 29 C.F.R. 1910.120 (b) (1) (i) 1996.

49. US EPA Designation of hazardous substances, 40 CFR 302.4. 1996.

50. US DOT Hazardous Material Table, 49 C.F.R. 172.101. 1996.

51. OSHA Hazardous Waste Operations and Emergency Response, 29 C.F.R. 1910.120 (3) (B) 1996.

52. OSHA Hazardous Waste Operations and Emergency Response, 29 C.F.R. 1910.120. 1996.

53. OSHA Appendix C, 29 C.F.R. 1910.120 (7) 1996.

54. OSHA Hazardous Waste Operations and Emergency Response, 29 C.F.R. 1910.120 (C) (7) 1996.

55. OSHA Hazardous Waste Operations and Emergency Response, 29 C.F.R. 1910.120 (b) (2) (B) 1996.

56. OSHA Appendix C, 29 C.F.R. 1910.120 (7) 1996.

57. OSHA Hazardous Waste Operations and Emergency Response, 29 C.F.R. 1910.120 (6) (I) 1996.

58. OSHA Hazardous Waste Operations and Emergency Response, 29 C.F.R. 1910.120 (6) (I) 1996.

59. OSHA Hazardous Waste Operations and Emergency Response, 29 C.F.R. 1910.120 (C) (7) 1996.

60. US EPA Test Methods for Evaluating Solid Waste, SW-846, (Washington DC, 1994) 4.1.

61. US EPA Test Methods for Evaluating Solid Waste, SW-846, (Washington DC, 1994) 3.1.

62. US EPA List of Hazardous Substances, 40 CFR 302.4

63. Sidell, Frederick R., et al. *Janes Chem-Bio Handbook.* p. 140. 1998.

64. Sidell, Frederick R., et al. *Janes Chem-Bio Handbook.* p. 143. 1998.

65. Black, R.M., & Read, R.W. Analysis of degradation products of organophosphorus chemical warfare agents and related compounds by LC/MS using electrospray and atmospheric pressure chemical ionization., *Journal of Chromatography,* A 794:233–244. 1998.

66. Ness, S.A. *Surface and Dermal Monitoring for Toxic Exposures.* Van Nostrand Reinhold, Chapter 7: Surface Sampling for Chemicals, p. 168. 1994.

67. Ness, S.A. *Surface and Dermal Monitoring for Toxic Exposures.* Van Nostrand Reinhold, Chapter 7: Surface Sampling for Chemicals, p. 168. 1994.

68. OSHA Technical Manual, Chapter 2: Sampling For Surface Contamination. 1999.

69. Ness, S.A. *Surface and Dermal Monitoring for Toxic Exposures.* Van Nostrand Reinhold, Chapter 7: Surface Sampling for

70. OSHA Technical Manual, Chapter 2: Sampling for Surface Contamination. 1999.

71. Ness, S.A. *Surface and Dermal Monitoring for Toxic Exposures.* Van Nostrand Reinhold, Chapter 12, Skin Sampling Methods, Part 1: Wiping, Swabbing and Washing, p. 296. 1994

72. Black, R.M. & Read, R.W. Analysis of degradation products of organophosphorus chemical warfare agents and related compounds by LC/MS using electrospray and atmospheric pressure chemical ionization., *Journal of Chromatography,* A 794:233–244. 1998.

73. US EPA Test Methods for Evaluating Solid Waste, SW-846, (Washington DC, 1995).

74. US EPA Test Methods for Evaluating Solid Waste, SW-846, (Washington DC, 1986) 9.2.2.7.

75. US EPA Test Methods for Evaluating Solid Waste, SW-846, (Washington DC, 1986) 9.2.2.7.

76. Moodie, M. L. & Nagler, G.W. The Utility of Sampling and Analysis for Compliance of Monitoring of the Biological Weapons Convention: Parameters and Procedures for Sampling and Analysis, Monterey Institute of International Studies p. 37 ñ 45. February 1997.

77. Klotz, L.C. Countermeasures for Possible Evasion Scenarios in Sampling and Analysis Under a Biological Warfare Compliance Regime. October 1996.

78. Ness, S.A. *Surface and Dermal Monitoring for Toxic Exposures.* Van Nostrand Reinhold, Chapter 8: Surface Sampling for Microorganisms, p. 213. 1994.

79. Ness, S.A. *Surface and Dermal Monitoring for Toxic Exposures.* Van Nostrand Reinhold, Chapter 8: Surface Sampling for Microorganisms, p. 212. 1994.

80. Miller, S.L., et al. Aerosol Science and Technology, Volume 30, Number 2, p.94, February 1999.

81. Sidell, Frederick R., et al. *Janes Chem-Bio Handbook.* p. 241. 1998.

82. Miller, S.L., et al. Aerosol Science and Technology, Volume 30, Number 2,p.96, February 1999.

83. American Industrial Hygiene Association Publications, Field guide for the Determination of Biological Contaminants in Environmental Samples, p. 54. 1996.

84. American Industrial Hygiene Association Publications, Field guide for the Determination of Biological Contaminants in Environmental Samples, p. 78. 1996.

85. American Industrial Hygiene Association Publications, Field guide for the Determination of Biological Contaminants in Environmental Samples, p. 78. 1996.

86. Miller, S.L., et al. Aerosol Science and Technology, Volume 30, Number 2, p.97, February 1999.

87. American Industrial Hygiene Association Publications, Field guide for the Determination of Biological Contaminants in Environmental Samples, p. 78. 1996.

88. US DOE Environmental Measurements Laboratory. HASL-300, 28th Edition. February 1997.

89. Ness, S.A. *Surface and Dermal Monitoring for Toxic Exposures.* Van Nostrand Reinhold, Chapter 9, Surface Sampling for Low level Radiation, p. 242. 1994.

90. American Nuclear Society: Criteria for emergency radiological field monitoring, sampling and analysis, 3.8.5. 1992.

91. US DOT Radioactive Materials Transportation Information and incident Guide, Chapter 6, Special Nuclear Materials and Weapons.

92. US DOE Radiological Control Manual. 1992.

93. Ness, S.A. *Surface and Dermal Monitoring for Toxic Exposures.* Van Nostrand Reinhold, Chapter 9, Surface Sampling for Low level Radiation, p. 229. 1994.

94. Brookhaven National Laboratory, Safety and Environmental Protection Division, Collection of Vegetation Samples, Procedure No. RAP-SOP-11, July 1992.

95. US DOE Environmental Measurements Laboratory, HASL-300, 28th Edition, February 1997.

96. US DOE Environmental Measurements Laboratory, HASL-300, 28th Edition, February 1997.

97. US DOE Environmental Measurements Laboratory, HASL-300, 28th Edition, February 1997.

98. US EPA Guide for Decontaminating Building, Structures and Equipment at Superfund Sites, EPA Washington DC 1985.

99. US DOE. Radiological Control Manual. 1992.

100. Ness, S.A. *Surface and Dermal Monitoring for Toxic Exposures.* Van Nostrand Reinhold, Chapter 9, Surface Sampling for Low level Radiation, p. 238. 1994.

101. US EPA Guide for Decontaminating Building, Structures and Equipment at Superfund Sites, EPA Washington DC 1985.

102. US DOE Radiological Control Manual. 1992.

103. US DOT Transportation , 49 CFR 171.8, Revised 10/1/98.

104. US DOT Transportation, 49 CFR 171.11, Revised 10/1/98; 49 CFR 171.12, Revised 10/1/98.

105. US DOT Transportation, 49 CFR 173.201 p. 471, 49 CFR 211 p. 473, Revised 10/1/98.

106. US DOT Transportation, 49 CFR 173.134 p. 446, Revised 9/26/96.

107. US DOT Transportation, 49 CFR 173.7, p. 152, Revised 10/1/98.

108. US DOT Transportation, 49 CFR 172.403, p. 309, Revised 10/1/98.

109. US DOT Transportation, 49 CFR 172.403, p. 309, Revised 10/1/98.

110. US DOT Transportation, 49 CFR 172.403, p. 309, Revised 10/1/98.

111. US DOT Transportation, 49 CFR 172.101, pp. 205–206, Revised 10/1/98.

112. Black, R.M. & Read, R.W. Analysis of degradation products of organophosphorus chemical warfare agents and related compounds by LC/MS using electrospray and atmospheric pressure chemical ionization. *Journal of Chromatography*, A 794:233. 1998.

113. Black, R.M. & Read, R.W. Analysis of degradation products of organophosphorus chemical warfare agents and related compounds by LC/MS using electrospray and atmospheric pressure chemical ionization. *Journal of Chromatography*, A 794:234,243. 1998.

114. Klotz, Lynn C. Sampling and Analysis Under a Biological Warfare Compliance Regime, October 1996.

115. Klotz, Lynn C. Sampling and Analysis Under a Biological Warfare Compliance Regime, October 1996.

116. Goldhaber, Judith. New Apparatus Doubles Speed of DNA Replication, July 28, 1995.

117. Levine, J. & Suzuki, D. *The Secret of Life: Redesigning the Living World*, Chapter 1, p. 26, 1993.

118. Klotz, Lynn C. Sampling and Analysis Under a Biological Warfare Compliance Regime, October 1996.

119. Klotz, Lynn C. Sampling and Analysis Under a Biological Warfare Compliance Regime, October 1996.

120. Barry, T. & Gannon, F. Direct genomic DNA amplification from autoclaved infectious microorganisms using PCR technology. PCR Methods and Applications, 1: 75.

Cold Springs Harbor Laboratory. 1991.

121. US DOT Transportation, 49 CFR 178.502 (a) 1996.

122. Douglass J., Livingstone, N. America the Vulnerable: The Threat of Chemical and Biological Warfare, Lexington, MA. 1987.

123. Bilbe, R.M., et al. An Improved Raman LIDAR System for the Remote Measurement of Natural Gas Releases into the Atmosphere, Measured Science Technology, UK, 1, pp. 495–499. 1990.

124. OSHA Appendix C, 29 C.F.R. 1910.120 (2) 1996.

125. OSHA Hazardous Waste Operations and Emergency Response, 29 C.F.R. 1910.120 (L) (1) 1996.

126. OSHA Appendix C, 29 C.F.R. 1910.120 (7) 1996.

127. OSHA Hazardous Waste Operations and Emergency Response, 29 C.F.R. 1910.120 (C) (7) 1996.

GLOSSARY

Absorption: The entry of a hazardous substance into a person's body by way of the skin.

Air sampling: The collection of samples of air to detect and measure the presence of radioactive material, particulate matter, biological organisms, or chemical compounds.

Airborne radioactive material: Radioactive material in any chemical or physical form that is dissolved, mixed, suspended, or otherwise entrained in air.

Alpha particle: A positively-charged particle ejected spontaneously from the nuclei of some radioactive elements. It is identical to a helium nucleus that has a mass number of 4 and an electrostatic charge of +2. It has low penetrating power and a short range (a few centimeters in air). The most energetic alpha particle will generally fail to penetrate the dead layers of cells covering the skin and can be easily stopped by a sheet of paper. Alpha particles are hazardous when an alpha-emitting isotope is inside the body.

Air Purifying Respirator (APR): Respiratory protection that removes particulate matter, gasses, or vapors from the air.

Ambient air: The general air in the area of interest (e.g., the general room atmosphere), as distinct from a specific stream or volume of air that may have different properties.

Arsenical: A chemical agent that contains arsenic.

Background radiation: Radiation from cosmic sources, naturally occurring radioactive materials, including radon (except as a decay product of source or special nuclear material) and global fallout as it exists in the environment from the testing of nuclear explosive devices.

Beta particle: A charged particle emitted from a nucleus during radioactive decay with a mass equal to 1/1837 that of a proton. A negatively-charged beta particle is identical to an electron. Large amounts of beta radiation may cause skin burns, and beta emitters are harmful if they enter the body. Thin sheets of metal or plastic may stop beta particles.

Chemical protective clothing (CPC): Specially designed clothing made of chemical resistant materials used to protect the skin and eyes from direct chemical exposure.

Cold zone: The area beyond the warm zone. The command post is usually established within this area.

Coliwasa tube: Composite Liquid Waste Sampler is a device used to sample free-flowing liquids and slurries contained in drums, shallow tanks, pits and similar containers. It is especially useful for

213

sampling liquids that consist of several separate layers.

Command post: The location at or near the incident from which incident operations are managed or directed.

Consequence management: Measures to protect public health and safety, restore essential government services and to provide emergency relief to governments, businesses, and individuals affected by the consequences of an act of terrorism.

Consolidated action plan: A verbal or written plan that includes strategic goals, tactical objectives, and support activities for an entire operational period.

Contamination: The deposition of unwanted chemical, biological, or radioactive material on the surfaces of structures, areas, objects, or people. It may also be airborne, external, or internal (inside components or people).

Continuous air monitor (CAM): An instrument that continuously samples and measures the levels of airborne contaminates on a "real-time" basis and has alarm capabilities at preset levels.

Control sample: A scientific sampling of a substance or area that is believed to be uncontaminated. The analytical results of which are compared to the suspect sample. A background soil sample.

Cross-contamination: A type of contamination caused by the introduction of part of one sample into a second sample during sampling, transportation, analysis, and/or storage of the evidence.

Crisis management: Measures to identify, acquire, and plan the use of the resources needed to anticipate prevent and/or resolve a threat or act of terrorism.

Crime scene coordinator: The criminal investigator at a WMD crime scene who coordinates all investigative and evidence-gathering activities.

Decontamination: The removal and/or neutralization of chemical, biological, or radiological contamination from personnel and equipment.

Daughter products: Isotopes that are formed by the radioactive decay of some other isotope. In the case of radium-226, for example, there are 10 successive daughter products, ending in the stable isotope, lead-206.

Degradation products: Chemical compounds that may be found after the original chemical agent has been exposed to water (hydrolysis products) and other environmental media.

Deoxyribonucleic acid/polymerase chain reaction (DNA/PCR): A biological analysis method that amplifies and identifies the DNA of biological organisms.

Digestion procedure: Introduction of an oxidizing acid solution into a sample prior to analysis.

Dipper: A glass or plastic beaker clamped to the end of a telescoping pole that serves as the handle. A dipper samples liquids and free-flowing slurries.

Dosimeter: A small portable instrument (such as a film badge, thermoluminescent, or pocket dosimeter) for measuring and recording the total accumulated personnel dose of ionizing radiation.

DOT date: A date that appears on certain hazardous materials containers which indicates the month and year the container was tested for its integrity.

Dye testing: The use of a vegetable dye to determine if two points are connected by a system of pipes or conduits.

Elute: To remove, wash out, or extract absorbed material from an absorbent by means of a solvent.

EOD: Explosive ordnance disposal. Bomb technicians, sometimes referred to as hazardous devices technicians.

Evacuation: Moving endangered subjects from a dangerous or potentially dangerous area to a safe area.

Extension augers: Consists of sharpened spiral blades attached to a hard metal extendible shaft. This device is designed to sample hard or tightly packed soils.

Field blank: Also known as equipment blank. A sampling quality control method in which a piece of sampling equipment is cleaned and then rinsed with distilled water prior to reuse. The rinse water is collected and analyzed later to insure that no preexisting contamination was present on the equipment.

Flame ionization detector: Chemical detector that detects the presence of organic compounds by using a hydrogen/air flame.

Frisk: The movement of a radiological survey instrument over a suspected contaminated area. This method may be used for locating areas to be sampled and for the checking of sampling equipment for any preexisting contamination.

Gamma rays: High-energy, short wavelength, electromagnetic radiation emitted from the nucleus. Gamma radiation frequently accompanies alpha and beta emissions and always accompanies fission. Gamma rays are very penetrating and are best stopped or shielded by dense materials, such as lead or depleted uranium. Gamma rays are similar to x-rays.

Gas chromatograph/mass spectrometer (GC/MS): An instrument used to detect the presence of, and determine the concentrations of, numerous volatile and semi-volatile organic chemical compounds in a sample.

Geiger-Mueller detector: Radiation detection and measuring instrument. It consists of a gas-filled tube containing electrodes, between which there is an electrical voltage but no current flowing. When ionizing radiation passes through the tube, a short, intense pulse of current passes from the negative electrode to the positive electrode and is measured or counted. The number of pulses per second measures the intensity of the radiation field. It is sometimes called simply a Geiger counter or a G-M counter and is the most commonly used portable radiation instrument.

Growth Culture Analysis: A biological analytical method based upon cell culturing. Microorganisms are placed into a growth medium and examined after specific periods of time.

Hazardous material: A hazardous material is a substance or material, that has been determined by the Secretary of Transportation to be capable of posing an unreasonable risk to health, safety, and property when transported in commerce. The term hazardous material also includes hazardous substances and hazardous wastes.

Hazardous materials response team (HMRT): A group consisting of specially trained and equipped personnel capable of mitigating incidents involving hazardous materials.

Hazardous substance: Any substance defined as a hazardous substance under CERCLA. Any biological agent or other disease causing agent which, after release into the environment and upon exposure, will or may reasonably be anticipated to cause death, disease, behavioral abnormalities, cancer, genetic mutation, physiological malfunctions, or physical deformation in a person or their offspring. Any substance listed by the U.S. Department of Transportation as a hazardous material or any hazardous waste.

Hazardous waste: By-products of a manufacturing process that can pose a substantial or potential hazard to human health or the environment when improperly managed. Possesses a least one of four characteristics (ignitability, corrosivity, reactivity, or toxicity) or appears on special EPA lists.

High volume air sampler: Sampling devise used to collect airborne radiological materials onto a filter medium.

Holding time: The recommended time period in which certain chemical and biological evidence should be analyzed. The time period is measured from the time of collection to the time of analysis.

Hot zone: Area immediately surrounding the release or threatened release of a hazardous material. Access is restricted to properly trained and equipped personnel.

Immediately dangerous to life and health (IDLH): An atmosphere that poses an imminent hazard to life or that may inflict immediate and irreversible negative effects on a subject's health.

Immunoassay: A biological analytical method which uses known antibodies that bind to an antigen allowing for identification.

Improvised explosive device: A homemade device consisting of an explosive and the firing components necessary to initiate the device.

Improvised incendiary device: A homemade device consisting of an incendiary material and the firing components necessary to initiate it.

Improvised nuclear device: An explosive device that contains special nuclear materials, conventional high explosives, and a triggering device.

Incident command system (ICS): The organizational arrangement wherein one person is in charge of an integrated, comprehensive emergency response organization and the emergency incident site, backed with resources, information, and advice by an emergency operations center.

Infectious substance: A viable microorganism, or its toxin, that causes or may cause disease in humans or animals. It includes agents listed in 42 CFR 72.3 and any other agent that causes or may cause severe, disabling, or fatal disease.

Ingestion: The entry of a hazardous substance into a person's body via the mouth.

Inhalation: The entry of a hazardous substance into a person's body via the respiratory system.

Ionizing radiation: Any radiation capable of displacing electrons from atoms or molecules, thereby producing ions. Some examples are alpha, beta, gamma, x-rays, neutrons, and ultraviolet light. High doses of ionizing radiation may produce severe skin or tissue damage.

Leaching pool: A waste containment system designed in such a way as to allow its contents to leach into the soil.

Level "A" protection equipment: Protection equipment that includes a positive pressure, full face-piece, self-contained breathing apparatus (SCBA); or a positive pressure supplied air respirator with escape SCBA; totally encapsulating chemical protective suit; inner and outer chemical resistant gloves; and chemical-resistant, steel-toed and steel-shank boots. This level of protection is selected when the greatest level of skin, respiratory and eye protection is required.

Level "B" protection equipment: Protection equipment that includes a positive pressure, full face-piece, self-contained breathing apparatus (SCBA); or a positive pressure supplied air respirator and escape SCBA; hooded chemical resistant clothing, inner and outer chemical-resistant gloves; and chemical-resistant, steel-toed and steel-shank boots. This level of protection is selected when the highest level of respiratory protection is necessary but a lesser level of skin protection is needed.

Level "C" protection equipment: Protection equipment that includes a full-face or half mask, air-purifying respirator; hooded chemical-resistant clothing; inner and outer chemical-resistant gloves; and chemical-resistant, steel-toed and steel-shank boots. This level of protection is selected when the concentration(s) and type(s) of air borne substance(s) are known and the criteria for using air purifying respirators are met.

Level "D" protection equipment: The normal work uniform that provides only minimal protection. It affords no respiratory protection and minimal skin protection.

Local emergency planning committee (LEPC): Local organization responsible for developing and maintaining a community's hazardous materials contingency plan.

Material safety data sheets (MSDS): A compilation of information required under the OSHA Communication Standard on the identity of hazardous chemicals, health, and physical hazards, exposure limits, and precautions.

Millirem: One thousandth of a rem (1 mrem $= 10^{-3}$ rem).

MOPP-4 protective equipment: Mission Oriented Protective Posture. Protective ensemble employed by military personnel consisting of an air-purifying respirator with a hood, adsorbent charcoal over-garment, butyl rubber gloves, and overboots.

Neutron: An uncharged elementary particle with a mass slightly greater than that of the proton and found in the nucleus of every atom heavier than hydrogen.

Onset time: The amount of time that it takes for a hazardous substance to begin affecting a victim.

OSHA: Occupational Safety and Health Administration.

Parts per billion (ppb): Parts (molecules) of a substance contained in a billion parts of another substance (or water).

Personal protective equipment (PPE): Specialized clothing and other equipment used to protect emergency response personnel from exposure to hazardous substances.

Photo-ionization detector (PID): A chemical detector which consists of an ultraviolet lamp and ionization chamber. This device is used to detect the presence of organic compounds.

Portable liquid sampler: Sampling device that allows for the automatic and timed sampling of liquid waste streams.

Pig: A colloquial term describing a container (usually lead or depleted uranium) used to ship or store radioactive materials. The thick walls of this shielding device protect the person handling the container from radiation.

Psychogenic illness: An illness that originates in the victim's mind.

Radiation: Ionizing radiation: alpha particles, beta particles, gamma rays, x-rays, neutrons, high-speed electrons, high-speed protons, and other particles capable of producing ions.

Radiation detection instrument: A device that detects and displays the characteristics of ionizing radiation.

Radiological survey: The evaluation of the radiological conditions and potential hazards incidental to the production, use, transfer, release, disposal, or presence of radioactive material or other sources of radiation. When appropriate, such an evaluation includes a physical survey of the location of radioactive material and measurements or calculations of levels of radiation, or concentrations or quantities of radioactive material present.

Radiation dispersion device: An explosive device that contains conventional explosives, a triggering device, and a radiological source.

Safety officer: The individual at a hazardous materials incident or WMD crime scene who is responsible for establishing and supervising any required safety protocols.

Sampling placard: A sign used to identify an individual sampling point through a systematic numbering system.

Sampling templates: A cut-out device which is laid over an area to be sampled. A surface wipe sample is taken from the inside area of the template. These devices are pre-sized.

Self contained breathing apparatus (SCBA): Respirator using a limited supply of air that is carried by the user offering the highest level of respiratory protection.

Science officer: The individual at a hazardous material incident or a WMD crime scene who provides scientific and technical advice as to the hazards present.

Sector officer: Individual designated by the incident commander to manage a specific function or geographic area.

Shelter in place: Also known as "protection in place," keeping people indoors in a secure atmosphere while an atmospheric hazard passes or dissipates.

Special nuclear materials: Certain radioactive substances such as μ-235, μ-233 and Pμ-239.

Specific gravity: The ratio of the density of a substance to the density of some other substance (i.e., water) taken as a standard when both densities are obtained by weighing in air.

Staging area: A prearranged area where personnel and equipment are temporarily maintained.

Stratified sample: A liquid sample that represents the complete strata (all levels) of the substance being sampled.

Supplied air respirator (SAR): Respirator having an airline that is connected to a remote air supply (i.e., air compressor, air cylinder).

Survey meter: Any portable radiation detection instrument especially adapted for inspecting an area or individual to establish the existence and amount of radioactive material present.

Tracer balloons: Balloons filled with air that are used to trace interior or exterior airflow patterns.

Trip blank: Sample container of distilled water and/or contaminant free soil which accompanies all sample containers to and from the field. Analysis of the trip blank will determine if any outside contamination occurred during handling and transportation.

Urticant: A chemical agent that causes irritation at the point where it contacts the victim.

Volatile organic compound (VOC): Any organic compound that participates in atmospheric photochemical reactions except those chemicals designated by the EPA as having negligible photochemical reactivity.

Warm zone: Area immediately beyond the hot zone. Decontamination is usually conducted in this area.

Weighted sampler: Sampling device consisting of a weight, stopper, line, and bottle. The line is used to raise, lower, and open the stopper allowing a sample to be taken. This device is used to sample liquids and free-flowing slurries.

Wipe sample: A sample taken for the purpose of determining the presence of removable radioactive contamination, biological microorganisms, or chemicals on a surface. It is also known as a swipe or smear sample.

INDEX

A

Adamsite (DM), precursor to, 21t
Agricultural terrorism, 9
ANSI standards, 99
Anthrax, 173f
    characteristics of, 18, 20f, 136f, 174
    exposure route, 9, 14, 20f, 137
    threat of use, 88
    treatment, 20f
Arsine, precursor to, 21t
Assassination, 8
Atlanta area, bombs, series of, 15
Atlanta Olympics bombing (1996), 5
Atmosphere
    flammability of, 111, 112
    monitoring/sampling, 100-101, 148-49
    oxygen deficient, 36, 39
    remote sampling, 176-77
    See also Detection devices

B

Bioaerosol sampling, 141-45
Biological agents
    bacteria, 10, 13, 14, 36
    detection of, 4, 13, 21, 26, 97, 135-37
    and etiological harm, 36
    evidence analysis, 163-66
    exposure routes, 13-14, 20f, 37-38, 52
    incubation period, 13, 18, 136f
    packaging/shipping, 157
    sampling protocols, 135-46, 205-06
    theft of, 173f
    toxins, 13, 14, 30, 36, 99, 174

    training for, 99
    types of, 13-14
    viruses, 13, 14, 36
Biological weapons
    delayed symptoms, 4
    manufacture of, 3-4, 137, 139-40, 166, 173-74
    materials recognition, 24-25
    See also Weapons of mass destruction
Black market, 174
Blister agents, 12
Blood agents, 11, 12-13
"B-NICE" acronym, 3, 45
Bomb building. *See* Device manufacturer
Bomb technicians
    debriefed as witnesses, 47
    for dissemination devices, 7, 17
    for explosive devices, 7, 28
    for military ordnance, 24
    at special events, 83
    specialized equipment, 86
    and tactical operations, 74
    for unactivated WMD device, 30
    See also Robotic bomb handler
Botulinum, 20f, 136f, 173f
Brucellosis, 136f, 174
Bureau of Alcohol, Tobacco, and Firearms
    (ATF), 81
BZ
    characteristics of, 13
    precursors to, 21-23t

C

Centers for Disease Control (CDC), 72
Chain of custody, 155

custodians of, 55, 118, 134, 146, 155
for facilities search, 194
laboratory protocols, 134, 146, 155, 161
standard operation procedure, 103, 203
training for, 100
Chemical agents
classifications of, 11-13
detection of, 4, 26, 48, 97
evidence analysis, 162-63
exposure routes, 12-13, 37-38, 52
"limited" releases of, 97
onset time, 11-12, 18
organic, in radiological sample, 155
persistence of, 11
precursors to, 21-23f, 101, 123, 125, 162, 168-70
for riot control, 13
sampling protocols, 126-32, 204-05
See also Clothing, protective; Sampling; Weapons of mass destruction
Chemical devices
materials recognition, 21-23t, 24-25
in public schools, 97
See also Weapons of mass destruction
Chemical sites, illegal, 167-73
fingerprint search, 112
materials in, 3-4, 133f
precursor container tracing, 168-73
sampling methods, 112, 176-78
searching, 179-95
Chernobyl incident, 147
Chlorine (CL)
characteristics of, 13, 19f
EPA response to, 72
Choking agents, 11, 13
Clothing, protective, 40-43
ballistic vest, 37, 87
body armor, 74
bomb suit, 86
chemical suit, 102, 103, 112, 180, 185
flashover suit, 41
fully encapsulating suit, 102, 103, 109, 180
levels of, 42-43
suspicious possession of, 25
for tactical operations, 74-76, 78-79, 87
See also Personnel protection
"Cold zone," as support/safe zone, 31-32, 43
Coliwasa tube, 113, 114f, 122-23, 126, 139, 148, 155-56
Commission on Accreditation for Law

Enforcement Agencies, 57
Communication links
with enforcement personnel, 10, 17, 83
with health care providers, 18-20
with news media personnel, 16
with private citizens, 16
Communications, radio, 42, 78, 186, 202
Communications systems
command post and, 70
for hot zone, 111, 202
interagency integration, 59-60
Logistics Officer and, 66
preplanning, 15, 78, 84, 186
response guidelines, 199
security of, 45
terrorist attacks on, 63
Confined space entry, 99, 100
Crime scene, 104-06
See also Incident site
Crime scene coordinator, 107f-08
evidence expertise of, 88, 105
for facilities search, 181f, 182, 186, 195
and interview reports, 106, 108
and sampling protocols, 108, 119
Crime scene notes, 115
Critical incident stress debriefing (CISD), 34, 95-96
Crowd control, 80, 84
Cyanide. *See* Hydrogen cyanide
Cyanogen chloride (CK)
characteristics of, 12-13, 19t, 126
precursor to, 23t
Cytotoxins, 14

D

Debriefing
critical incident stress, 34, 95-96
threat recipient, 47
witness, 47
Decontamination
after facilities search, 184
with biological hazard, 21
federal resources, 72, 73
HazMat personnel for, 90
of incident personnel, 21, 34, 55, 102, 109, 113
Safety Officer and, 108
site, 15, 16f, 31, 37, 104
of SWAT personnel, 76, 77, 78
of victims, 21, 31, 34, 49, 54-55, 106

Decontamination team, 109
Dengue fever, 20f
Deoxyribonucleic acid/polymerase chain reaction. *See* DNA/PCR analysis
Department of Defense (DOD), 73
Department of Energy (DOE), 72-73, 150, 155, 157, 166
Department of Health and Human Services (DHHS), 72
Department of Transportation (DOT), 156, 158f, 171-72f
Detection devices, 100-101
   atmospheric flammability meter (LEL), 103, 111, 112, 180, 185
   for biological agents, 26, 103
   canine detectors, 4, 26, 48
   for chemical agents, 26, 48, 105f, 112
   direct reading devices, 26, 101
   for explosive materials, 4, 26, 48
   field testing units, 105
   Geiger-Mueller detector, 103, 146
   ion detection devices, 4, 101, 129
   oxygen monitors, 36, 39, 100, 102, 103, 180
   for radiological agents, 25, 26, 48, 102, 111, 148
   radiological dosimeters, 77, 86, 103, 180
   remote air sampler, 176-77
   suspicious possession of, 25
   training for, 99, 100-101, 102
   See also Robotic bomb handler
Dissemination devices, 6-9
   "binary," 8-9f, 126
   breakable container, 7-8f
   dart or syringe, 8, 10f, 38
   explosive/bursting, 7f
   radiation dispersion, 146, 149-50, 151f, 154
   remotely activated, 7
   spraying, 6-7, 27f
   time-delayed, 7
Dissemination methods
   aerosols, 6, 13, 26, 27f, 37, 45, 100
   mechanical ventilation systems, 4, 174
   natural airflow, 4, 6, 100-101, 149
   vector contamination, 8-9, 38
DNA/PCR analysis, 137, 143, 163, 165-66, 179
"Dry land drowning," 13

E

Ebola, 20f, 173f

Emergency medical services (EMS)
   for facilities search, 184
   HazMat-trained, 109
   Logistics Officer and, 66-67
   on-site maintenance of, 66-67
   secure conditions for, 50
   for tactical operations, 76
   for victim treatment, 21, 27
   See also Response personnel
Environmental agencies, and perimeter guidelines, 34
Environmental crimes, 87-88, 99-100
Environmental Protection Agency (EPA), 72, 91, 99-100
EOD teams (Explosive Ordnance Disposal), 24, 81
Epidemiological Intelligence Service (EIS), 72
Equipment, 84-87
   for facilities search, 180
   for hot zone, 111, 202
   investigative, 85, 102-03
   post-incident critique of, 94-95
   for sampling, 101, 114f, 119-30, 137-45, 147-48f
   for tactical operations, 26-29, 76-79, 86-87
   training with, 85, 87, 90, 100-101
   weapons, 50, 74, 76, 78, 79
   See also Detection devices; Personnel protection; Weapons
Evidence
   analysis for, 161-66
   contaminated, 55-56, 77, 106, 109
   dissemination device, 6, 10, 16f, 17
   forensic, 71, 74, 84, 88, 98
   in "hot zone," 30, 88, 92, 97, 107, 111-17
   identification/collection, 103
   traditional, 6, 17, 103, 110, 112, 170
   transport methods, 6, 156-60
   unexploded devices, 15, 126
   videos and photos, 17, 77, 103, 105-06, 112, 134
   See also Chain of custody; Manufacturing sites; Sampling
Evidence, preservation of
   access restrictions, 17, 49
   in containment pig, 148, 150, 158, 175
   labeling for containers, 134-35, 145-46, 149, 156
   preplanning for, 80
   storage, 135, 146, 156, 166, 203
   suspect clothing, 151

victim clothing, 17, 55, 126-27, 140
Explosive devices
  for agent dissemination, 7f, 149-50
  and B-NICE acronym, 3
  hazards of, 7, 36
  ordnance, 24, 81
  pipe bombs, 5
  undetonated, 15, 126
  vehicle bombs, 29
Explosives
  accident risk for bomb builder, 3-4
  for agent dissemination, 7f
  detection of, 4, 26, 48
  shipping category of, 156
  terrorist preference for, 3, 86
  variety of, 25f
Exposure routes, 20f, 37-38, 52
  absorption, 37-38
  for biological agents, 13-14, 20f, 37-38, 52
  for chemical agents, 12-13, 38, 52
  ingestion, 37, 38
  inhalation, 37, 38-40
  injection (or open skin or vector), 37, 38

F

Facilities search, 179-95
  equipment for, 180
  personnel, 181-83
  staging area, 186-87
FBI
  Evidence Response Team, 71
  Hazardous Materials Response Unit (HMRU), 71
  incident team model, 45
  as lead agency, 71, 81, 97
  notification recommendations, 81
Federal Bureau of Investigation. *See* FBI
Federal Emergency Management Agency (FEMA), 71-72, 91
Field testing, 88, 100, 104, 105, 110, 112
Field/trip blanks, 120-22, 131, 147, 155
Finance Section, 67
Fingerprints, 6, 17, 103, 112f
Footprints, 6, 17, 103, 112
French and Indian War (1754-1767), 8

G

Gas chromatography/mass spectometry

(GC/MS), 128, 162-63, 179
GF, precursors to, 22-23t
Growth culture analysis, 163, 164

H

Hazardous materials
  transport of, 156-60
  See also Evidence; Sampling
Hazardous Materials Response Unit (HMRU), 71
Hazardous materials technicians, 90
  capabilities of, 90
  training courses, 91, 98-102
  See also HazMat teams
Hazardous wastes, 98-102, 109, 156-60, 177-78, 180
HazMat teams
  debriefed as witnesses, 47
  FBI, 71
  for immediately dangerous materials, 24
  notification of, 29, 81
  and perimeter guidelines, 34
  protective actions, types of, 37, 53
  response to incident, 104
  safety team as backup, 108
  and tactical operations, 74-75
  and TRACEM acronym, 36
High volume air sampler, 148, 149, 150f
Hostage taking, 3
"Hot zone"
  equipment for, 111, 202
  evidence in, 30, 88, 92, 97, 107, 111-17
  as restricted zone, 28, 30, 34, 52-53, 54
  tactical operations in, 74-79
Hydrogen cyanide (AC)
  characteristics of, 12-13, 19t, 126
  EPA response to, 72
  minor release of, 97
  packaging/shipping, 157
  precursor to, 23t

I

IDLH (Immediately Dangerous to Life and Health), 24
Immunoassay, 163, 165
Improvised explosive devices (IEDs), 29, 37
  See also Explosive devices
Improvised nuclear device (IND), 146, 149-50
Incapacitating agents, 11, 13

Incendiary weapons, 3
Incident Command System (ICS), 57-61
   action plans, consolidated, 61, 63-64
   command staff, 68-70
   command structure, unified, 60-61, 62
   incident facilities, 62-63
   modular organization, 59
   preplanning for, 84, 92
   resource management, 63, 64, 65, 66-67
   span of control, 61-62, 64, 65
   for special events, 83
   terminology use, common, 58
   training on, 102
   See also Incident management
Incident Commander
   command staff under, 68, 70
   investigator coordination with, 104
   and media relations, 69
   and perimeter control, 31
   post-incident critique, 93
   prioritization by, 63
   responsibilities of, 63-64
Incident log, 35f
   at command post, 34
   record of personnel present, 34
Incident management, 57-70
   assistance, sources of, 71-73
   command post and, 34, 69-70, 83
   consequence management, 71-72
   crisis management, 71
   functional roles, 63-69
   staging areas, 31, 65, 66f, 83
   See also Incident Command System
Incident site, 104-06
   evacuation of, 29-30f, 32-33, 47, 49, 50, 82
   evidence collection at, 6, 30, 55-56
   law enforcement assessment of, 14, 44-48, 63
   people, contaminated, 21, 52-54
   personal protective devices at, 6
   sheltering in place, 33
   site, contaminated, 7, 16f, 52-54
   See also Evidence; "Hot zone"; Response
     personnel; Response systems
Incident site, securing
   factors to consider, 33-34
   perimeter establishment, 28, 29-30f, 31-32f,
     48-49, 63
   search for device, 26-27, 47-48, 72
   second event, possibility of, 15, 17, 27, 34,
     48, 52

structures, stabilization of, 15
   See also Decontamination
Incidents
   information sharing during, 10, 16-20, 45,
     59-60, 83
   magnitude of casualties, 4, 15
   recognition of, 14-15, 18-20, 28, 44-45, 89
   response team components, 45
   threat reports, 10, 26, 45, 47, 88
   See also Incident site
Industrial toxicology, 99
Information Officer, 68-69
Intelligence units, 81, 89, 136-37
Interagency activities
   communications integration, 59-60
   mutual aid agreements, 83, 95
   post-incident critique, 93-95
   response planning, 88-92
   training, 90-91, 94
International Air Transport Association (IATA),
   156
International Civil Aviation Organization
   (ICAO), 156
International Maritime Dangerous Goods code
   (IMDG), 156
Interviewing
   at incident site, 104, 201
   as investigative skill, 98
   of response personnel, 106
   of victims, 45-46f, 50, 106
   of witnesses, 47, 63, 106
Investigation
   criminal, 80, 87, 97
   post-event initiation of, 15-17, 65
   preplanning, 87-88, 97-103
   remote sampling techniques, 176-78
   standard operating procedures, 103, 201-05
   training for, 6, 75, 87-88, 92, 98-102
   See also Evidence; Incident site; Sampling;
     Witnesses
Investigative team, 107f-10
   for facilities search, 181f, 182, 183
   hot zone, 110, 111-17, 202
   See also Crime scene coordinator

K

Kidnapping, 3

L

Laboratory team, 109, 181f
Lassa fever, 20f, 173f
Law enforcement
    countersnipers, 50
    on "inevitable" terrorism, 3
    investigative personnel, 6
    materials recognition by, 21-22t, 21-26
    preventative activities of, 6
    and site searches, 10, 26-27, 47-48
    special weapons teams, 50
    See also Incidents; Investigation; Response
        personnel
LEPC plan, 81
Lewisite (L)
    characteristics of, 12, 19f
    degradation products, 133f
    precursor to, 21t
Liaison Officer, 68, 70
Liquid chromatography-mass spectometry
    (LC-MS), 162-63
Local Emergency Planning Committees.
    See LEPC plan
Logistics Officer, 66-67, 85

M

Manufacturing sites
    accident risks in, 3-4
    biological, 3-4, 137, 139-40, 166, 173-74
    facilities search, 179-95
    materials recognition, 24-25
    radiological, 154, 155, 174-75
    SWAT teams and, 74
    See also Chemical sites, illegal
Marbug fever, 20f
Mass spectometry (MS), 128, 162-63, 179
Material Safety Data Sheets (MSDS), 184
Metropolitan Medical Strike Teams, 72
MOPP-4 protective equipment, 78-79
Mustard, Nitrogen (HN1), precursors to, 21t, 23t
Mustard, Sulphur, distilled (HD)
    characteristics of, 12, 19f, 126
    decontamination process, 55
    precursors to, 21t, 23t
Mustard (H; HN)
    characteristics of, 12, 19f, 38, 126
    degradation products, 133f

N

NAERG guide, 18, 19f, 32f, 33-34, 199
National Fire Academy, 91
National Institute for Occupational Safety and
    Health (NIOSH), 99, 131
National Institute of Standards and Technology
    (NIST), 147
Nerve agents, 11, 12, 36
Neurotoxins, 14
    biological agents, 20f, 36
    chemical nerve agents, 12, 36
    exposure route, 14
News media personnel
    information releases to, 16, 64, 69
    as information source, 16
Night vision equipment, 77
NIOSH standards, 99, 131
North American Emergency Response Guidebook.
    See NAERG guide
Nuclear Emergency Search Team (NEST), 72
Nuclear weapons, DOE response to, 72-73

O

Occupational Safety and Health Administration.
    See OSHA
Oklahoma City bombing (1995), 3, 36
OPD Chemical Buyers Guide, 171
Operations Officer, 61, 64-65
Oregon salmonella incident, 10
OSHA
    and Incident Command, 57
    Respiratory Protection Standard, 38
    sampling protocols, 98, 131
    training courses, 98-99
    training mandates, 57, 85, 92

P

Personnel protection, 36-43
    glasses or eye shields, 38
    at incident site, 6, 103, 111
    preplanning for, 84, 91
    sheltering in vehicles, 33, 37, 77f
    See also Clothing, protective; Respiratory
        protection
Personnel protection, levels of
    Level A, 16f, 42, 75, 78-79, 112-13f, 184

Level B, 42, 75, 79, 184
Level C, 42-43, 79, 184
Level D, 43
Phosgene (CG)
  characteristics of, 12, 19f, 126
  packaging/shipping, 157, 159
Phosgene Oxime (CX), characteristics of, 12, 19f
Plague
  "Black Death," 14
  characteristics of, 20f, 136f, 174
  pneumonic plague, 14
  treatment for, 20f
Planning, response, 80-92
  interagency, 88-92
  by local governments, 81
  notification procedures, 29, 81, 83, 95
  personnel preparation, 4-5, 57
  post-incident critique of, 95
  threat assessment, 4-6
  vulnerability assessment, 82-83, 85, 88, 91
  See also Targets, potential
Planning Officer, 65-66
Post-incident operations, 93-96
Psychogenic illness, 49

Q

Q fever
  characteristics of, 14, 20f, 136f
  treatment for, 20f

R

Rabbit/deer fly fever, 14
Radiation
  background, 147
  ionizing, 99
Radiation dispersion device (RDD), 146, 149,
  150, 152f, 154, 174
Radiological Assistance Program (RAP), 72
Radiological materials
  contamination by, 21, 37, 150-51
  delayed symptoms of, 21
  dispersion devices, 146, 149-50, 151f, 174
  DOE response to, 72-73, 150, 155, 157, 166
  evidence analysis, 166
  injuries, source of, 36
  "limited" exposure to, 97
  manufacture of, 154, 155, 174-75

  materials recognition, 24-25, 99, 151f
  official regulation of, 24-25, 72, 174
  organic chemicals in, 155
  packaging/shipping, 156
  sampling protocols, 146-55, 206
  training for, 99, 102
  types of particles/rays, 146
  See also Detection devices
Raman Light Detection and Ranging (LIDAR),
  178
Rescue
  from "hot zone," 30, 52-53
  personnel involved, 50, 52-53, 65, 71
  Safety team and, 108-09
  "scoop and run," 52-53
Respiratory protection
  air-purifying respirators (APR), 38-39, 42-43,
    74, 103, 180
  as HazMat shielding devices, 37
  powered air purifying respirators (PAPR), 39
  Safety Officer and, 34
  self-contained breathing apparatus (SCBA),
    38, 39-40, 42, 74, 102, 103, 111, 180
  supplied air respirator (SAR), 38, 40
  suspicious possession of, 25
  for tactical operations, 74, 87
  training for, 85, 99
  types of, 38-40
Response personnel
  "first responders," 14, 44-51
  "freelancing" by, 65, 68
  guidelines for, 18, 199
  in hospital assignments, 17, 50, 106
  medical surveillance of, 96
Response systems
  epidemiological principles of, 18
  fire departments, 50, 60-61, 76, 81, 104
  health care providers, 18-20
  monitoring system for, 19
  notification of, 29, 81, 83
  public health departments, 45, 47, 50, 72, 81,
    104
  See also Incident management
Ricin, 173f
  characteristics of, 14, 20f, 174
  treatment for, 20f
Rickettsia, 14, 173f
Rift Valley fever, 20f, 173f
Robotic bomb handler, 15, 30, 77, 86f, 91

S

Safety Officer, 64, 68, 107f
 and decontamination method, 109
 for facilities search, 181f, 182-83
 and hot zone management, 34, 108, 202
Safety team, 108, 181f, 182
Salmonella, 10
Sample team, 109, 181f, 183, 194
Sampling, 118-60
 for biological agents, 135-46
 for chemical agents, 126-32, 189f, 191-93,
  204-205
 for degradation products, 132, 133f
 equipment, 101, 114f, 119-30, 137-45, 147-48f
 equipment protocol, 204-06
 preplanning, 88, 184-85
 quality control, 132, 147
 for radiological evidence, 146-55
 record keeping, 110, 113-17, 124
 surreptitious methods, 176-78
 training, 91, 100
 See also Detection devices
Sarin, Ethyl (GE), precursor to, 21t
Sarin (GB)
 characteristics of, 12, 19f, 126
 degradation products, 133
 EPA response to, 72
 precursors to, 21-23t
 surface sampling for, 131
Scene log. *See* Incident log
Schools, public, 97
Science officer, 110
Search warrants, 106, 177, 179, 186
Simple Triage Rapid Treatment (START), 53
Smallpox, 173f
 characteristics of, 136f, 174
 dissemination methods, 8, 14
 treatment for, 20f
Snake venom, 14
Soman (GD)
 characteristics of, 12, 19f
 degradation products, 133f
 precursors to, 21-23t
Soman (GF), precursor to, 23t
Special response teams, 81
 See also EOD teams; HazMat; SWAT teams
Specific gravity, 122, 123f, 171
Standard operating procedures, 103, 201-05
Staphylococcal enterotoxin B, 136f

Superfund Amendment and Reauthorization Act
 (SARA), 81
Surveillance, remote, 176-78
Suspects
 dermal/surface sampling of, 131-32, 151
 evidence collection from, 140
 identification of, 49-50, 63, 105-06, 173
 SWAT teams (Special Weapons and Tactics),
  74-79

T

Tabun (GA)
 characteristics of, 12, 19f
 degradation products, 133f
 precursors to, 21t, 23t
Tactical operations, WMD
 equipment for, 76-79
 "hot zone," 74-79
"Target hardening," 4
Targets, political, 97
Targets, potential
 "false alarms" at, 62
 identification of, 85, 88
 lists of, 5-6, 82
 notification of, 81
 site searches at, 10, 26-27, 47-48
Technical Instructions for the Safe Transportation of
 Dangerous Goods by Air, 156
Terrorism
 "agricultural," 9
 and "B-NICE" acronym, 3
 false alarms, 50, 62
 See also Incidents
Terrorists, 10
Thermal imaging devices, 77
Three Mile Island incident, 147
Tire impressions, 6, 17, 103, 112
Traffic control, 48, 80, 84
Training, 89-90
 Awareness level, 6, 11, 69, 90
 with equipment, 85, 87
 Hazmat, levels of, 90, 92
 interagency, 90-91
 for investigation, 87-88
 OSHA mandates for, 57, 85
 special WMD, 26, 81, 89-91, 98-102
Trip/field blanks, 120-22, 131, 147, 155, 204
Tularemia
 characteristics of, 14, 18, 20f, 136f, 174

treatment for, 20f
Typhoid fever, 14

U

Unabomber, 10
U.S. Army Military Research Institute for
    Infectious Disease (USAMRIID), 73
U.S. Army Technical Escort Unit (TEU), 73
U.S. Marine Corps Chemical Biological Incident
    Response Force (CBIRF), 73
Urban Search and Rescue Teams (USAR), 72

V

Vehicles, sheltering in, 33, 37, 77f
Venezuelan equine encephalitis (VEE), 173f
    characteristics of, 14, 20f
    treatment for, 20f
Vexicants, 12
VG, precursors to, 23t
Victims, 52-56
    deceased, 53
    dermal/surface sampling of, 131-32
    evidence gathering from, 17, 140
    identification of, 16, 17, 105, 201
    initial assessment of, 45, 63
    injured, 49, 52-53, 65, 71-72
    interviews of, 45-46f, 50, 106
    seeking safety for, 27, 29, 30-34, 49
    transportation routes for, 48
    See also Decontamination; Rescue

Viral hemorrhagic fevers, 173f
    characteristics of, 14, 20f, 136f
    treatments for, 20f
    types of, 20f
Volitile organic compounds (VOCs), 163
VS, precursor to, 21t
VX
    characteristics of, 12, 19f
    degradation products, 133f
    precursors to, 21-23t

W

"Warm zone," as limited access zone, 31, 54
Weapons, law enforcement, 50
    "less lethal," 76
    tactical operations, 74, 76, 78, 79
Weapons of mass destruction (WMD)
    assessment questions, 45
    interdiction techniques, 167-78
    recognition of, 21-23t, 24-26, 28-29, 89, 101
    signs/symptoms of, 17-21, 20f
    sources of assistance, 71-73, 97
    types of, 11-14
    See also Dissemination methods; Incidents
Weather and wind, 31-32f, 33, 45, 140, 185-86
Witnesses
    identification of, 16, 49-50, 63, 104, 105
    interviews/debriefing of, 47, 63, 106
WMD. *See* Weapons of mass destruction
World Trade Center bombing (1993), 3
World War I, chemical agent use, 13